PROBLEMS
IN
DECIPHERMENT

BIBLIOTHÈQUE DES CAHIERS DE L'INSTITUT
DE LINGUISTIQUE DE LOUVAIN — 49

PROBLEMS
IN
DECIPHERMENT

PEETERS
LOUVAIN-LA-NEUVE
1989

D/1989/0602/29 ISBN 90-6831-177-8

Bondgenotenlaan 153 Place Blaise Pascal 1,
B-3000 Leuven B-1348 LOUVAIN-LA-NEUVE

Printed in Belgium

BCILL 49 : *Problems in Decipherment*, 7-8.

PREFACE

Preliminary versions of the articles in this volume were delivered as invited papers at the 11th Burdick-Vary Symposium in honor of Emmett L. Bennett, JR., held at the University of Wisconsin–Madison on April 8-9, 1988 under the sponsorship of the Institute for Research in the Humanities and the Department of Classics. The organizing committee for the symposium thought that papers on the topic "Problems in Decipherment" would be timely, because of advances in current research on scripts, undeciphered and deciphered, of the ancient Mediterranean and pre-Columbian Americas. The organizers also hoped that the presentation of such papers would be a particularly appropriate way to honor a scholar whose exacting epigraphical and analytical work had contributed so much to Michael Ventris's decipherment of the Mycenaean Greek script Linear B, still acknowledged as one of the extraordinary intellectual achievements of the twentieth century. Their hopes were fully realized.

Following the success of the symposium, it was decided to publish these separate studies in a single volume. Since publication of the papers was not planned in advance, the editors wish to thank all the contributors for making a firm commitment to transform their talks into proper written texts. In this volume, readers will find critical assessments of work in progress on all branches of prehistoric Aegean and Cypriote scripts and ancient Etruscan. For each area of research, the authors have focused on the particular problems which have been or still must be overcome. Two papers deal with principles of decipherment as they were applied by Ventris and as they were developed and practiced by earlier European scholars. We keenly regret that unforeseen circumstances prevented Linda Schele from producing a survey of the exciting advances in the study of Mayan inscriptions. Fortunately we can refer readers to the series of articles on Mayan script and language in the journal *Antiquity* 62:234 (March 1988) 122-172.

The editors wish to thank David C. Lindberg, director of the Humanities Institute, Barry Powell, chair of the Classics Department, and Loretta Freiling, as usual the omnificent spirit of Institute activities, for making us take the first steps toward this volume. Philip Freeman, research assistant in the Program in Aegean Scripts and Prehistory, helped with text formatting. Finally we thank Emmett L. Bennett, JR., for doing more than merely tolerating a second *Unfestschrift*.

Yves Duhoux *Louvain–la–Neuve*
Thomas G. Palaima *Austin*
John Bennet *Madison*

BCILL 49 : *Problems in Decipherment*, 9-23.

MICHAEL VENTRIS AND THE PELASGIAN SOLUTION

Emmett L. BENNETT, Jr.
Institute for Research in the Humanities
University of Wisconsin—Madison

My original intention for this paper was to discuss what Michael Ventris actually did as he worked toward his successful decipherment of the texts from Knossos and Pylos in the "Minoan" Linear B script.[1] That subject is, I think, particularly interesting because of the great difference between what he expected to find, a Minoan language, and what he did find, Mycenaean Greek. I would have presented the subject as a commentary on the notes in which he recorded the stages of his progress in the critical period of 1951-52. I intended to supplement these by drawing upon his correspondence with me, and by relying as much on hindsight as on my memory of those exciting times. The paper of my intention is not yet written, however, and I should like to write it someday. The fact is that I succumbed to the antiquarian's question, "How did it all start?" and have put off to a distant tomorrow the practical question, "How did he do it?"

I shall start by attacking this question bibliographically. The obvious beginning is in 1958, in John Chadwick's excellent account of *The Decipherment of Linear B* (CHADWICK 1958, 1967).[2] But we may be able to see more of Ventris' own view of his work in his account of the decipherment for the book on which he and

---

1 It will be apparent that this paper was prepared for oral presentation, with no expectation of a prompt publication. I have changed as little as possible of the form in which it was delivered. The principal cause of change is the fact that in presenting comparanda I relied then not on footnotes, but on extracts of certain publications copied and put into the hands of the audience. These extracts were taken from Evans' *Palace of Minos*, Ventris' "Introducing the Minoan Language," Ventris' *Languages of the Minoan and Mycenaean Civilizations*, and Ventris' first *Work Notes on Minoan Language Research*. As for bibliographical references, I solved that problem then by holding up a copy of each item as I mentioned it, and here append a bibliography, in the preparation of which I have been greatly helped by GRUMACH 1963 and 1967. Now, a year after this was read as a paper, we can start with materials written and privately circulated by Ventris, and available in the convenient volume edited by Anna Sacconi, VENTRIS 1988.

2 I fear that I made little use of the further account of the decipherment offered by Chadwick, CHADWICK 1973 = VENTRIS 1988, 371-396.

Chadwick had collaborated in 1956, *Documents in Mycenaean Greek* (VENTRIS and CHADWICK 1956, 1973). A bit earlier there is their briefer account in the article which announced their remarkable results, "Evidence for Greek dialect in the Linear B texts," in the *Journal of Hellenic Studies*,[3] and still earlier there is "Deciphering Europe's earliest Scripts on the Cretan Tablets," the announcement Ventris himself made in July 1952 on the BBC (VENTRIS 1952 = 1988, 363-367). All of these describe, in effect, a *fait accompli*, and they tend to put selected steps in his workings into a rational, and not necessarily historical, order. When we try at last to answer the question, "how did he do it?," we will find more helpful, since they are closer to the workings, the *Work Notes on Minoan Language Research* (VENTRIS 1951 = 1988, 135-333). Of these there were 176 typed pages dating from January 1951 to June 1952. Ventris composed, duplicated, and circulated these in about a dozen copies, on an average of once a month. I was privileged to receive the *Notes* promptly, and, since I was writing to him frequently during that period, there are a fair number of additional remarks he entered on my copy. It is from this period that I have many of his letters to me, though I have not yet used them extensively in this study, while I have none of my letters to him.

Important as these *Notes* are, they obviously do not describe the beginnings of the process of decipherment. We must go farther back to 1950, when he had prepared a remarkable collection of notes, or small essays, which were actually the responses to a questionnaire he had composed and distributed at the end of 1949 for the 50th anniversary of Evans' work at Knossos in 1900, when the first inscribed tablets were excavated. This was *The Language of the Minoan and Mycenaean Civilizations, New Year 1950*, and he called it *Mid-Century Report* (VENTRIS 1950 = 1988, 29-132). The authors of the notes were correspondents whom he knew to be interested in, or actively working on, the problems of the Linear B script, and he added his own views in a summary and critique of the rest. It may be good to quote his introductory sentence. "At the end of 1949 I sent out copies of the following questionnaire to a number of scholars who have been working in recent years on the problems set up by the language and writing of the prehistoric Aegean, suggesting that we might make New Year 1950 the occasion for an informal exchange of views, reviewing the position reached at the end of the half-century"(VENTRIS 1951, 2 = 1988, 32).

But this also was not his beginning. Ten years before that there was the startling announcement of his decipherment of Linear B, an article in the *American Journal of Archaeology*, which he called "Introducing the Minoan Language"(VENTRIS 1940). Yet he made it clear that it was not to be understood as a claim of a completed decipherment, but of progress toward one with apparently excellent chances of a successful completion.[4] I intend, then, to look at

---

3 VENTRIS *and* CHADWICK 1953. I fear I have made little use of the additional account offered by Ventris himself, VENTRIS 1953.

4 "The excursions which I have here described form only the prelude to the work that lies ahead." VENTRIS 1940, 519.

that article to see if it shows anything of his resources and methods. This "decipherment" may now be looked upon as a curiosity, for we do not, as he did then, think the language of Linear B is something like Etruscan, and besides, it does not meet the criteria we all have been setting for worth-while decipherment. But I prefer to see how much of what he was then doing contributed directly to his eventual success. Perhaps this is, after all, the real beginning of the decipherment we recognize as correct.

The fascinating problem of the decipherment of the Linear B script started at Knossos, in 1900, and it is now safe, I think, for me to ask the question, "*how* did it all start?" That is why I mentioned Ventris' resources; if we identify them we can see how he transformed the problem. Ventris' chief resource was actually Sir Arthur Evans, whose contribution to the successful decipherment is large. Of course, it was Evans who had found inscribed clay tablets in the ruins of the complex of buildings he uncovered on the hill of τοῦ Τσελεβῆ ἡ Κεφάλα, and which he decided to name the "Palace of Minos" at Knossos. The first tablets were found in the campaign of 1900. As soon as the digging was over, and in preparation for his first prompt report of the first season of excavation in *Annual of the British School at Athens*, he drew most of the substantial tablets or fragments. "I have copied over nine hundred of these tablets which I hope carefully to revise with the aid of the originals on my return to Crete. The retention of the tablets in Crete itself is naturally a hindrance to study." He also had photographs taken of many of the more photogenic tablets and he published the photographs of 14 of them (containing about 68 sign-groups).[5] A good many more were found in 1904, and a few even later.

Already in 1900 Evans had taken the first important step toward the decipherment of the tablets. He discovered that the system for writing numbers was decimal, and pointed out that the signs standing for numbers were used in connection with others for weights and measures to express quantities of particular things.[6] He prepared a list of the signs employed in the script, assigning each a number,[7] and eventually drew up tables showing their varieties as they

---

5 EVANS 1900. Drawings: the first example, "Linear Tablet referring to Chariot and Horses and, perhaps, Cuirass," EVANS 1900, 58, fig. 12. The corpus of the drawings is found in EVANS 1952. Quotation: EVANS 1900, 58, note 2. Photographs: "Tablets with Linear Script," "Large tablet with Linear Script," three photographic plates reproduced, EVANS 1900, plates 12, 13. The corpus of the photographs is found in EVANS 1952.

6 "The system is decimal. The units, consisting of upright lines, are practically the same as the Egyptian." EVANS 1900, 57. Examples: "Numerals of Classes A and B," taken from EVANS 1935, 691, fig. 676, and "Ideographic Signs connected with Agriculture and Cereals," EVANS 1935, 721, fig. 705.

7 "About seventy characters seem to have been in common use. Besides these there exists another smaller group used exclusively in connexion with numerals and apparently in some cases indicating weights and measures. A certain number of quasi-pictorial characters also occur which seem to have an ideographic or determinative meaning." EVANS 1900, 57. The first list seems to have been offered in WEILL 1903, 221, fig. 2. A second appeared in SUNDWALL 1914, 5-6, Tab. 1-2. Evans' first list may be "Comparative Table of Signs of the Hieroglyphic and Linear Scripts," EVANS 1921, 643, fig. 477.

appeared in the writing of one or another person.[8] Thus a numerical transcription would be possible, but he preferred the more elegant solution and had a handsome font of type prepared, and eventually used it for the publication of *Palace of Minos*. He observed that if tablets were grouped into classes characterized by the commodity signs in them, something of the meanings and functions of those signs could be reasonably inferred. Tablets in such groups often enough also agreed in the arrangement of their text, in the shape and size of the tablet, and in the area of the excavation where they were found.[9] As he continued his work on the tablets he numbered and renumbered them, shuffling them about to present each group more or less as a unit, and placing the groups in a fairly rational order.

All of this was aimed toward the goal he set for himself of publishing a corpus of all the prehistoric inscriptions of Crete, not only those he found at Knossos, but those the Italians had found at Haghia Triadha, and those on the Cretan seal stones he had been collecting and writing about since 1894. The intended program of publication began to be realized in 1909 as *Scripta Minoa* I, containing the monuments of what I stubbornly persist in calling the pictographic script. The second and third volumes were then planned, to deal with the Linear A and B inscriptions.[10] But they did not appear in that form after all. There were very few Linear A tablets at Knossos, and the many from Haghia Triadha, though surely available for his inspection in the Museum, were not soon published. So Evans' account of Linear A, and not his corpus, appeared in 1921 as a chapter in the general account of Minoan archaeology, the *Palace of Minos*.[11]

Although there was quite enough material for a corpus of Linear B, it was rather a general and descriptive account which appeared in 1935, and this was published in the *Palace of Minos*, volume 4, part 2 (EVANS 1935). Until that publication it was very hard indeed to do any serious work on Linear B; the number of documents available before was only about 60. But they were not readily available; more than half were published only in photographs, rather small and not too clear. About ten were not actually published, but could be seen, I think, in a small collection of casts in a few museums;[12] some of the actual tablets

---

8 "Synopsis of Linear Signary B and comparisons with Class A," EVANS 1935, fig. 666, inserted opposite p. 684. In this list, as in his earlier list and in those of Weill and Sundwall, we now recognize that several signs have been conflated and put under a single number. Alice Kober pointed out that Evans' signs 23, 41, 44, 49, and 50 must each be divided into two distinct signs, *a* and *b*. KOBER 1944, 65, note 2.

9 Examples: "'Percentage' Tablets," EVANS 1935, 692, fig. 677, and "Specimens from 'Chariot Tablets' Deposit," EVANS 1935, 788, fig. 763.

10 "The remaining Volumes—II and III—of this work will be devoted to the detailed publication of the documents of the advanced Linear Scripts of Crete, of both Classes (A and B)." EVANS 1909, x. Sealstones: EVANS 1894. Further materials listed in GRUMACH 1963.

11 "MM III. The Linear Script A and its sacral Usage." EVANS 1921, 612-646.

12 The inventory numbers of those in the Metropolitan Museum of Art begin with "13.", and there is mention of casts in SUNDWALL 1914, 4: "Zu diesem Material kommen noch Kopien, die ich dank dem Entgegenkommen der Herren Hatzidakis und Xanthudidis im Museum zu Kandia machen konnte, und hier für meine Zwecke ausgenutzt habe, ohne natürlich in irgenwelcher Weise deren Veröffentlichung durch ihre Entdecker vorgreifen zu wollen. Es sind 12 Täfelchen aus Hagia Triada in A-Schrift und 30 aus Knosos in B-Schrift".

must have been on display in the cases of the Archaeological Museum in Iraklion. From the sixty published objects about 350 sign-groups could be collected. And of course all but one or two of these inscribed objects were obviously accounts, since they included about 325 examples from the large repertory of signs for the commodities being accounted for, plus the numbers used with them.

With the appearance of *Palace of Minos* IV, the stock of Linear B increased by almost 200 documents, including some inscribed stirrup jars found not in Crete but on the mainland of Greece;[13] their inscriptions included some sign-groups found at Knossos and perhaps suggested more strongly the idea that a widespread linguistic, an essentially Cretan, Minoan, community was represented by Linear B.[14] The 200 documents were a more or less representative sample, and in them, or sometimes only in citations without their contexts, were about 500 sign-groups, and about 250 commodity signs. These were also much more readily examined; almost all the new documents were represented by Evans' drawings of their texts. But, most important, they were shown in such a way that the considerable progress Evans had made in understanding the documents was evident.

I must return to the sketch of what Evans had learned about the texts. Among the things he learned from two of the larger tablets, one dealing with lists of men, the other with lists of women, was the observation that in them a repeated pattern of text could be observed.[15] The pattern is of a sign-group, a commodity sign more or less human in appearance, and the numeral stroke meaning one. By genuine instinct he called the one a "man" sign and the other a "woman" sign, and with equal good sense decided that in each case the sign-group was the name of the person counted. As he was doing this he noticed an interesting uniformity: certain signs occurred frequently at the end of men's names; different ones were frequent endings for women's names. This led him to collect also pairs or triplets of sign-groups with identical beginnings and different endings, thirty-two shown as "Name-groups of Linear Script B associated with 'Man' sign", and fourteen as "Name-groups of Linear Script B associated with 'Woman' sign."[16]

As we look back at what he accomplished we can see that, although he had access to at least 1600 tablets, he was not very discriminating in his table of identified and numbered signs, and he did not systematically exhaust the possibilities of studying such uniformities and variations in the sign-groups he considered to be names. He seems not to have done much more investigation in that line; but he rightly supposed that these phenomena were important for an eventual decipherment, and

13 "Stirrup Vases from Tiryns, with Painted Inscriptions," EVANS 1935, 743, fig. 726 and p. 740, fig. 724a. Notices first appeared for the inscription from Orchomenos in 1903, from Tiryns in 1910, from Thebes in 1921, from Mycenae in 1922, from Eleusis in 1935. GRUMACH 1963, 76-79. Very few illustrations appeared before the publication of EVANS 1935.

14 "Comparative table showing correspondence of Mainland name-groups with Knossian of Class B", EVANS 1935, 751, fig. 734.

15 Drawings: "Large Tablet showing Lists of Men," EVANS 1935, 703, fig. 686, and "Tablet of 14 Lines containing two Lists of Women and, apparently, Children, with signs of Addition," EVANS 1935, 707, fig. 689.

16 EVANS 1935, 710, fig. 693A for sign-groups with the 'Man' sign, and fig. 693B for groups with the 'Woman' sign.

that they deserved a place in his treatment of the Linear B script for the *Palace of Minos*. The correct and generous judgment I can quote directly from Ventris' article, to which I am about to turn: "The real and valuable work on the Minoan inscriptions has so far consisted almost entirely of research into the method rather than the meaning. A great deal of labor has gone into classifying the signs and tracing their varying forms throughout the successive systems, in sorting out the records according to certain recurrent ideographs, and in the detection of that large element consisting of proper names. All this we owe to the untiring energy of Sir Arthur Evans. No further progress would be possible without it."[17]

Michael Ventris' first public essay on our subject was the ambitious article "Introducing the Minoan Language" (VENTRIS 1940 = 1988, 494-520). I shall pass over quickly what he may well have thought the real substance of it. This was a elaborate statement and defence of his primary assumptions; that in the pre-Greek Aegean there was a widespread linguistic community, whose parts were referred to by the later Greeks under several names, among them "Minyans" and "Pelasgians." He assumed that the language of this community should be ascribed to an "Asianic" group, and that it included especially the inhabitants of Bronze Age Crete, whom Evans called Minoans, as well as other peoples of the Aegean area, all conveniently referred to as Pelasgians. Finally he was sure that this community included the Etruscans of Italy, whose language was preserved, or should I say hidden, in alphabetic inscriptions. His conception was of "the unity of Minoan and Etruscan within a single 'Pelasgian' language" (VENTRIS 1940, 519). These opinions were not entirely new, but Ventris had read widely, wrote well, and he made it seem plausible that they could be fitted together.

Naturally, then, his conclusion was that he had found reasonable evidence in the Linear B texts of linguistic features characteristic of Etruscan texts. To get to that point he had first to determine how speech was represented by the script, and second he had to find a set of values for a good number of the signs. Most of those who had considered what type of script was used in the Aegean scripts, and Evans himself, thought that it would follow the models of Egyptian pictographic or Mesopotamian cuneiform scripts; but Ventris, considering at least the number of signs in the repertory, preferred the model of the Classical Cypriote syllabic script. This script was used in Cyprus for writing Greek texts when the other Greeks had the alphabet; there were about 55 signs; these represented syllables such as *a e i o u, ta te ti to tu*, &c. The first of the inscriptions in this script had been deciphered in the 1870's, and the rules according to which the syllabic signs were combined to represent words were already fairly clear.[18]

I quote his statement: "there can be no doubt that [the Cypriote syllabary] was adapted directly from a form of the Minoan Linear script. A large proportion of

---

[17] VENTRIS 1940, 495. I may add the concluding footnote from VENTRIS 1940, 520: "In conclusion I must record my deep indebtedness to Sir Arthur Evans, not only in respect of the enormous groundwork covered in his publications, but also for very valuable personal help in the earlier stages of this research."

[18] MASSON 1983: Le déchiffrement du syllabaire, 48-51; La structure théorique du syllabaire, 51-57.

the signs correspond exactly with letters of Linear B" (VENTRIS 1940, 503). In other words, a few of its signs do closely resemble Linear B signs, and it seemed reasonable that when Linear B and Cypriote signs had similar shapes the values of the Linear B signs could be identified as the same. These would form a nucleus of the list of Linear B syllabic values, to which others could be added as they were discovered by other means. Again he assumes that: "we are justified in regarding Linear B, in its literary use, as a regular phonetic system, accurately and simply recording the contemporary pronunciation, syllable by syllable" (VENTRIS 1940, 508). So Ventris' next assumptions were that Linear B (and Linear A, too) followed the model of the Cypriote script and that he could recognize 14 Linear B signs as common in shape and value with Cypriote signs. He presented these in a table with columns for Evans' numeration, for the Linear B form, for the cognate Linear A form, and for a phonetic value, with an indication of forms paralleled in the Cypriote syllabary.[19]

But by the end of the article his assumptions included the values of 28 signs, or twice as many as Cypriote shapes suggested to him. With these he should have been able to substitute values for every sign in almost 200 of the sign-groups occurring in the published texts. How did he get them? A journal article is not place for a detailed account of all one has done on its subject, especially the many things that turned out to be unproductive. But Ventris even avoided the practice, frequent in such "decipherments", of reporting how, one by one, the discovery of each value led to the next one. He has instead modestly said that "the values of certain others have suggested themselves from internal evidence" (VENTRIS 1940, 509). It is not important here to find out how he got them, but one might start by taking all the inscriptions he had available, and setting aside the sign-groups which consisted entirely of the 14 solid Cypriote values and examining those with the signs whose values he considered less certain.

What is important is that he found the confirmation of his guess that the Linear B texts were recognizably like Etruscan, not in a message like that in Edgar Allan Poe's *The Gold Bug*,[20] but in the structure of those sign-groups which could be recognized as proper names. Evans had been able to recognize a considerable number of proper names, and observed in several cases that a name was plainly related to others, sometimes even a man's with a woman's, in that they began with the same sequence of two, three, or four signs, but had different endings. And he had, of course, identified the particular signs which frequently ended men's names, and the largely different set of signs which came at the end of women's names. He was brought to this, clearly enough, by the two large tablets, one with

---

19 Examples: the table of signs and suggested phonetic values, some marked with a question mark, some marked with a C to indicate validation by a parallel form in the Cypriote syllabary, and six others suggested on other grounds. VENTRIS 1940, 510. I found that the addition of forms from the Cypriote syllabary was helpful to the audience. Ventris might have seen them in DEECKE 1884. Three additional values (*ni*, *ri*, and *ro*) are introduced, VENTRIS 1940, 512, 518, and at least one other (*no*, in the name-radical *no-no* [?]) is mentioned without identification, VENTRIS 1940, 514.

20 POE 1843. The first reprinting, POE 1844, was a new edition, partially corrected. KAHN 1967, 789-792.

42 women's names, followed by a woman sign and a numeral one,[21] the other with 65 men's names, followed by a man sign and numeral.[22] And both had totals at the ends of series of names. Ventris added to these a few more names, until he had a list of some 250 proper names.[23]

To examine the structure of these names, he followed Evans' lead; he identified suffixes in the last signs (or pairs of signs) of names, and found 45 masculine and 15 feminine suffixes, simple and complex.[24] Five of the simple suffixes were the vocalic parts of syllabic signs, most were single signs, but a few included two signs. The compound suffixes were all made up of two or three complete syllabic signs. I repeat a few of them here:

Masculine: *-a -e -i -o -u, -ce -lo -ně -ta -va, -s -v(e) ...*
Feminine: *-i, -iě -ito, -ce -ri -ši, -liě -tiě -viě ...*
Masculine: *-celo -valo -lině -tipe -pupa -nito, -lav(e) -θev(e) ...*
Feminine: *-veni -nito*

With the suffixes removed, he could make a list of the first parts of the names, and he called them "name-radicals." I repeat a few of them:

Lal-, Pat-, Ral-, Ran-, šep-, Tir-, Vit-, θel-; šeli-, š(e)ne, θ(e)ve-

To discover what were the sign-groups and texts in which these suffixes and name-radicals and names were found, I reassembled all the texts published whole, or in quoted sign-groups, before 1939. I transcribed them, first using the numbers Evans' had assigned, and then substituting Ventris' suggested values wherever I could. It is possible I overlooked some texts known to Ventris; it is very possible that I failed to transcribe some texts as Ventris did, by transcribing them as I would today. But I can recognize almost everything he refers to, and identify its source. Then I made an index to find all the sign-groups beginning with the name-radicals, and another to find all those ending with the suffixes.

Now among his simple suffixes, he had not identified any signs corresponding only to the vowels *a, i, o, u,* so that eight of these suffixes must have begun with the vocalic part of syllabic signs, e.g., *(v)a, (t)i, (l)o, (p)u.* And the consonantal parts of those signs might (but need not) belong to "name-radicals." And in fact the majority of the "name-radicals" identified end in the consonantal part of a syllabic sign, and only seven of those were pairs of complete syllables.[25]

---

[21] Now KN Ap 639. EVANS 1935, 707, fig. 689.

[22] Now KN As 1516. EVANS 1935, 703, fig. 686.

[23] VENTRIS 1940, 511, starting perhaps from EVANS 1935, 710, figs. 693A, 693B, and 751, fig. 734. I am not sure that I can identify them all.

[24] Examples: a list of simple suffixes, masculine and feminine, VENTRIS 1940, 514; a list of compound suffixes, masculine and feminine, and a list of Name-radicals, VENTRIS 1940, 515.

[25] Examples: VENTRIS 1940, 515.

A name-radical of the type of **Šeli-**, where the division falls between syllabic signs, can give us no indication about the syllables involved in the transition between name-radical and suffix.[26] The more common type, that of **Lal-**, **Lap-**, &c., does divide within a syllable. But with the second type, as in **Šep-**, he did find the transitional syllables *p-u* and *p-a*, and could know that they had the same consonant. From the following table it can be seen that, if the sign-groups I have identified and counted actually are names and begin with the name-radicals,[27] we can identify four groups of signs (with Evans' numeration) each beginning with the same consonant: in items 1-5, *49b * 54 * 25*; in 6-8, *44a * 60 * 47*; in 9, *30 * 46*; in 10-11, *58 * 2 * 59*.

	Name radical	final syllable realized as				
1	**Lal-**	la 1/0	=	li 2/1	lo 0/#	=
2	**Pal-**	la 1/0	=	li #/1	lo 1/1	=
3	**Šal-**	la 0/0	=	li 1/0	lo 1/0	=
4	**Θel-**	la 1/#	=	li 7/3	lo 0/0	=
5	**Vil-**	la 3/2	=	li 3/2	lo 0/1	=
6	**Lap-**	pa 0/0	pe 1/0	=	=	pu 1/1
7	**Šep-**	pa 6/1	pe 0/1	=	=	pu 4/3
8	**Vip-**	pa 2/0	pe 1/0	=	=	pu 3/1
9	**Tir-**	ra 2/4	re 1/0	ri 0/0	ro 0/0	=
10	**Šet-**	ta 1/0	=	ti 1/2	to 0/0	=
11	**Vit-**	ta 0/0	=	ti 2/1	to 5/3	=
12	**Ral-**	la 0/0	=	li 0/0	lo 0/0	=
13	**Val-**	la 0/0	=	li 2/0	lo 0/0	=
14	**Ran-**	na 0/0	ne 3/0	ni 0/0	=	=
15	**Šar-**	ra 2/1	re 0/0	ri 0/0	ro 0/1	=
16	**Ver-**	ra 0/0	re 0/0	ri 1/0	ro 0/0	=
17	**PeŠ-**	=	Še 0/1	Ši 0/0	=	=
18	**Pat-**	ta 0/1	=	ti 1/0	to 0/1	=

[26] The examples A-E in VENTRIS 1940, 516, from EVANS 1935, 710, figs. 693A, 693b, and EVANS 1935, fig. 734, are all of the type with endings occupying complete signs; none of them includes one of Ventris' name-radicals.

[27] The frequencies are for sign-groups with both name-radical and suffix, and for those with only a name-radical. In line 5, **Vil-** 3/2 represents 3 groups beginning with **Vil-** and ending with suffixes, and 2 more without identified suffixes; in line 4, **Θel-** represents 1 name-radical-suffix group, and 1 or more groups with only the name radical, but found or published only after 1939. It will be clear from the numbers for the name-radical **Ral-** in line 12 that I found no instance of any such sequence at the beginning of a sign-group, and that I do not know why.

19	**ʒat-**	ta 0/2	=	ti 0/0	to 0/0	=
20	**ʒeθ-**	=	θe 8/0	=	=	=
21	**ʒiev-**	va 1/0	ve 0/0	vi 0/0	=	=

This phenomenon appears as a consequence of the assumptions that the script follows the pattern of the Cypriote syllabic script and that Linear B personal names are regularly compounds of radicals and suffixes. I feel sure Ventris noted it, but I think he did not attach much importance to it. Yet it was to become of great importance in his later work. The other aspect of this work to become of equal importance is the practice of classifying sign-groups by their apparent function within their context. Here names are clearly distinguished from non-names; later other distinctions are insisted on.

However, there probably would not have been any later work at all along these lines, although he was sure he had laid excellent foundations. "Beyond this point all that is required is hard work, and the collaboration of all workers in this field. Thus can we make up for the energies which, through a lack of direction, have been squandered on the elaboration of so many misguided interpretations"(VENTRIS 1940, 520). But, of course, there was a significant discovery while the article was in press.

In the spring of 1939 Carl Blegen found a large number of tablets inscribed in Linear B, not in Crete, but at Ano Englianos, near Pylos, on the mainland of Greece. Some were immediately published in the *Illustrated London News* (Blegen 1939), and others by the end of the year in *American Journal of Archaeology* (Blegen and Kourouniotis 1939). It was apparent then that with a little patience there might soon be an abundance of material with which he could confirm his decipherment, so he had a good motive for continuing. This discovery may also have suggested to Sir Arthur Evans the advantages of prompt publication of all the Linear B texts from Knossos, that is, his proposed *Scripta Minoa* II. But in 1941 Evans died, and the work was entrusted to his executor.

The situation in the mid-forties, then, was this. Ventris could work on the 200 texts Evans had published, plus half a dozen from Pylos. I was given by Carl Blegen the opportunity of preparing a preliminary publication of the Pylos texts, and from 1940 on could work on all of them, plus Evans' 200. By 1947 I had completed a preliminary transcription and examination of the texts. Sir John Myres had actively taken up the task of publishing *Scripta Minoa* II. He was very ably assisted in this by Alice Kober, of Brooklyn College. She, like Ventris, had started with a review of the linguistic context of the Bronze Age Aegean, and Evans' 200 texts, and also had paid great attention to the proper names. She published in 1945 in the *American Journal of Archaeology* her contention that the spelling variations gave evidence of nominal inflection, and not of the morphology of stem and suffix that Ventris had suggested (KOBER 1945). By 1947, at latest, Alice Kober had prepared a working transcription of all the Knossos texts, and knew the half-dozen Pylian ones. It was the end of 1948, I think, that she and I finally exchanged copies of our preliminary transcriptions.

Toward the end of 1949 Ventris noticed that the 50th anniversary of Evans' discovery of the Knossos tablets was coming up. He distributed a questionnaire (reprinted in VENTRIS 1950, 4-5 = 1988, 34-35). He then printed answers from twelve correspondents, and circulated them to about thirty.[28] It may be of interest to notice some of his own answers.

In his answers to questions 1-7, primarily eliciting opinions of the identity of the Minoan language,[29] he is still very much convinced of the existence of his Pelasgian language and of its use in Linear B. In his answers to 11 and 12, on the relationships of the Cypriote syllabary,[30] he is still sure that Cypriote is the right pattern for Linear B, but a little less sure about some values and spelling rules; he is firmly convinced that the spelling system is purely phonetic, and not logographic.

He may not yet have been convinced about the evidence for inflection, but he does hold, in his answer to question 14,[31] that the discovery of phonetic relationships among the signs, namely that some pairs share the same consonant, that other pairs share the same vowel, is a necessary step toward decipherment.[32]

Ventris' next, still informal, and most important, publication is the *Work Notes on Minoan Language Research*, started in January 1951, for private circulation (VENTRIS 1951). Let me first indicate what he was working with. Formal discussion of the whole set of Knossos and Pylos tablets was not possible until they were published, for Pylos until a bit later in 1951 (BENNETT 1951)[33] and for Knossos until 1952 (EVANS 1952). The most important section of the first *Note* is a collection of fifty-one sets of sign-groups from which the evidence for declension could be gathered. More textual material had been published since 1939, and he makes good use of it. He cites some Pylos texts for evidence of declension, and at least once he refers to Kober and to a Knossos text not yet published and only available in Kober's transcription (KOBER 1948). She may have given him a copy as soon as the end of 1948.

When he composed this note he had been convinced, undoubtedly by the work of Alice Kober, that much of the variation in the structure of names that he had worked with in the beginning was due to inflection rather than to the morphology of names.[34] He now not only sees the possibility of using those variations to establish the relationships of the still unknown phonetic values of the syllabic signs

---

28 Ten correspondents are listed in the title page; the reply of the eleventh, Alice Kober, is interesting for its brevity as well as for her opinion, much elaborated in KOBER 1948. VENTRIS 1950, 2 = 1988, 32.

29 Examples: answer to question 2, VENTRIS 1950, ii-iii = 1988, 88-89; answer to 4, VENTRIS 1950, v = 1988, 91.

30 Examples: to questions 11 and 12, VENTRIS 1950, xiv = 1988, 102.

31 "There is some evidence that the following groups of signs share the same consonants." VENTRIS 1950, xvi = 1988, 104. But in fact there is earlier evidence to the same effect, in the question itself: "What phonetic or other values (or alternative experimental values) do you assign to the common signs of the Linear B signary? What series of signs appear to share the same consonants or the same vowels?" VENTRIS 1950, 5.

32 Other examples: answer to question 1, VENTRIS 1950, i-ii = 1988, 87-88; to 10, VENTRIS 50, xii-xiv = 1988, 98-102; to 14-15, VENTRIS 50, xvi = 1988, 104.

33 I had given him a copy of my transcription in July 1950.

34 Discussion of cases for sign-groups, VENTRIS 1950, 2 = 1988, 136.

(e.g. in his figure 1 he shows the signs "ag" and "aj" with the same consonant) — not only that, but the necessity of marshalling the evidence for that relationship, and of guaranteeing the strength of that evidence. For that relationship "ag" - "aj" he shows the spelling alternations which give the necessary evidence in items 2, 3, and 7; for the relationship of "om" - "av" in items 2, 11, and 13; for the relationships of "od" - "ok" - "ez" in items 6 and 47 (VENTRIS 1950, 3-10 = 1988, 137-148; 1950, fig. 1 = 1988, 143).

Before I offer my conclusion, let me say three things about the much reprinted "'B' Syllabary Phonetic 'Grid'" (VENTRIS 1951, fig. 1 = 1988, 143). First of all, it can be forgotten that of the relationships shown by pairs of signs in the same row or in the same column, some are right, some are quite wrong, some are a little misguided. Second, we can ignore his suggested values with question marks, but on the other hand there is hardly a remnant of the "Pelasgian" values. He is 2/3 right about "t" in row 1, in row 4 he's 1/5 right about "n," and 3/5 right about "s," and, if I didn't so very much like to quibble about r's and l's, I'd admit he's really right about row 6. For the columns he is 5/8 right about "o" in vowel 1, he is 5/13 right about "i" in vowel 2. My third comment is that I wonder very much why the word 'GRID' at the top of the page is in quotation marks. Is it because he has invented the application of that term to this diagram, and isn't sure whether it will be accepted, or is it a bit of arcane jargon such as cryptanalysts might have been using?

I was going to start my paper with this *Work Note*, and my discussion by showing how and why Ventris got some signs in the wrong row or column of this 'grid', and how in later *Work Notes* he gradually got them almost all right. But I am quite content to draw all my conclusions from *Work Note* 1. For, of course, I read it when I received it 36 years ago. I believed then that as soon as he was able to work with all the texts, Knossos and Pylos together, it was inevitable that he would construct a "grid" whose elements were more numerous and more secure; it would be so nearly complete and secure that any suggested phonetic value would have to satisfy not only the word which suggested it, but the many words in which there occurred the three or four other signs with the same consonant, and the nine or ten other signs with the same vowel. At the top of the page he identifies this as the "State as at 28 Jan 1951 : before publication of Pylos inscriptions," which implies that it will soon change. To be sure, it would require a lot of work, and that is what is to be found in the other *Work Notes*.

As for the word "Pelasgian" in the title of this talk, I haven't precisely identified the evidence, but I may assure you that in the first *Work Note*, and in all except the last, he had no doubts; he was confident that when Linear B was finally deciphered he would find the language of the Linear B texts in the "Pelasgian solution."

REFERENCES

BENNETT, E. L., Jr.
1951 *The Pylos Tablets, a Preliminary Transcription.* New Haven, Yale U.P.

BLEGEN, C. W.
1939 Nestor's Palace at Pylos yields the first Mycenaean inscribed Tablets ever found on the Greek Mainland. *Illustrated London News*, 3 June 1939, 979-981.

BLEGEN, C. W. *and* KOUROUNIOTIS, K.
1939 Excavations at Pylos, 1939. *American Journal of Archaeology* 43, 563-570.

CHADWICK, J.
1958 *The Decipherment of Linear B*[1]. Cambridge, C.U.P.
1967 *The Decipherment of Linear B*[2]. Cambridge, C.U.P.
1973 Linear B. *Current Trends in Linguistics* 11, edited by Thomas A. Sebeok, Mouton, 537-568. Reprinted in VENTRIS 1988, 371-396.

DEECKE, W.
1884 Die griechisch-kyprischen Inschriften in epichorischer Schrift. Collitz, H., *Sammlung der griechischen Dialekt-Inschriften* I, 1-80, with table of the signary.

EVANS, A. E.
1894 Primitive Pictographs and a Prae-Phoenician Script, from Crete and the Peloponnese. *Journal of Hellenic Studies* 14, 270-372.
1900 Knossos 1900, *Annual of the British School at Athens* 6 (1899-1900), 3-70.
1909 *Scripta Minoa,* I. *The Written Documents of Minoan Crete with Special Reference to the Archives of Knossos.* Oxford, O.U.P.
1935 *The Palace of Minos*, vol. 4, part 2.
1952 *Scripta Minoa,* II. *The Archives of Knossos*, edited by J. L. Myres. Oxford, O.U.P.

GRUMACH, E.
1963 *Bibliographie der kretisch-mykenischen Epigraphik.* München, C. H. Beck.
1967 *Bibliographie der kretisch-mykenischen Epigraphik*, Supplement I. München, C. H. Beck.

KAHN, D.
1967 *The Codebreakers. The Story of Secret Writing.* New York, Macmillan.

KOBER, A. E.

1944 The "Adze" Tablets from Knossos. *American Journal of Archaeology* 48, 64-75.
1945 Evidence for Inflection in the "Chariot" Tablets from Knossos. *American Journal of Archaeology* 49, 143-151.
1948 *Tentative Arrangement of Linear B Inscriptions from Knossos according to Content.* New York, hectograph, for private circulation, 29 November, 1948.
1952 The Minoan Scripts: Fact and Theory. *American Journal of Archaeology* 52, 82-103.

MASSON, O.
1961 *Les inscriptions chypriotes syllabiques*[1]. *Études Chypriotes*, 1. Paris, de Boccard.
1983 *Les inscriptions chypriotes syllabiques*[2]. *Études Chypriotes*, 1. Paris, de Boccard.

POE, E. A.
1844 The Gold Bug. *Dollar Newspaper*, June 21, 28, 1843. Reprinted 1845 in *Tales*, New York, Wiley & Putnam.

SUNDWALL, J.
1914 Über die vorgriechische lineare Schrift auf Kreta. Ein Beitrag zur Geschichte des ägäischen Gebietes im zweiten Jahrtausend v. Chr. *Öfversigt af Finska Vetenskaps Societetens Förhandlinger* (B. *Humanistika Vetenskaper*) 56, 1913-1914, 1-36

VENTRIS, M.
1940 Introducing the Minoan Language. *American Journal of Archaeology* 44, 494-520.
1950 *The Language of the Minoan and Mycenaean Civilizations, New Year 1950*, (cover title: *Mid-Century Report*). London, for private circulation. Reprinted in VENTRIS 1988, 29-132.
1951 *Work Notes on Minoan Language Research.* London, for private circulation. Reprinted in VENTRIS 1988, 135-333.
1952 Deciphering Europe's Earliest Scripts on the Cretan Tablets. *The Listener*, 10 June 1952. Reprinted in VENTRIS 1988, 363-367.
1953 A Note on Decipherment Methods. *Antiquity* 27, 196-200.
1988 *Work Notes on Minoan Language Research and other unedited Papers*, edited by Anna Sacconi. *Incunabula Graeca* 90. Roma, Edizioni dell'Ateneo.

VENTRIS, M. *and* CHADWICK, J.
1953 Evidence for Greek Dialect in the Mycenaean Archives. *Journal of Hellenic Studies* 73, 84-103.
1956 *Documents in Mycenaean Greek*[1]. Cambridge, C.U.P.
1973 *Documents in Mycenaean Greek*[2]. Cambridge, C.U.P.

WEILL, R.
1903 La question de l'écriture linéaire dans la Méditerranée primitive. *Revue Archéologique,* sér. 4, t. 1, 213-232.

Institute for Research in the Humanities
Old Observatory
University of Wisconsin—Madison
Madison, WI 53706
U.S.A.

BCILL 49 : *Problems in Decipherment*, 25-37.

VENTRIS'S DECIPHERMENT — FIRST CAUSES

Maurice POPE
Oxford

First my text — Henry James as he might have been on a radio chat-show.

> *Presenter:* I wonder if anybody on the panel has any thoughts on corkscrews ? Yes, Henry ?
>
> *James:* Curious, is it not, how this small spiral device could never have been invented by the ingenious mind of man, were it not that the same ingenious mind had already devised... the wine-bottle - which itself ...required the prior invention not only of glass but also of fermented grape-juice. ... The corkscrew is at the end of a chain of so many inventions. But, and this is the question which puzzles me, whither does the corkscrew lead ?
>
> Miles Kington *The Independent* (11/1/88).

Emmett Bennett was not, like the rest of us at this congress, an *epigonos* of Michael Ventris, but a *progonos*. His accurate and orderly transcription of the Pylos Tablets provided the immediate material cause of the decipherment. I shall not dwell on the qualities, industry and ingenuity of course, but also integrity and faith, which it needed to become the Linnaeus of Mycenaeology. It would be embarrassing and unnecessary. What I am here for, what I have been asked to do, is to hymn *tous tou progonou progenesterous*, or, to use a fashionable metaphor, to delve for the roots of the decipherment. Particularly in the time of Leibnitz. The assignment may at first seem a little remote from present-day problems of decipherment and somewhat unexciting since one moral of the story is how slow. But there is a more encouraging way to look at the matter. There were not just a few men who did it all but a great many who each made a significant contribution.

I begin with Bennett's own precursors. Even the idea of accurate transcriptions needed precedent. Thomas Hyde, speaking in 1700 with the full authority of an Oxford academic about the Persepolis inscriptions, said (Hyde, 1700, 517) "There can be such things as trivial problems which are laboursome to solve and not worth the labour" *(Nugae aliquando sunt inventu difficiles et inventae nil prosunt).* On this view a short specimen of them, approximately copied, would have been enough to "put a period to all further curiosity" — a phrase from an article on Persepolis in *Philosophical Transactions* of 1693[1]. Luckily it was not this lazy, cost-accountant's, view that triumphed, but the opposite, Leibnitz's. "Always have your line out — the fish will be where you least expect it" *(Semper tibi pendeat hamus : Quo minime reris gurgite piscis erit)*[2]. And ever since there have been men who have sacrificed their time and energy to publish unintelligible material in the faith that it will one day become intelligible. Cornelis de Bruin and Carsten Niebuhr did this for Persian cuneiform; Niebuhr and after him the members of Napoleon's Expedition d'Égypte for Egyptian; Mecquenem for Proto-Elamite; Virolleaud for Ugaritic. Many more too. And of course the tradition still continues, witness the immaculately tailored new edition of Linear A that goes under the name of GORILA.

And there has been more than just hard work. There has been a whole staircase of technical improvement — photography, lithography, copper-plate, woodcuts, movable type.

The earliest full publication of a script, De Bruin's copperplates of Persepolis cuneiform was greeted by Leibnitz in 1715 (in the same letter as the one I have just quoted) as "an excellent work" which might one day lead to a solution *velut Cryptolytica arte,* by code-breaking means. This is nearly the first-ever mention of decipherment, but not quite. In 1677 Thomas Herbert called the Persepolis inscriptions "well worthy the scrutiny of those ingenious persons that delight themselves in the dark and difficult Art or Exercise of deciphering". No such hope is expressed by any earlier writer as far as I can discover[3].

But though Herbert scored a first here, he offered no plan of attack. Leibnitz did. In the same essay of 1715 he called for an accurate transcription of the corpus of the Palmyra inscriptions so that an alphabet could be drawn up and the character of the language eventually recognised *(Inde fortasse constitui Alphabetum posset et linguae indoles tandem cognosci).*

For obviously an alphabet can only be established after a full publication. A specimen is not enough.

This brings me to Bennett's other great contribution as *progonos* — the establishment of the Pylos Linear B signary.

---

1 *Philosophical Transactions* vol. XVII, n° 201 by F.A. Esq. The author is speaking of Chardin's specimen publication of the Persepolis inscriptions.

2 Leibnitz 1715, quoting Ovid *Ars Amatoria* 3. 425-6.

3 There is no mention of decipherment in the first edition of Herbert's book in 1634.

Needless to say Linear B was a much more complicated affair than the Palmyrene alphabet of twenty-two or so letters. It had well over a hundred different signs, all *sui generis*. Neither Bennett nor anybody else could have made any sense out of them of it had not been for a whole chain of prior discoveries. These made it highly probable that the script, like our own, consisted of logographic signs (including numerals) standing for whole words or ideas, and phonetic signs standing for whole syllables. A double helix, and if we follow the strands back to their origin — who first had the idea of an ideogram and who first had the idea of a syllabary — we shall get back to the time of Leibnitz and beyond.

I shall begin with the ideogram. Writing on the art of writing, Hermanus Hugo (1617, 37 and 61-2) pointed with approval to the specialized modern hieroglyphs used by astronomers and mathematicians, and believed that a general hieroglyphic system, as in China and Japan, might be best. Mastering 70 - 80 thousand different signs (the alleged size of the Chinese signary) would be well within the capacity of the learned, he said, and the ignorant could easily make do with fewer. One advantage would be no more language barrier. But that was a spin-off. Hieroglyphs were intrinsically superior. Nor was Hugo the only person to think so. Long before, Plotinus (*Enneads* 5, 8. 6) had said that an Egyptian priest could, by contemplating them, immediately apprehend reality without having to labour through letters, words and sentences; and this view had a great following in the renaissance among neoplatonists, among the creators of emblem literature, even in the Royal Society which encouraged attempts to invent a system of universal writing by means of "real characters".

In the years around 1660 over half a dozen separate attempts were published, culminating in a massive book brought out in 1668 by the Royal Society itself and written by its first secretary, John Wilkins, Bishop of Chester and former Master of both Wadham College Oxford and Trinity College Cambridge. The new system was to be better than either Egyptian or Chinese, the product not of accidental factors but of reason. It failed — the world has not adopted it — but its failure made two truths apparent. The first was that bricks did not automatically make a building. In the Lord's Prayer you could have logograms for FATHER, HEAVEN, BLESSING, NAME, KINGDOM, ARRIVAL, WILL, ACTION, and so on but there would be no understanding them unless they were bonded together grammatically. The second was that you could not write names at all or foreign words (like "amen") unless you had a class of phonetic signs.

This is where the two strands interlace. For the phonetic system which Wilkins invented to supplement his ideographic script was a syllabary. He presents it in a table with the vowels across the top of the page and the consonants down the left. A grid therefore, though not quite like Ventris's. It allowed for both open and closed syllables, and the symbols were more rational. The vowel signs were adjuncts to the consonants, like accents or diacritic marks, and attached on the left for closed syllables, on the right for open ones. The number of different symbols came to 174 for the open syllables, the same again for the closed ones, 29 bare consonants and 6 pure vowels — in all a repertoire of 393 signs.

Wilkins published in 1668. Even so we are not yet at the beginning. There was a grid seven years older, Wilkins's model[4]. This is a table of the Ethiopian signs by Jobus Ludolfus in 1661 in his *Grammatica Aethiopica*. It shows the 202 signs of the script arranged as an open syllabary with the vowel-adjuncts across the top and the consonants down the left. What is more, Ludolfus in his text refers to the table as a syllabary. He was the first to do so. The Ethiopians themselves, I am informed, never presented their signary in this way.

In earlier Latin the word *syllabarius* does occur[5], but it means a schoolboy in second grade who has mastered the names of the letters (as an *abecedarius*) and is now engaged in learning the syllables. In English the first use of the idea, though still not the actual word, that I have come across, is by Thomas Herbert, who remarks (1677, 141) that the Persepolis characters may stand for words or syllables "as in the Brachygraphy or Shortwriting we familiarly practise".

So here it looks as if we have the root of the "grid", with one tendril stretching towards Abyssinia and the Amharic script; one towards Utopia and "philosophic writing"; and another, less exalted, towards shorthand and cryptography.

Once the concept of a syllabary is in the air, diagnosing it is an easy step — or it ought to be. All you need do is count the separate signs in a script and draw your conclusion. A low number means an alphabet, an intermediate number a syllabary, and a very high number hieroglyphics. But easy or not the step was two hundred years in the taking.

For Egyptian indeed it was only ever half taken. In 1743 Pococke wrote that the number of separate hieroglyphs should be counted to see if their variety is so great "as to exceed the number of letters in any language". In 1790 Bruce did so and counted 514 separate signs — a distressing result. It was too many for "letters", far too few for a one-sign=one-word system except perhaps, Bruce suggested, if it were confined to a strictly specialized subject like astronomy. In 1797 Zoega counted 958, but pointed out that it was still possible to save the theory of a general-purpose ideographic script. Each sign could stand for more than one idea, determined by context; and paired signs might take on an altogether new meaning. Eventually Champollion (1824, 266) made good use of a sign-count, but a relative, not an absolute one. The 486 words of the Greek text of the Rosetta stone were represented by 1419 hieroglyphic signs, of which only 66 were different. This count made it impossible to go on supposing that the hieroglyphs were straightforward logograms, and was therefore a major staging-post in Champollion's decipherment.

---

4 Nevertheless a model that was not uncritically accepted. Wilkins (1668, 14) says that "all the Ethiopian characters are exceedingly complicated and perplexed", and claims that his own proposals are much less difficult.

5 In Petrus Damianus, *Lib. VI, Epist.* 17 IV.

In cuneiform the first sign-count was made by the Danish traveller Carsten Niebuhr in 1774. He produced a list of 42 signs for the simplest of the three Persepolis scripts, but did not commit himself to any conclusion.

That was to take another generation. In 1802 Grotefend drew a conclusion, but a wrong one. The signs, he said, were far too few for a *Zeichenschrift,* or even for a syllabary. They must be alphabetic, *Buchstaben,* and the reason for the rather large number must be that the script had signs for both long and short vowels. This was bad luck rather than bad theory. In fact Persian cuneiform is not a lavishly equipped alphabet but an economically equipped syllabary.

Rawlinson's decipherment of it in the 1830's made this clear; and the ensuing decipherments of other cuneiform scripts gave plenty of evidence about syllabaries of various sizes. Even so when Hyde Clarke in 1872 proved by a distribution curve that the Hama script (what we now call Luwian) was genuine writing because out of a known corpus of three hundred characters only 59 of them were different and occurred with different frequencies just like the signs of any phonetic script, he did not conclude that 59 characters must mean an open syllabary but suggested values as if he expected them to be alphabetic.

Cypriot writing, which had been discovered a few years before, was rapidly recognized as syllabic. But this was was because of a biscript, five signs representing the eight Greek letters of *Karyx emi,* and not because there were 55 signs. At least I cannot find anyone who argued for a syllabary on this basis.

But the step was about to be finally taken. A.H. Sayce, reading a paper on the Hama inscriptions to the Society of Biblical Archaeology in May 1876, stated firmly that 56 different characters were too many for an alphabet, too few for a complete system of hieroglyphics, "and this, coupled with the fact that the separate words consist of several characters, proves clearly that we have to deal with a syllabary", plus perhaps some determinatives and some ideograms. He was right, and the decipherment proceeded, slowly but successfully, for the next fifty years on this assumption.

And within twenty years the same assumption was made by Evans in his very first publication on Cretan writing, a letter to the *Athenaeum* in April 1894, where he says that the number of 80 separate signs (for what we now call the first palace script) makes it certain to have been a syllabary, probably related to the "asianic" and to the Cypriot.

When he discovered the later scripts, which he labeled Linear A and Linear B, Evans was equally certain that they contained syllabaries because of the number of the signs. This certainty was taken over by Kober and by Ventris (Ventris, 1953, 85), and it was an essential stepping-stone to the decipherment.

There would seem nothing very complicated about it. But laying it took over 200 years and at least twelve distinct operations.

Another great feature of Ventris's decipherment which filled the layman with awe and the hierophant with knowing pride was the labio-velar. The knowingness was, for many of us I fear, a recent acquisition. Archaeologists and run-of-the-mill classicists of my generation were not taught in any detail about Indo-European Languages. That was "philology". But it was neighbouring territory and accessible. When we explored it we could at once see how obvious it was that there must have been a common origin for the sounds in *-te* and *-que*, and in *pente*, *funf* and *quinque*.

But obvious or not finding it had taken a long time. Here again there were many stages, many spirals in the cork-screw. As far as I can see the word labio-velar was created by Karl Brugmann in 1885. Curtius in 1862 had used "labialism" and "dentalism" and had given a slightly different account of the phenomena. And the problem had been worked on by at least four other German scholars since Bopp first raised it in 1833. What made a precise explanation necessary was of course "Grimm's Law" and the discovery that sound-changes in language followed regular patterns. And what prompted this was the discovery of language groups. This is normally attributed to Sir William Jones, the friend of Dr Johnson, who went out to Calcutta in 1783, learned to "converse familiarly in Sanskrit", was "astonished at the resemblance between that language and both Greek and Latin"[6], and went on to argue (as a proposition "capable of incontestable proof") that the Persians and Indians, the Romans, Greeks, and Goths "originally spoke the same language"[7]. Equally "undisputed and undisputable", he said, was the existence of a second "family of nations" that included the Jews, Arabs, Assyrians, Syriac-speakers, and numerous tribes of Abyssinians. A third family probably included all the other inhabitants of Asia, "and consequently, as it might be proved, of the whole earth, sprung from three branches of one stem". These are, as you would expect from an eighteenth century scholar, the sons of Noah, but they are the sons of Noah scientifically considered. Jones works out that a few thousand years is far more than enough to populate the world "to its present state of luxuriance" if one assumes that each person has two children, and that indeed "the earth would not now have room for its multiplied inhabitants" but for the devastations of wars and plagues and famines and floods. [The calculation is correct: all one needs is a maintained increase of 10 % a generation, counting a generation as 25 years.]

Now this is where the standard account of the pedigree of the idea ends. However Jones was by no means the first to recognize elements in common between German and Greek or even German and Persian. Lipsius in 1598 commented on the remarkable parallels in vocabulary between Persian and German (Lipsius, 1602, letter 44); so did Joseph Scaliger, who died in 1609 (Scaliger, 1666, 239). Boxhorn, in 1654, pointed to the remarkable similarities borne by Welsh both to German and Persian and to Latin and Greek (Boxhorn,

---

6 Letter to Thomas Caldicott, Sept 27th 1787.

7 In his Ninth Anniversary Discourse to the Asiatic Society of Calcutta, delivered on 23rd February 1792.

1654, chapter 6). And this was accepted by Wilkins and by Leibnitz and by everybody else. What distinguished Jones was not his view of the closeness of these languages or even of an extinct common source for the common factors in them — that is in Boxhorn — but his view of linguistic families. The 17th century view of a language was that it was like a muesli. What made one different from another was that its elements were mixed in different proportions. Thus Wilkins, in his chapter on linguistic change (Wilkins, 1668, chapter 2), speaks entirely about vocabulary. He never mentions grammar at all.

Leibnitz had the same view. Though be is well aware of the strong similarity between, for instance, Celtic and Greek numerals, he attributes it to borrowing[8]. Persian is simply a more mixed language than many others, while Lithuanian is a veritable "Mischmasch"[9]. No more than Wilkins does he ever mention the idea of grammatical structure as being the essence of a language or a common grammatical structure being able to link languages into a family.

Yet this is the position that Jones assumes, and since he assumes it without argument he must have inherited it from a predecessor, not constructed it for himself. But who was this predecessor ? As far as I know the vacancy has never been advertised, let alone filled.

I should like to propose a candidate for it who seems to me very well qualified, Dr William Wotton. Born in 1666 to a father who had lived for a long time with Meric Casaubon, and who brought him up on Casaubon's principles, he showed himself to be an infant prodigy, being admitted to Cambridge at the age of 10 and graduating at the age of 13. Thereafter be pursued a moderately successful career in the church as a learned divine. He was a friend of both Newton and Bentley and on one occasion a co-author with Leibnitz. It is this occasion which interests us. Leibnitz and Wotton each contributed an essay to an ambitious book by John Chamberlayne publishing over 150 versions of the Lord's Prayer in different languages. Leibnitz's essay was the one in which he suggested proper names as the proper starting point for a decipherment. Wotton's was on the Confusion of Tongues at Babel[10]. It was intended to support the interest of true religion by proving that the miracle must have taken place as and when the Bible says it did, as against "the Freethinkers of this Age *(libertini huius saeculi)* who wish to throw

---

8 See Leibnitz's letter to M. Pezron, written in February 1699. The first person I know of to argue the case that shared numerals must indicate affinity, not borrowing, is James Parsons, who claims the idea as his own (Parsons, 1767, XVIII).

9 Leibnitz's own word — see the proposals he put forward to Peter the Great in 1712.

10 After Wotton's death his executors published his essay in English on the grounds (perhaps rather exaggerated) that the original Latin had been printed "with great Disadvantage both to the Author and the Reader. The frequent Mistakes committed <in> it, were so obvious that they could not escape without Censure". The English and the Latin texts are closely parallel, but neither is a consistent, let alone a slavish, translation of the other and I would judge that they are both from Wotton's own hand.

aside the Mosaic History and give Credit to the most fabulous Accounts of other Nations which boast of the greatest Antiquity". The cause was destined to be lost, but it was an important one at the time and espoused by eminent men. Wotton thought he had discovered and could bring to bear a totally new argument. This was the classification of languages by grammar.

The most obvious deduction to be drawn from the specimens of the Lord's Prayer printed in Chamberlayne's book, Wotton argues, is that new sub-species of language can readily emerge. The Romance languages had a common mother in Latin, the Germanic languages had a common mother in Teutonic[11], "and there are several such common originals in the World (*multae communes originales*)". "The Gradation and Derivation of different Dialects from a common Stock" is not to be denied. But this is not the same as "the actual Formation of some essentially different Tongue". Different classes of language "tho' they may have some few Words in common, yet have a quite distinct Frame and Make (*forma*) from others; and this Frame and Make runs through (*percurrit*), and is manifestly visible in their Subdivisions, and has been so from all Antiquity". Thus in the "western and northern" languages (by which he means Latin, Greek, German, etc.) nouns are varied by their termination, verbs have two voices, active and passive, prepositions can be prefixed to verbs, possessive pronouns are distinct words, adjectives have comparatives and superlatives: all these things are different in the Hebrew-related languages.

The confirmation of this is what happens when words are borrowed. *Dharaba* is an Arabic word. We borrow it as "drub", and then treat it as an English word, so that we can be drubbed, give drubbings, and so on.

"In a word the essential Difference of one Language from another is to be taken from their respective *Grammars,* rather than from their *Vocabularies".*

We now come to the point. In respect of grammar all languages of which we know enough history to judge have remained stable or at least mutually recognizable for two or even three thousand years. What is more there is a great number of other languages — in Europe Finnish, Estonian, Lettish and Hungarian; elsewhere the multitudinous languages of China, of the Far East, and of America. For them all to go back to a common beginning either the freethinkers must be right and the world immeasurably old or "we must recur to Moses" and acknowledge that the different classes of language ("I enquire not how

---

[11] The descent of the Teutonic languages, including English, from an original "Gothick" had recently been argued in detail by George Hickes *(Institutiones Grammaticae Anglo-Saxonicae et Moeso-Gothicae* 1789 and *Linguarum veterum septentrionalium Thesaurus grammatico-criticus et archaeologicus* 2 vols. 1705). Wotton was so impressed by the *Thesaurus,* a massive work, that he compiled and published a Latin summary of it in 1708. However the concept of grammar as the form or essence of a language does not seem to be foreshadowed either by Hickes or in Wotton's summary. Wotton must have developed it entirely between 1708 and 1714 (the completion date of his essay *de confusione linguarum* to Chamberlayne).

many") were "formed at once in the Confusion of Babel by the same Almighty Hand that taught Adam and Eve to speak at the Creation and empowered the Apostles to speak with new Tongues at the great Pentecost".

The idea was undoubtedly Wotton's own. His purpose was to prove a point of divinity not of linguistics, and it would have helped his case if he could have pointed to a predecessor. Moreover he says clearly that he did not have one, explicitly calls the idea his own, "this notion of mine" *(opinio mea)* and tells us not only that it was sparked by Chamberlayne's project but also that he had apprehensively consulted others about it.

However Wotton's idea, like Hilaire Belloc's Miss Charming, "is now accepted everywhere". It would seem right therefore for his name to be included among the fathers of the Indo-European hypothesis and *a fortiori* of the Indo-European labio-velar.

I have now followed some of the spirals of the corkscrew some of the way. But I shall go no further. To trace the Trojan War back to the twin egg or the Argonauts' expedition to the axe that cut down the first fir-tree on Mt Pelion is the classic mark of a bore[12]. Instead, let me end with the question I began with. Whither does the corkscrew lead.

It is obviously a twisty problem. Nobody at a higher point in the spiral could have predicted the next step after their own contribution. Looking back all one can say is that the ideas have constantly taken a new turn. But was each new turn inevitable ? Would somebody else have deciphered Linear B by now if Ventris had not ? Would the signs have been classified by somedoby else if it had not been for Emmett Bennett ? And so on. Each new idea certainly came as a single spy and not in a battalion, but did it come on a chain of necessity ? Or was each step taken because of time and chance and human personality ?

It would seem to me absurd to suppose that each tiny step was pre-destined — even more absurd to suppose that the journey was pre-destined but not the steps. On the other hand the destination was manifestly pre-destined ! Linear B could only be deciphered as an early form of Greek, the Egyptian hieroglyphics as an

---

[12] Already in 1194 Giraldus Cambrensis in his *Descriptio Cambriae,* I vi and I xv (Rolls Series vol VI, 177, 194), had noted some Welsh words, including the numerals five *(pûmp)* and ten *(dec),* which bore a striking resemblance to their Greek or Latin equivalents. With what would now be considered highly commendable restraint he simply notes that the languages conform *(conveniunt)* in these particulars and erects no hypothesis on the observation.
Roger Bacon may also claim precursor status in the field. He classed what we now call the Romance languages as "idioms" *(idiomata)* of Latin, just as English and Teutonic, he says, are "idioms" of each other, also Hebrew and Chaldee (*Gram Gr.* 26-7, *Op. Maius* 89, *Op. Tertium* 90, *C.S. Phil.* 438). I should like to thank Dr David Howlett and Richard Sharpe of the *Dictionary of medieval Latin from British Sources* for showing me these yet-to-be-published references.

early form of Coptic, and so on. But we can go back to the other hand again. For the destination need not have been reached. The train might never have started. It needed curiosity. So perhaps the very First Cause of the decipherment was a desire to know the truth.

But it is not my purpose to argue, like the devils in Milton, of fate, freewill, and knowledge absolute or to lose myself in wandering mazes. I merely wish to point out that the corkscrew has a philosophic bent.

It also has a practical one. Our own value to the world. Three personal experiences make me feel that we have been far too shy about this in the past and that we should trumpet the achievements of our subject. Or at least get them heard of in schools. The first of these experiences concerns Erasmus. When I was working on the *de Pronuntiatione* (the earliest decipherment ever published because its subject is the forgotten values of the Greek and Roman letters), people, educated people, used often to say to me "But we don't really know how Latin was pronounced, do we ?" And this was 450 years after Erasmus had given a popular account of the matter — the scholarship had been done twenty or thirty years earlier. People do not go up to astronomers like this and ask "But we don't really know, do we, whether it is the sun that moves or the earth ?" My second experience was when a son of mine was in Iran, and people, educated people, used to come up to me and ask if he had been posted there because he speaks Arabic. They had never heard of Persian being Indo-European, or indeed of Indo-European at all, and as for the concept that it was possible to use an Arabic script for a non-Arab language, well, they would politely agree but it was obvious they did not believe it. My third experience is even closer to our present concern. We are all decipherers, and 80 % of us successful ones. But up to 20 % of people fail to solve the problem and risk being labeled dyslexic. Not so long ago I found myself interested in this and spent some two months reading books and articles on dyslexia by medical men, psychologists, educationists, and ophthalmologists. The result, if not to freeze the blood, to harrow the soul and to make one's two eyes start from their spheres, was at least to raise the eyebrows. One of the causes given for dyslexia (and I was reading the learned literature not popular magazines) was the inability to master "man's last acquired accomplishment". As if a person who could not read was somehow stranded half-way between human-being and orang-utang ! Another alleged cause was "developmental immaturity" in not being able to proceed from left to right. Fall out both Hebrews and Arabs ! Most articles assumed that the English alphabet was the only one: writers who had heard of Greek or Russian letter-forms or of Hebrew and Arabic sinistroverse scripts stood out as Apollos of enlightenment. Almost nobody knew of the word phoneme, let alone understood what it meant. There was talk of "enunciating letters", of "visually recognizing word-patterns", and of "phonically irregular words". (This last not meaning "foreign-sounding" but "spelt surprisingly".) And although all the tangible evidence points to mirror-image letters (like lower-case p and q, b and d) being a prime cause of difficulty, none of the authors I read who discussed this fact ever showed any awareness that there are scripts (including our own capital letters) where this problem does not exist or asked themselves whether this might or might not make any difference[13].

Now I do not mean to imply that we should all abandon our researches on ancient scripts and devote ourselves to the betterment of primary education as Champollion once very nearly did. But we should stand up for ourselves and point out to the public that while it is no doubt desirable to be numerate it is just as important if not more so to be literate: and that at the present time they are not literate, but a hundred years or two hundred years or even four hundred years out of date. And that we grammatologists can help them.

The claim may sound arrogant, but it is in the spirit of Leibnitz, who once drew up a memoir telling Peter the Great what he ought to do.

BIBLIOGRAPHY

BOXHORN, Marcus
1654 *Originum Gallicarum liber,* Amsterdam.

BRUCE, James
1790 *Travels to discover the Source of the Nile,* Edinburgh.

BRUGMANN, Karl
1885 *Griechische Grammatik,* Munich.

BRUIN, Cornelis de
1698 *Reizen, etc. etc.* Delft.

CHAMBERLAYNE, John
1715 *Oratio Dominica in diversas omnium fere gentium linguas versa,*

CHAMPOLLION, Jean-François
1824 *Précis du système hiéroglyphique des anciens Égyptiens,* Paris.

---

13 My reading on the subject of dyslexia, though intensive, was inevitably not exhaustive. There may therefore exist literate treatments of the subject that I have missed. If so I should like to apologise pre-emptively to their authors, and in any case to exempt specifically one book, *Dyslexia or Illiteracy ?,* C. Young and P. Tyre, Milton Keynes, 1983, from my general condemnation.

CLARKE, Hyde
1872 Notes on the script of the Hama Inscriptions, *Unexplored Syria* by Richard Burton and Tyrwhitt Drake, London, 1972, vol. 1, 352-60.

CURTIUS, Georg
1862 *Grundzuge der griechischen Etymologie,* Leipzig.

EVANS, Arthur John
1894 Letter from Candia, *The Athenaeum,* June 23rd.

GROTEFEND, G.F.
1802 Praevia de cuneatis, quas vocant, inscriptionibus Persepolitanis, legendis et explicandis relatio, *Göttingen gelehrten Anzeiger,* 3, 1481-7.

HERBERT, Thomas
1677 *A Description of the Persian Monarchy,* 3rd ed., London.

HUGO, Hermanus
1617 *De prima scribendi origine et universa rei litterariae antiquitate,* Antwerp.

HYDE, Thomas
1700 *Historia religionis veterum Persarum,* London, 1700.

JONES, sir William
1821 *Letters,* 2 vols, London.

LEIBNITZ, G.W. von
1715 see CHAMBERLAYNE 1715.
1768 *Opera Omnia,* ed. Dutens, Geneva.

LIPSIUS, Iustus
1602 *Epistolarum Selectarun Centuria Tertia ad Belgas,* Antwerp.

LUDOLPHUS, Job
1661 *Lexicon Aethiopico-Latinum... cui accessit Authoris Grammatica...,* London.

NIEBUHR, Carsten
1774 *Reisebeschreibung nach Arabien...,* Copenhagen.

PARSONS, James
1767 *Remains of Japhet: being historical enquiries into the affinity and origin of the European languages,* London.

POCOCKE, Richard
1743 *A Description of the East,* London.

RAWLINSON, Henry Creswick
1846 The Persian cuneiform inscription at Behistun deciphered and translated, *Journal of the Royal Asiatic Society,* 10, London.

SAYCE, A.H.
1876 The Hamathite Inscriptions, *Transactions of the Society of Biblical Archaeology,* 5, 22-32.

SCALIGER, J.J.
1666 *Scaligeriana sive Excerpta de ore J. Scaligeri per F.F.P.P.,* ed. Vossius, The Hague.

VENTRIS, Michael and CHADWICK, John
1953 Evidence for Greek Dialect in the Mycenaean Archives, *Journal of Hellenic Studies* 1953, 84-103.

WILKINS, John
1668 *An Essay toward a real Character and a philosophical Language,* London.

WOTTON, William
1715 *De confusione linguarum Babylonica,* v. CHAMBERLAYNE 1715.
1731 *A Discourse concerning the confusion of languages at Babel; proving it to have been miraculous... contrary to the opinion of Leclerk and others. With and enquiry into the primitive language before that remarkable event,* London.

Elmwood
26, Lathbury Road
Oxford OX2 5AU
England

BCILL 49 : *Problems in Decipherment*, 39-58.

THE POSSIBLE METHODS IN DECIPHERING THE PICTOGRAPHIC CRETAN SCRIPT*

Jean-Pierre OLIVIER

National Fund for Scientific Research (Belgium)

First of all, the title of my communication—which was suggested to me by the organizers and which I accepted too quickly—has to be slightly modified.[1] I shall speak about "The *problems* in deciphering the *hieroglyphic* Cretan script." Of course, a close examination of these problems—or 'difficulties', if you prefer—will automatically lead us to speak about some methodological approaches towards a decipherment. In fact, there are quite a lot of these problems when we study the so-called 'first Cretan script'.

We can sort these problems into three general categories, arranged in order of increasing complexity:

I. The *first category* has a unique item. It is the problem of *terminology*; and it is relatively simple to define, if not to resolve satisfactorily.

II. The *second category* contains the *practical* problems. There are many of them. Some are solvable, others are not—in the present stage of our documentation, at least—but they are certainly difficulties which can be surmounted. And at the end of the work now underway, we probably shall be able to say "such is the *status quæstionis*" and "such are the possibilities."

III. The *third* category consists in *methodological* problems; and, under this pompous heading, are in fact hidden all the unsolvable questions, which means, of course, the serious ones.

---

* I would like to express my thanks to Miss Patricia Robins who kindly corrected my English.

1 In figures I use the following abbreviations: H = Cretan hieroglyphic; A = Linear A; B = Linear B; MA = Mallia; KN = Knossos; PH = Phaistos.

I. TERMINOLOGICAL PROBLEM

This problem concerns the very name of the script itself. The discoverer of the script, A.J. Evans, christened it 'hieroglyphic'. But he spoke also of 'conventionalized pictographs' for its signs; and some people, among whom we may include our honoree, Emmett L. Bennett, JR., prefer to call it 'pictographic' according to Evans' alternative appellation.

The honorable gentleman who spoke before me at the Burdick-Vary symposium proposed, in 1967 at the First International Congress of Mycenology in Rome, that we name the script which we are here discussing the 'First Cretan Palatial Script'. He had a very good reason: he stressed that the appellations 'hieroglyhic' and 'pictographic' misrepresent the script, because it is a phonetic script, in the same degree as its two relatives Linear A and Linear B, being, like them, an open syllabary. And he demonstrated this fact very convincingly and definitely. I wish to add, that he also brought forward evidence that the inscriptions on seals and the inscriptions on accounting documents are of a different nature one from the other and are, therefore, to be taken into consideration separately. We shall return to this crucial point later.

To quote Maurice Pope in his own words: "To call the script 'hieroglyphic' suggests a dubious analogy with Egyptian; to call it 'pictographic' may be misleading, and is certainly question-begging. The name that I would suggest, in default of better candidate, is 'First Cretan Palace Script'." This attractive suggestion was proposed more than twenty years ago, and we can now consider two points: (1) how it was received by people working in the field; and (2) whether it still holds up in the light of more recent evidence.

In regard to the first point, we can say categorically that it was not generally adopted: scholars are keeping to their old habits. CHADWICK 1987, for instance, in his recent succinct introductory survey of Aegean scripts, still uses the terms 'hieroglyphic inscriptions'; and Emmett Bennett himself, in his letters concerning this meeting, still prefers 'Minoan pictographic script'. So the proposed usage did not become widespread; and the old—and false or at least ambiguous—appellations remain.

In regard to the second point, unless we concentrate on 'archives' documents (hereafter 'archival') only—which is not unthinkable, but not really possible—we have now a sure attestation of our script *before* the palatial period (which traditionally begins at the MM I B [ca 1900 B.C.]). I am making an allusion to the so-called 'Arkhanes script' which appears on seals at the beginning of MM I A [ca 2050 B.C.]. Even if, as is probable, the 'Arkhanes Script' is not a true script in its own right but rather an ancestor of our 'hieroglyphic-pictographic' script, doubt is still permissible. In conclusion, 'palatial' certainly has to be rejected as a proper designation of the 'hieroglyphic-pictographic' script; and 'first' probably also should be rejected. Of course 'first palatial', taken together as a unit, is perhaps not untrue, but it seems a little too risky and misleading in my opinion.

Personally, since there is no ideal solution nor consensus, I am tempted to practice the politics of expediency. I propose to continue calling the writing system under discussion 'hieroglyphic'. We do at least know that it has nothing to do with hieroglyphic Egyptian. This applies equally to the origin of its signs—this is absolutely certain—and to the nature of the language it represented—this is not yet completely demonstrable, but nevertheless is highly probable. Lastly, it is certain that this script has nothing especially 'sacral' about it.

So, let's keep the less adequate and the most popular terminology, but let's make an effort always to add 'Cretan' in front of it, in order that other scholars be certain about the object of our discourse.

II. PRACTICAL PROBLEMS

These are of two kinds, *quantitative* problems and *qualitative* problems.

1) The quantitative problems:

In fact, there is only one problem of this type: *the quantity of our documentation* is, and seems to have a tendency to remain, dramatically poor. The paucity of the material can be illustrated by quoting some figures which are to be compared with the corresponding figures for Linear A and B. You will see the details in figure 1.

For the Cretan Hieroglyphic Script, we have 270 documents and 1537 signs, representing respectively 4% and 2% of the whole collection of data for Cretan-Mycenaean writing.

But we shall see later that from these 270 documents, 150 are seals or impressions of seals (with 560 signs) and must be used only with great caution.

Not only is the number of documents low, but the rate at which they are being found is slowing down significantly, especially in comparison with the period of the first discoveries at the end of the last century. Cf. figure 2.

Evans found the first archives in Knossos in 1900. It represents 61 inscriptions with 615 signs.[2] Incidentally, an erratic tablet—and only one—in hieroglyphic script was found in 1901 at Phaistos[3] (moreover, some people think it is written in Linear A). After that we have to wait until 1923, when Renaudin and Charbonneaux found in the Palace at Mallia 24 inscriptions with 189 signs.[4] Next we have to be patient until 1968 for the beginning of the next significant batch of

2 Published by himself in 1909.
3 It was published along with the Knossian pieces by Evans.
4 Published by CHAPOUTHIER 1930.

discoveries: 21 inscriptions with 79 signs excavated by Poursat in the *Quartier Mu of Mallia*;[5] the ultimate document of this series appeared in 1977.

These are the three landmarks. You can see that the interval between discoveries is becoming longer every time and that every time also the finds are becoming less significant in the number of documents as well as in the number of signs. Of course, it is perhaps a mere coincidence, but if we extrapolate the trend, we shall be dealing with negative numbers in 1992.

I hope it is only a joke, and nobody can say what will happen tomorrow. But we have been waiting since 1977 now, and MM II destruction levels —the good period for hieroglyphic—were excavated in Mallia again, at Monastiraki, in NW Crete and elsewhere, but without yielding hieroglyphic inscriptions; on the other hand, perhaps significantly, some bits of Linear A are found almost every year.

Perhaps we should assume that it is not just a coincidence that the hieroglyphic inscriptions are so rare. Looking for probable reasons for this scarcity of finds, we can propose two:

1. the more ancient a level at a Minoan site, especially a continuously inhabited palatial site, is, the more it has a chance to have been destroyed by the successive occupations. As a matter of fact, neither the pieces of archives from Knossos nor the ones from Mallia Palace were found *in situ*, but mixed with earth in fillings associated with more recent structures;

2. the nature of the documentation, as we shall soon see, is perhaps in a significant manner different from the the nature of documentation in Linear A and Linear B. Consequently it might be that the extent of literacy, on clay at least, was different, too. But the hieroglyphic script was fortunately not only written on clay (and seals): we have one lapidary inscription of 16 signs (from Mallia; it was found by a peasant in his field) and about a dozen inscribed vases (generally from Mallia too). (See figure 3.) So we are permitted to entertain some hopes.

The average of signs per document for the three Cretan scripts is about 10. Thus we can see no significant difference between these scripts (but it has to be noticed that the difference between the kind of support of the script plays an important role).

In conclusion, a serious problem exits here; we only have about 1000 signs in 'Cretan hieroglyphic' (1500 if we include signs on seals). According to large typewriting standards, this total represents less than a single page (1800 signs and blanks) of our normal roman signs (in my hieroglyphic font, displayed in 9 point, 1800 signs and blanks are just kept on one page: fig. 4). Of course, I am not forgetting that the hieroglyphic script is a syllabary, so that two or three times more information can be concealed by a single sign than in an alphabet, but this is a matter of detail. Half a page, one page, two pages . . . what difference? (On the

---

5 Published by GODART and OLIVIER 1978.

same basis, Linear B 'weighs' more than thirty pages, and Linear A a little more than seven pages.) This problem is certainly the most serious which confronts us, and there is no substantial hope for an 'intellectual' solution: only more lucky excavations, quickly published, can change this picture.

2) The qualitative problems

I refer, first, to the quality of the documentation itself and, second, to the quality of the editions at our disposal. So we are not speaking about the same kind of quality. In the first case the term 'nature' would probably be more appropriate. But I hope my meaning will be clear.

a) The documentation itself

1°) As a whole:

There is here a real problem, and not a recent one. Indeed, Evans left for Crete to search for seals with pictographs, or with 'hieroglyphic script', if you prefer. Incidentally, he also excavated the Palace of Knossos and found there not only an archive in Linear B and a few tablets in Linear A, but also documents in hieroglyphic script (not an archive really, but remains from an earlier deposit).

Here it must be stressed that his whole conception of the Cretan scripts was strongly influenced by the views he had about the hieroglyphic seals he first studied. Therefore, he presented the evidence in such a way that many people are still convinced that the most important and most numerous part of the hieroglyphic 'Corpus' is the group of inscriptions on seals and sealings. It is true that we have more seals than other documents (150 against 120 for the moment); but the seals bear only *ca.* 560 signs vs. 977 on the other documents. Moreover, quite a lot of the seals bear the same sign-groups, alone or in combination with other sign-groups, so we have only *ca.* 300 *useful* signs on the seals (and this figure is a maximum). The conclusion is that, quantitatively speaking, we have about three times more useful evidence on archival documents than on seals.

But is the value of the two sets of documents *qualitatively* equal? Maurice Pope, in the same communication in Rome to which I have already referred, cast a strong suspicion on the documentary value of the 'inscriptions' on seals, as I previously mentioned. He spoke of 'dubious' writing, and he was quite right. In most of the cases we are confronted with an 'ornamental' or 'decorative' writing and the main purpose of the seal (or, more exactly, of the sealing) was not to be read, that is, it was not intended to convey a 'legible', 'unique' and 'unambiguous' meaning. Pope wrote, very sensibly, "We cannot tell whether the seal inscriptions communicated awe, prestige, or pleasure, but they are unlikely to have conveyed serious information."

Without going so far (some information, sometimes serious, was probably conveyed; but we are quite unable to say exactly in what measure), we have to convince ourselves that all scientific study of the Cretan hieroglyphic script must start from the real inscriptions, that means the archival inscriptions mainly (plus the few vase inscriptions and the unique stone inscription). For palaeographical studies, of course, we have to consider, without fear, the seals, on the condition that we make a careful distinction between the signs of the script and the signs which are not of the script (the latter being 'emblematic' or more simply 'decorative'). Such a distinction is sometimes far from evident, but, once made, given that the signs on the seals are generally more 'monumentally' executed than on the clay documents, the results are often very useful. Here I must emphasize that, when I use the term 'monumental', I do not mean to imply that the script of the archives is, in contrast, a 'real cursive': the link between the two is almost always evident, which is not the case when we are in front of a real cursive script, e.g., Egyptian hieratic, in contrast to a real monumental script, e.g., Egyptian hieroglyphic. In the case of the Egyptian writing systems, the link between them is not evident at all, except to extremely well trained specialists; and we can speak of two different scripts. This is absolutely not true of the Cretan hieroglyphic on seals and on archival documents, where we still have one, and only one, script.

So the seals prove useful in palaeographical studies, if we always start, of course, from the point of view of the archival documents and not vice versa. But also the seals are useful in comparative studies, too, because some sign-groups (probably less than a dozen) appear both on the seals and on the other documents. In this we are rather fortunate because in order to understand—we could perhaps say 'to decipher'?—our material, it is essential to have bridges between the two sets of documents, even though, and perhaps because, they are so different.

But let us not get ahead of ourselves. In any case, no study can start—as Evans did and many people after him have—from the seals. It will always be better to risk missing a small piece of evidence than to introduce a distorted, or even a completely wrong bit of evidence, in an edition first, and secondly in an analysis of the material.

Enough said about the seals. Anyway, it is unlikely that I shall save anyone from the temptation of overestimating the value of the seal documentation by any such discussion or demonstration. In the same way, it will always be more tempting for some people to rotate tables or even the Phaistos disk than to take serious trouble in studying dusty and broken pieces of archives. This is all that there is to say about the *quality* of the documentation as a whole.

2°) The archival documentation

N.B.: The quality of the stone inscription and of the vase inscriptions is obvious, but the total textual material they provide is too limited to give us many clues. Some difficulties can be encountered in the stone inscription because no word-dividers are marked, but that is another problem.

By saying 'quality' I mean 'quality' in comparison with the material we have in Linear A and Linear B.

As far as we can judge, we have in front of us extremely difficult material; and this is one of the reasons why study of it has made such little progress between 1909 and today.

The difficulties we confront in studying this material are as follows:

a) a lot of documents are not complete;

b) some of them, even complete, bear very few signs;

c) we are not always able to say in what direction the sign groups, complete or incomplete, are to be read. Of course, there is the so-called 'initial cross' but its function, although becoming clearer and clearer, is not always unambiguous. So this cross is not always a help to us in determining the direction in which an inscription is to be read.

d) we are not always able to say how a document, even if complete, has to be 'taken', in the real sense of the term 'taken into the hands'. This is a practical, let us say a 'pinacological', question; and the most frequent answer is that a lot of these complex documents (the quadrangular 'bars' for instance) were written in several steps, perhaps by different people, while they were hanging by a thread from a container or something of this sort. So the process of writing was not especially easy, nor was the process of re-reading, nor is the process of editing the texts now.

And, last but not least, though the scribes were not writing a real cursive, they were certainly writing rather hastily (you can see this, for instance, in all the signs with dots at the end of some lines: the dot and the line ought to touch each other but in many cases there are a few millimeters between dot and line); and, let us repeat, the scribes were writing rather carelessly in the case of the bars (which represent almost half of our archival documentation in number of documents, but more than 70% in terms of total textual material), due to the particular circumstances of writing. We certainly have all had in our adventurous lives the opportunity of writing something on a hanging label or tag which was tied by too short a thread to a badly positioned object, a suitcase for instance. So my meaning is easily understood. Remember, too, that, in the case of the hieroglyphic scribe, the bar was made from crude clay, so he had to treat it gently so that he would not press his fingers on a part previously inscribed, or accidentally deform its shape, or even accidentally detach the bar from the object to which it was connected.

Fortunately for the Minoans and the Mycenaeans, these complex suspended documents written on clay are only attested in 'hieroglyphic' times. And even in these times, 'normal' bars, i.e., bars without a hole for suspension, were used in Knossos and Mallia. I think they were used for conveying another type of information, much closer to the information given by the majority of the Linear A and B documents. This last type of document (the unperforated clay bar) is still attested in Linear A, but only at Mallia, in a deposit where we find hieroglyphic and Linear A together. Elsewhere it is absent, as it is in Linear B.

Are these phenomena to be related to the general tendency towards simplification which we observe in the whole history of the Cretan scripts (such a tendency is very obvious in the system of notation of the numerals and also apparent in the layout of the documents)? Or do we have, in the Knossian hanging bars, something special and, given the paucity of our material, perhaps over-represented, due to the hazards of excavation?

I presume that there is some degree of truth in these two suppositions, but any proof is out of the question for the moment. If this is so, we should not expect the quality, or more exactly the nature, of the greater part of the documentation written on clay archives in Cretan hieroglyphic to be exactly the same as the documentation written on clay archives in the other scripts. Nor should this be surprising. There are still rather strong suspicions that the Linear A and Linear B documents of archives which we have do not convey exactly the same kind of registration: the information seems to be more local for Linear A, more central (that is 'palatial') for Linear B. What kind of differentiation is to be found on the clay hieroglyphic bars? I have some ideas about this question, but they are not pertinent to the subject of this paper.

b) The editions

The quality of the editions is probably the most important problem after the problem of the paucity of the documentation. And the two are ineluctably tied together, because the rarer the data the more difficult they are to edit, independent of the peculiar difficulties they present in and of themselves. Of course, everybody knows that without correct and complete editions—accompanied by accurate and complete tables of signs—no serious work is possible at all. And, for the moment, right now, I must confess that no serious work is possible on the Cretan hieroglyphic script for the very obvious reason that we have at our disposal only the editio princeps for each of the three batches of finds (EVANS 1909 for Knossos, CHAPOUTHIER 1930 for Mallia-Palace and GODART and OLIVIER 1978 for Mallia-Quartier Mu) and nothing else (as for seals: if they are not in EVANS 1909, you have to go hunting for them in dozens of publications).

The basic table of signs which people are obliged to use—simply because no other one exists—is to be found in EVANS 1909, 232-233. It is pointless noticing that it is eighty years old and not exact in many ways: in spite of all this it is the only one on the market!

But how is one to work well with a table of which about 30 of the 135 entries are not signs of the syllabary but decorative motives on the seals, among which a dozen or so have to be deleted because they are the same as others in the list (and this fact is not exactly balanced by the absence of a more or less equal number of signs improperly assimilated to others in the list)? How is one to work without the approximately twenty signs which have appeared at Mallia, before and after the Second World War? One cannot dismiss them by saying that more than half of them seem to be unique: to ignore a unique sign in a corpus like ours of about one thousand signs would be like ignoring the 20 signs of linear B [20 out of 87] having a frequency of less than 0.10%—among which 8 are perfectly readable! Incidentally, a detail like this one shows immediately the kind of problems, and difficulties, arising from the paucity of the material: we cannot discard the smallest piece of evidence, even if highly dubious. There are 31 unique signs—out of a total of 96—in the last stage of my tentative list of the Cretan hieroglyphic syllabograms. Some of them are, or were, really unique; but which ones are they? We really have no objective means to reach definitive conclusions.

To go back to Evans' list—even 'corrected' and completed by Chapouthier's and Godart-Olivier's lists—we have to admit that it is no longer usable. We need a new global edition, a 'corpus', and a new list of the signs. This is a clear and simple statement.

Fortunately—or unfortunately?—I am not in a very good position to say which, since, as is known, I have been in charge of this corpus, since 1969 exactly, when the German Archaeological Institute transmitted to me this part of the scientific heritage of Ernst Grumach. Ernst Grumach was a brilliant humanist but he had not yet reached the critical point of understanding what a Cretan script of the second millenium B.C. ought to look like. A direct consequence of this statement is that his archives were not entirely ready for printing. It is not offending his memory to say that he was not convinced at all by Ventris' decipherment of Linear B—though liberally permitting the publication of articles not in agreement with his own views in *Kadmos*, the journal which he founded—and that he was much more interested—like Evans!—in hieroglyphic seals than in archival material and, finally, that palaeography was not among his main preoccupations. All that perhaps explains why, in his posthumously published contribution to the *Handbuch der Archäologie* (GRUMACH 1969), there is no table of signs of the hieroglyphic script (just as there is no table of Linear A; but, rather ironically, one can find, on p. 261, a table of the Linear B signs taken from VENTRIS and CHADWICK 1956).

In fact, in order to produce a good edition of the Cretan hieroglyphic script, one has to try, first of all, to master Linear B and Linear A palaeography. This condition is certainly not sufficient, but it is absolutely necessary. In 1969 I had not finished working on the editions of Linear B in transliteration (I nonetheless took pictures of all the hieroglyphic archival material kept in the Iraklion Museum) and until 1984—not full time of course: I had, for instance, the opportunity of publishing in 1978 the hieroglyphic material from the Quartier Mu of Mallia—I was mainly working on the edition of the corpus of Linear A. I put the manuscript of the fifth volume of GORILA in the hands of the director of the French School of Archaeology at Athens on Friday 14th of September 1984 and went off to Crete to work for one week on a new arrangement of the Linear B tablets in the reserves of the Iraklion Museum, in the company of John Killen, having in mind, after that, to devote most of my time to the corpus of the hieroglyphic script; but, on Thursday 20th of September, John and I found the unexpected (or, more exactly, two of the guards showed us what they had found some time before): namely about three thousand fragments of Linear B tablets coming from Evans' excavations of 1900, wrapped inside pages of the *Times of London* dated 1902 and unseen by anyone since that time.

It would be an understatement to say that this discovery changed our working plans slightly; the publication of *CoMIK* which was felt by us to be more or less a formality, became instantaneously an extraordinarily difficult enterprise, and not only from the epigraphical point of view. With quite a lot of good fortune and hard work, we succeeded in publishing *CoMIK* I two years ago and *CoMIK* II will be issued this year; the preparation of *CoMIK* III and IV is now well advanced, so we can think seriously again at the *Corpus Hieroglyphicarum Inscriptionum Cretae*. Its acronymic abbreviation is *CHIC*. Now you certainly suspect my real reason for keeping the term 'hieroglyphic' instead of 'pictographic': *CPIC* is unpronounceable.

In fact, two years ago, I found the opportunity for correcting all the drawings (made by Louis Godart) of archival documents in the Iraklion Museum (and there are only four of them elsewhere, namely in the Ashmolean Museum, in Oxford). Louis Godart has still personally to check about one half of his own drawings previously corrected by me, but it will take only one or two weeks.

The real problem we now are confronted with is drawing of the faces of those seals that we decided are bearing hieroglyphic inscriptions. (I did not say 'isolated signs': for these, unless of exceptional palaeographical interest, we shall only give photographs.) Incidentally, this was not an easy decision to make; and the selection is still not completely finished, but it is now a resolved problem. Still the difficulty of drawing accurately a face of a seal which bears an inscription should not be underestimated. The drawing itself takes an average of five hours. The correction takes more or less the same time: it is one of the rules of the game, true for Linear A and Linear B, too. Given that there are about 150 inscribed seals and that some of them have three or four faces (one of them has eight, but it is an exception), there are about five hundreds faces to draw and the calculation of the time required is easy to do. Well, I am glad to announce that Godart has promised the completion of the job for the end of this summer. So, we can hope to finish it next year. And the *CHIC* itself ought to be given to the printer at the end of 1989. There will certainly be further delays, but we are reaching the end of the process.

But an up-to-date and accurate table of signs will be the last thing we will produce: all the verifications and corrections are to be made, indeed, before this is done. This is the reason why the only thing I can give you here is a provisional list of the syllabograms in the sign groups appearing in the archival documents, on the vases and on the Mallia stone, classified according to their frequency in these documents. We have not yet decided what will be the final order of the signs in the signary we will publish. There are quite a lot of possible alternatives. None is completely satisfactory. We are still open to suggestions, since the process of attributing definitive order to the signs can be undertaken almost at the last moment: the computer will rearrange them in the lists easily and reprint them in any numerical transcription very quickly.

In the list in figure 5, the ideograms (I personally prefer the term 'logogram') are not present (at least the ones which are not equally a sign of the syllabary). This list is certainly far from being correct: for instance, some signs are perhaps only logograms; some are perhaps displayed twice (for example 10 and 26, 15 and 24, 22 and 25 and probably others); and some are certainly missing.

But we have to wait for the study of the most accurate drawings possible of the 'monumental' signs on seals. This will certainly give us new clues (we refrained from using this material until now) and open other questions (for instance, it is fairly certain from new evidence from the peak sanctuary of mount Iouktas that at least one sign exists which is used in sign groups attested for the moment on seals only; but there are possibly two or three more signs in this situation).

So I ask you to be patient. It would be a pity to give you an imperfect tool, having waited now so many years.

And, once again, I repeat that the slowness for producing this corpus is due in part to external factors, but mainly to internal factors, namely the paucity of the material and its extremely complex nature (I hope I have convinced you on this point). So I do not say "let us hope"; I say "let you hope." As far as we are concerned, we shall advance as quickly as possible, but it would be a pity to try to gain some months, to scamp the work, after so many years.

III. METHODOLOGICAL PROBLEMS

You will remember the background: about 1,500 signs on less than 300 objects. Ventris, when he succeeded in deciphering Linear B, had at his disposal about 30,000 signs on 2,000 documents. What methods can one try to use on this material? I shall just permit myself some statements:

A. A linguistic method seems excluded:

We do not know the language which the Cretan hieroglyphic script represented and we have no means of knowing it.

Even if someday we read 80% of the texts written in Linear A and if at that moment we understand the language written by Linear A—by this I mean that we shall be able to link the language we shall be reading with some other relatively well known language—(all that is perhaps possible, but it will not take place tomorrow, I'm afraid; and I suppose that Yves Duhoux has not told us anything very different in this volume), even if we do all this, there is absolutely no compelling reason that we should have the slightest idea about the language noted by the hieroglyphic script.

Hieroglyphic and Linear A are two different scripts. They were living side by side, in a relatively small island, for at least several centuries and we can say that—with the serious exception of the seals, it is true—they were written on more or less the same categories of objects, probably for the same functional reasons.

More than that: I think we can confidently exclude the risky hypothesis that hieroglyhic script would be a 'monumental' script and Linear A the corresponding 'cursive' script; if you say that, the onus of the proof is yours. Why would archives on clay have been written in the so-called 'monumental' script? Why would 'monumental' inscriptions (on metal objects for instance) have been written in the so called 'cursive' script? And, what is most difficult to explain, why were the two scripts, 'monumental' and 'cursive', found together in the same deposit (in the Palace of Mallia), both written on clay archives ?

I know that the relationships between monumental and cursive scripts are generally not easy ones, because there are so many interactions possible between each of them. But that is true in abundantly attested scripts, over long periods of time. Here the two scripts are very badly attested—and on only some of their supports—during a very short span of time: altogether less than half a millenium. The case is far from being classic, and the comparisons with other systems are really dangerous.

So, it is highly improbable that the two different scripts were used to note the same language, or even two more or less slightly different forms of the same language. According to my personal opinion, there is a greater chance that Linear A was used to note two different languages or two different forms of the same language than that hieroglyphic script and Linear A were used for noting one and the same language. Consequently, in our approach to the problem, a possible 'reading' of Linear A would be of no use at all.

B. A *palaeographical method* seems excluded too, at least for the moment:

Even if we have very limited data, there are enough to establish with a satisfactory level of certainty that the signary of the hieroglyphic script consisted of between 80 and 100 signs and that we have most of them, even if some are attested only once.

There are rather clear relationships between the forms of about one third of the signs appearing in sign groups, or syllabograms, of the hieroglyphic script and of the Linear A.

I don't think there is enough evidence to say that the latter is derived from the former, as we can safely state for Linear A and Linear B. In their case, two thirds of the signs are closely similar. Please note that I am speaking about similarities of forms and these do not imply at all similarities of phonetic values.

Incidentally, it makes no matter which signs we judge 'similar'. You will find in VENTRIS and CHADWICK 1973, 33, a table of formal correspondences between Linear A on one side, hieroglyphic and Linear B on the other side. There are 31 of them given between Linear A and hieroglyphic; but some are pure fantasy, in my opinion. Others are match-ups with signs which appear only on seals as decorative motifs (like the cat's head which is a syllabogram in Linear A and B, but not in hieroglyphic). On the other hand, since the starting point is Linear A, some evidence is omitted when it concerns only hieroglyphic and Linear B: for instance, the sign resembling 'crossed arms' is clearly attested as a syllabogram in both the Cretan hieroglyphic and Linear B scripts, but it is absent in Linear A. Finally, I have noticed other similarities which exist between Cretan hieroglyphic and Linear A, but which were not taken into account by the authors of *Documents*. But, as I said, it does not matter. The global result will always be almost the same, and for negative reasons: a large hard core of forms exists which are not susceptible to being thought similar in the two scripts. One example will suffice. At least five distinctive forms exist for the 'tree branch' in hieroglyphic and only one in Linear A.

Although great caution is required until a full comparative study of the forms of the signs in the three writing systems will be achieved, I do think it is virtually impossible to say that linear A is a writing system issued from Cretan hieroglyphic. Once we have rejected the simplest, and therefore undiagnostic, forms (cross, eye, etc.), and once we have dismissed the overly clever comparisons, we are in front of similarities which are not numerous enough to prove any filiation. Common inspirations, certainly. Influences (probably reciprocal), of course! Filiation, very improbable (even if it is more or less the *communis opinio* from Evans' times onwards).

C. The *internal method* seems perhaps more promising:

But it has its limits. The *arithmograms* (the signs for numbers) are identified from Evans' studies. The *klasmatograms* (the signs for fractions) are less well defined; and their system is not really understood, probably because their attestations are so rare. But progress is probably still possible. The logograms (or ideograms, if you prefer) seem to be relatively infrequent, too, in the documents we have. But slow progress has been made (so it is a good thing that the sign Evans took for the representation of a boat is now admitted by everybody to be the logogram for WINE, with the same fundamental form as in Linear A and B). The sign groups are at the same time more and less promising: more, because the more exact readings of the 'corpus' will open the way to new investigations; less, because the paucity of the material and the lack of evident relationships, both at the level of the script and at the level of the language, with Linear A and B will exclude systematic comparisons. Nevertheless, some of the sign groups will some day be identified, with a variable level of certainty, as toponyms, anthroponyms, function or kinship names.

But all these results will remain theoretical if no parallels are found in Linear A or even Linear B (for the toponyms, and even for some anthroponyms, it is not impossible at all to imagine parallels with the Linear B texts of Knossos). But results in this field, even if reasonably secure, do not necessarily bring us very far. We know the sign group for 'total' in Linear A (and probably even for 'grand total' too), and where does it lead us? It brings us the bare statement: "we know the sign group meaning 'total' in linear A" and nothing else, at least for the moment (it was the same in Linear B before the decipherment and it did not help very much in deciphering). Incidentally, we still do not know the sign group for 'total' in hieroglyphic (unless + + ☐ would fit in KN P 110e, a conjecture which is far from certain). Some people claim to have found the sign group for 'son' in hieroglyphic. Very well, but we need more claims of this kind—and convincing ones—in order to be a little happier and more optimistic.

D. Finally, the *statistical methods* will probably be the most satisfactory.

First, because they are independent of the language noted and from the forms of the signs (once the signary is correctly established, of course). Second, because their combination with the study from the inside can prove fruitful, as happened in Linear B.

Two conditions are to be fulfilled: that the editions are correct (and this will be soon realized) and that the material is quantitatively sufficient (this is probably not yet the case, but we do not have control over this parameter).

We shall not speak here about elaborate statistics, because this kind of research can only be performed on the three 'corpora' together, each of them divided and subdivided into various categories after internal analysis. This sort of work will be done sometime, probably with appreciable results, but the work of 'dressing' the material for this kind of statistical analysis will be much longer than the analysis itself, whatever the method used.

As a concluding example, let us take a phenomenon visible at once and manageable by the means of an ordinary pocket calculator. It is the phenomenon of *reduplication*, in this case of *syllabic* reduplication; and, at first sight, it looks rather different, quantitatively speaking, in the three Cretan scripts:

In *Linear B*: out of 65,000 signs, 75 different reduplications of signs are found or 0.11% (if we also take into account the ca. 30 genitive endings in *-jo-jo* we will reach 0.16% and the difference will not be really significant);

In *Linear A*: out of 7,500 signs, 25 different reduplications, namely 0.33%. We can just make the statement that this phenomenon is between two and three times more frequent than in Liner B;

In *Cretan hieroglyphic*: out of 1,500 signs in the whole corpus, we have 10 reduplications, that is 0.66%. It seems at this time a phenomenon much more important than in the two other scripts. But if we concentrate on the sign groups on material other than seals and sealings (thus excluding from our account the initial crosses, the identified logograms, the numbers, and the fractions) we are left with 711 signs, and we find 8 certain and different examples, namely 1.12%.

In this latter case we have nearly three and a half times more reduplications than in Linear A and seven times more than in Linear B.

Is this rather significant result merely the product of chance? I would think not, since these reduplications are more or less equally present in the beginning (and/or the end: it is not always easy to determine) and in the middle of the sign groups and appear equally at Knossos as at Mallia Palace or at Mallia Quartier Mu (in that latter case we even have a triplication, but we still had one in linear B). But what is exactly the signification of this, since our sample is so tragically reduced? Chapouthier supposed that the final reduplication would indicate the dual, as in Egyptian. But this phenomenon is not always a final one (three examples are a maximum); and there is no special reason for having so many duals in our archive, nor is there a special reason for looking for an Egyptian explanation (if not Evans' Egyptomania). But I quoted Chapouthier just to show where we are obliged to stop: just after the bare establishment of a phenomenon, perhaps relevant, but whose signification escapes us or whose signification is probably invalid like, for instance, the unexpectedly high frequency of the sign 09 in the Linear A material from Zakros, where it represents about seven percent of our documentation (14 attestations of the sign on a total population of 52 in sign groups, i.e., 26%!).

Of course, especially in the case of reduplication, more detailed investigations are possible, but without much hope of achieving something really interesting. It is a pity. But so are the facts.

REFERENCES

CHADWICK , J.
1987 *Linear B and related scripts,* London.

CHAPOUTHIER, F.
1930 *Les écritures minoennes au palais de Mallia,* Paris.

CoMIK CHADWICK, J., GODART, L., KILLEN, J.T., OLIVIER, J.-P., SACCONI, A. & SAKELLARAKIS, I.A., *Corpus of Mycenaean Inscriptions from Knossos,* vol. I, Cambridge & Rome, 1986.

EVANS, A.J.
1909 *Scripta Minoa,* vol. I., Oxford.

GODART, L. & OLIVIER, J.-P.
1978 Écriture hiéroglyphique crétoise, *Le Quartier Mu,* vol. I., 29-220, Paris.

GODART, L., OLIVIER, J.-P. & POURSAT, J.-Cl.
(forthcoming) *Corpus Hieroglyphicarum Inscriptionum Cretae,* Paris.

GRUMACH, E.
1969 Die kretischen und kyprischen Schriftsysteme, *Handbuch der Archäologie*, 234-288, Munich.

POPE, M.W.M.
1967 The First Cretan Palatial Script, *Atti e Memorie del 1° Congresso Internazionale di Micenologia,* vol. I, 438-446, Rome.

VENTRIS, M. *and* CHADWICK , J.
1956 *Documents in Mycenaean Greek* [1], Cambridge.
1973 *Documents in Mycenaean Greek* [2], Cambridge.

Square Coghen 38
B-1180 Bruxelles
Belgique

FIGURES

SCRIPT	NO. of Docs.	% of TOTAL	NO. of SIGNS	% of TOTAL
H	270	± 4%	1537	±2%
A	1427	±22%	7362	± 11%
B	4765	±74%	57398	±87%
	6462		66297	

Figure 1. Cretan scripts

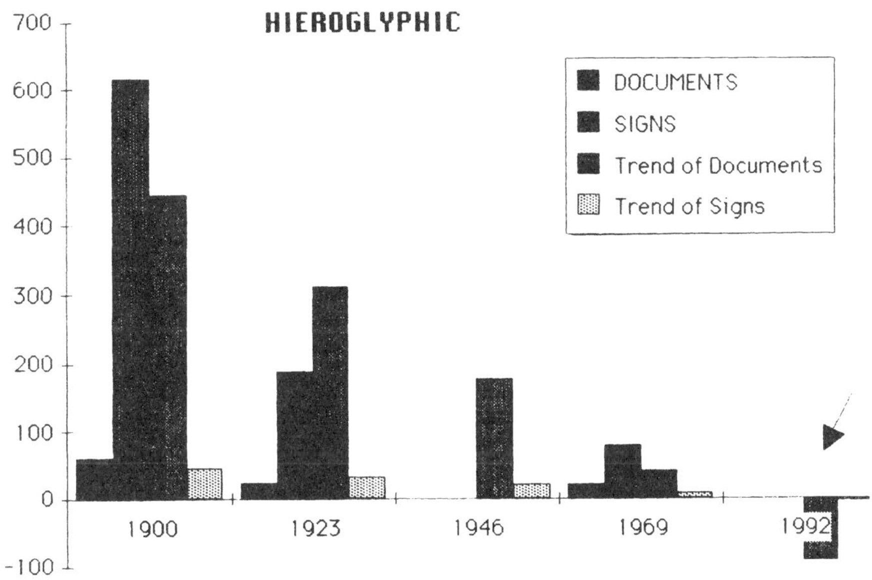

Figure 2.

	INSCRIPTIONS	SIGNS
KN	61*	615
MA (Palace)	24*	189
MA (Mu)	21*	79
PH (erratic)	1	28
vases (MA)	12	50
stone (MA)	1	16
	120	977

* **Altogether:** 42 bars, 26 sealings, 36 labels, 2 cones [=883 signs]

N.B. : Average number of signs per document: 8.30 (from 10 at KN to 3.76 at MA (Mu).

Cf. general average in *Linear A*: 5.15 (but without cretulae and roundels: 15); general average in *Linear B*: 12.3 (KN: 7.7; PY: 25).

Figure 3. Cretan hieroglyphic script (without the seals)

Figure 4. ±1500 signs in the Cretan hieroglyphic script (=1800 signs and blanks in font "Mallia-9")

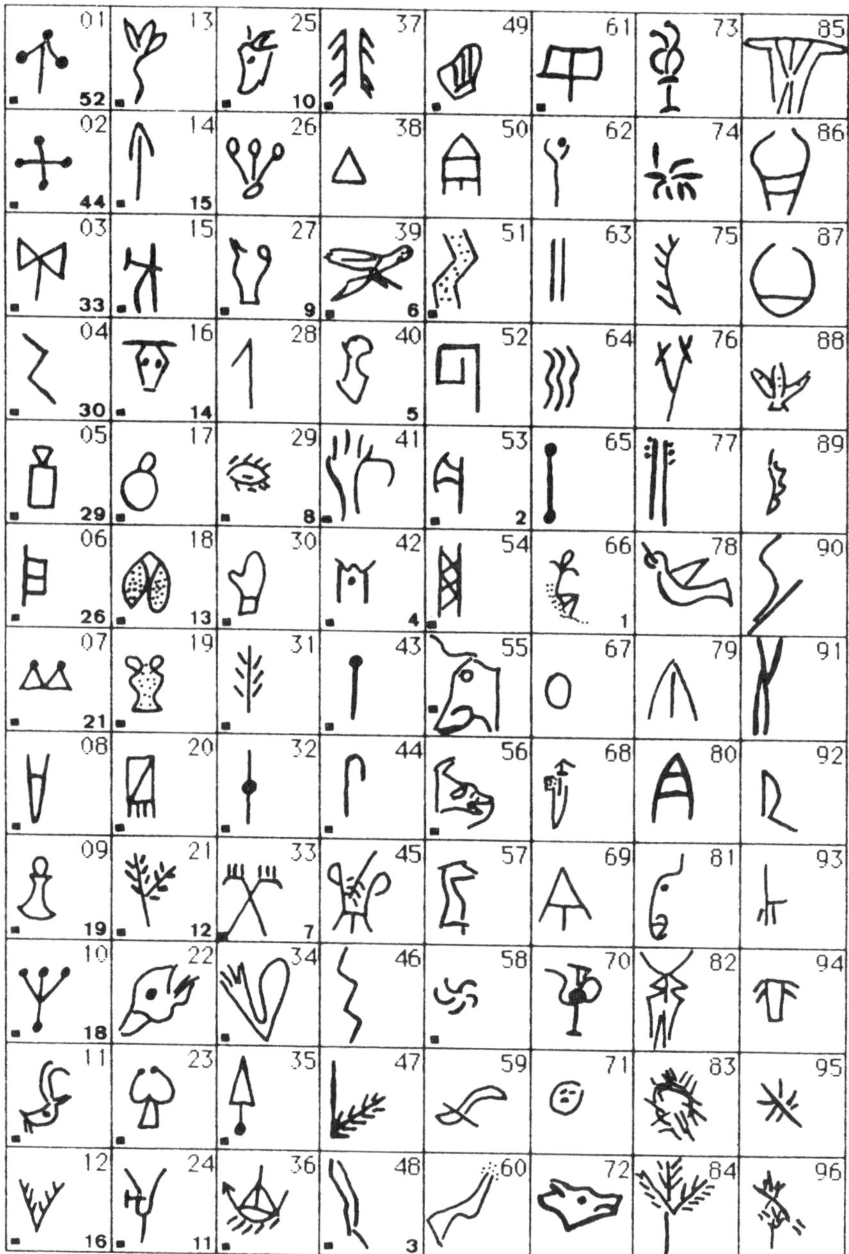

Figure 5. Tentative list of the syllabograms of the Cretan hieroglyphic script following the number of attestations in the clay documents (a black square indicates the presence in sign groups on seals)

BCILL 49 : *Problems in Decipherment*, 59-119.

LE LINÉAIRE A : PROBLÈMES DE DÉCHIFFREMENT

Yves DUHOUX
Université Catholique de Louvain

1. GÉNÉRALITÉS

1.1. *DÉFINITION*

On appelle linéaire A, depuis A. J. Evans[1], une écriture particulière, distincte des autres systèmes graphiques égéens du IIe millénaire avant J.-C. : les écritures non linéaires[2] («hiéroglyphique» crétois[3], écritures du disque de Phaestos et de la hache d'Arkalokhori) et le linéaire B. Le linéaire A est étroitement apparenté à

---

1 C'est A.J.Evans qui a découvert le premier texte connu en linéaire A (la «table à libation» PS Z 2 de Psychro, trouvée en avril 1896 : EVANS 1909, 13-16) et a donné son nom à l'écriture (EVANS 1902-1903, 52).

2 Je propose ce terme (que je crois être un néologisme) pour désigner l'ensemble des écritures crétoises de l'âge du bronze autres que les linéaires A et B. Je remercie Maurice Pope, avec qui j'ai pu utilement discuter de cette question.

3 Ce terme n'est pas approprié, et devrait être remplacé par «écriture crétoise des premiers palais» (voir POPE 1968), mais je le conserve conventionnellement ici. Sur cette question, voir en dernier lieu OLIVIER 1989.

l'une de ces écritures, le linéaire B, et a tout un groupe de signes communs avec l'«hiéroglyphique» crétois (fig. 1)[4].

1.2. *GÉOGRAPHIE* (fig. 2)

La quasi-totalité des textes linéaires A connus vient de Crète (1.419 textes sur 1.432 : 99 %)[5]. En Crète même, un seul site, Haghia Triada, a fourni plus de 70 % de tout le *corpus* (1.039 textes; 59,7 % de l'ensemble des signes).

Il existe seulement 13 textes provenant d'ailleurs. Ils attestent une diffusion du linéaire A vers le Nord : douze viennent des îles de Cythère, Théra, Milos et Céa; le dernier vient du Sud du Péloponnèse (Haghios Stéphanos)[6]. Il n'existe que deux sites non crétois qui aient livré des tablettes, et où l'on soit donc assuré que le LA était écrit sur place : Milos et Céa. À Théra, un vase, de fabrication apparemment locale, a été incisé avant cuisson (TE Z 2), ce qui va dans le même sens. Dans les deux autres sites, on ne peut exclure que les objets inscrits en LA soient de simples importations.

1.3. *CHRONOLOGIE*

Lorsqu'ils sont datés, les documents linéaires A s'échelonnent entre le milieu du XIXe siècle et le milieu du XVe siècle avant notre ère (depuis la transition du MM IIa vers MM IIb - aux environs de 1.850 - jusqu'à la fin du MR I - vers 1.460 ou 1.440). Un texte a été trouvé en contexte MR II (fin du XVe s. : KN Z 32).

1.4. *TYPE DE DOCUMENTS*

Plus des 9/10 des textes (1.338/1.432; 6.579 signes) sont des documents administratifs, écrits sur argile crue. On les répartit, d'après leur format, en tablettes, scellés, nodules[7] et rondelles[8] (fig. 3).

---

[4] Sauf indication contraire, les textes linéaires A seront cités d'après RAISON-POPE 1980. Pour les documents non édités par ces auteurs, voir GODART-OLIVIER 1976-1985; KARETSOU - GODART - OLIVIER 1985; KARETSOU 1987. La numérotation des signes LA est celle de RAISON-POPE 1977.

[5] Sur ces chiffres, de même que sur ceux qui suivent, voir OLIVIER 1987. J'ai actualisé ces données d'après les publications de nouveaux textes LA qui m'étaient connues au 31 décembre 1988.

[6] OLIVIER 1988, 255, 262-263 vient de publier un tesson de Tyrinthe (poterie locale), trouvé en contexte HR III B2 et portant deux signes où il propose de reconnaître du linéaire A. Il se pourrait toutefois qu'il s'agisse de simples marques de fabrication ou de propriété.

[7] Nodules : boulettes d'argile prismatiques ou ovoïdes. Sur la fonction de ces objets, cf. WEINGARTEN 1986.

[8] Rondelles : galettes d'argile aplatie.

Les 94 textes restants sont écrits sur vases (76 ex.) ou sur supports variés (stuc, terre cuite, pierre, métal : 18 ex.[9]) : fig. 4. Ces textes comportent 817 signes.

Dans les textes administratifs, le LA est inscrit dans l'argile molle avec un fin stylet. Ailleurs, il est gravé ou peint. Les textes peints attestent l'existence d'une forme cursive de l'écriture, ce qui fait penser qu'il a dû exister des documents linéaires A sur matière périssable (parchemin, papyrus, etc.). On pourrait avoir un témoignage de l'existence de tels documents grâce aux empreintes laissées sur des scellés de Zakro, qui pourraient avoir été apposés sur des documents en parchemin[10] - bien entendu, on ignore quelle(s) écriture(s) y étai(en)t utilisée(s).
Le sens de l'écriture LA est presque toujours dextroverse, bien que l'on ait quelques exemples d'écriture boustrophédon, sinistroverse, ou même divergente (←|→) [11].

2. DÉCHIFFREMENT DE L'ÉCRITURE

2.1. *CONDITIONS NÉCESSAIRES*

Le déchiffrement de l'écriture LA demande que soient remplies au moins les trois conditions suivantes :

2.1.1. ÉDITIONS RIGOUREUSES

Cette condition est remplie. Ces trente dernières années ont vu paraître d'importantes publications de l'ensemble du matériel : BRICE 1961, qui est désormais remplacé par les éditions de GODART-OLIVIER 1976-1985 et de RAISON-POPE 1980, - ce dernier volume sera bientôt remplacé par RAISON-POPE 1990.

2.1.2. RÉPERTOIRES DE SIGNES BIEN ÉTABLIS

Cette condition est également remplie, puisque RAISON-POPE 1977 et GODART-OLIVIER 1976-1985, vol. 5 ont fourni des répertoires à jour de l'ensemble des signes linéaires A.

---

9 On a ainsi du LA inscrit sur : haches (votives et fonctionnelles), lingots, bijoux (bague et épingles), jetons, poids/pesons, statuette, socle, pierre et murs.

10 WEINGARTEN 1983.

11 DUHOUX 1985, 59 n. 25; PALAIMA 1988, 310-313. Le sens d'écriture divergent est attesté en IO Za 9 (texte n° 20, § 3.2.2).

2.1.3. QUANTITÉ SUFFISANTE DE TEXTES

Les 1.432 textes édités comportent 7.396 signes, c'est-à-dire l'équivalent d'environ dix pages dactylographiées de texte continu. Une quantité de ce type est certainement suffisante pour découvrir une série de caractéristiques intéressantes de l'écriture utilisée. Est-ce assez pour la lire ? La réponse serait certainement positive[12] si nous connaissions la langue du LA. Ce n'est toutefois pas le cas (§ 4.3), ce qui complique évidemment la recherche.

2.2. *STRUCTURE DE L'ÉCRITURE*

Théoriquement, une écriture peut être soit purement idéographique, soit purement phonétique, soit mixte (idéographique et phonétique)[13]. En fait, le LA semble bien appartenir au type mixte, comme la plupart des écritures connues.

2.2.1. COMPOSANTE IDÉOGRAPHIQUE

Il est évident que les éléments suivants sont idéographiques (fig. 5) :

A) chiffres (en système décimal). Ce système est identique à celui du LB. Il comporte des signes spécifiques pour les unités, dizaines, centaines et milliers. Il n'existe pas de chiffre pour «zéro».

B) signes fractionnels : la fonction de ces signes ne fait pas de doute; ce qui est discuté, ce sont leurs valeurs relatives - bien qu'il soit clair qu'il s'agit de fractions de type «égyptien», où un nombre fractionnel complexe est exprimé par une séquence de fractions décroissantes (ainsi, 4/5 pourrait être exprimé en système de type égyptien par 1/2 1/4 1/20)[14]. Ces signes sont inconnus du LB.

---

[12] La formule de l'*unicity distance* de C.E. Shannon permet d'estimer le minimum de longueur au dessus duquel doit se situer un texte pour que la lecture phonétique de son écriture puisse être démontrable ou réfutable (cf. BARBER 1974, 203-205; sur la notion d'*unicity distance,* voir KAHN 1967, 750-751). Dans le type d'écriture du LA (§ 2.2), on arrive à une longueur d'environ 225 signes.

[13] Dans ce qui suit, je définis comme «phonétique» tout signe rendant un élément en lui-même dépourvu de sens (ainsi, en écriture française contemporaine, la lettre *a* sert à noter le phonème /a/, lui-même sans signification); «idéographique», tout signe rendant un élément pourvu de sens (ainsi, le signe *1* signifie, en lui-même, la notion de «un»). On peut aussi dire qu'est «phonétique» tout signe représentant un phonème ou une syllabe (ainsi, dans l'écriture française contemporaine, les cinq signes suivants : *a b c d e;* en LB, les cinq signes transcrits par: *da de di do du);* est «idéographique» tout signe ne représentant pas des phonèmes ou des syllabes (ainsi, en écriture française contemporaine, les cinq signes suivants : *1 2 , ? +;* en LB, les cinq signes transcrits par : *GRANUM ROTA VAS VIR T).* Il peut, bien entendu, se produire que certains signes phonétiques soient utilisés comme idéogrammes. C'est le cas des abréviations - ainsi, en écriture française contemporaine, M. (= Monsieur), etc.; en LB, *ME,* abréviation de *me-ri,* μέλι, «miel»; etc. Sur la terminologie relative à la description des écritures, voir par exemple GELB 1963, 248-253; sur le LB, voir en particulier BENNETT 1963.

[14] Sur les fractions linéaires A, voir spécialement BENNETT 1950, 1980, 1985.

C) ponctuation : il s'agit presque toujours d'un petit point ou trait vertical séparant des groupes de signes. Cette ponctuation se retrouve en LB.

D) idéogrammes représentant des objets ou des êtres vivants. Une partie d'entre eux se retrouve en LB. Leur identification est parfois évidente en raison du caractère naturaliste des dessins (ainsi, les idéogrammes de l'«homme» ou de la «femme»). Souvent, toutefois, le signe utilisé n'est pas directement évocateur pour nous (ainsi, les idéogrammes LA *146, 185* ou *187).*

Dans certains cas, il existe des associations structurées que l'on retrouve à la fois en LA et en LB. Ainsi, les trois idéogrammes suivants : LB *NI* [abréviation de la «figue»] = LA *60;* LB GRA [idéogramme du «froment»] = LA*42;* LB VIN [idéogramme du «vin»] = LA *82a.* En LB, ces idéogrammes sont associés comme suit : *NI* ~ GRA; GRA ~ VIN; *NI* ~ VIN. Or, cette triple association se retrouve en LA : LA *60 ~ 42; 42 ~ 82a; 60 ~ 82a.* Ceci fait penser que les idéogrammes en question ont probablement la même signification dans les deux écritures[15]. Sur LA*60,* «figues», voir § 2.2.2.2.1.c.3.

2.2.2. AUTRES SIGNES

2.2.2.1. Type d'écriture

Le nombre de signes dont il n'est pas possible de prouver le caractère idéographique se monte à une centaine[16]. Ces signes présentent la particularité de s'associer généralement en groupes, séparés par des blancs ou des diviseurs.

Une centaine de signes, fournissant à eux seuls des milliers de caractères, permet d'exclure que l'on se trouve devant des idéogrammes, car on attendrait - à moins d'attribuer aux rédacteurs du LA une indigence intellectuelle sans parallèle dans l'histoire humaine - un nombre de signes infiniment plus élevé. De même, il semble très peu probable que l'on ait affaire à un alphabet, qui n'a généralement que quelques dizaines de signes. En revanche, ce nombre s'harmonise bien avec ce que l'on attend d'un syllabaire.

Parmi les syllabaires, il faut distinguer les syllabaires *lourds*, à syllabes fermées, ou bien ouvertes et fermées (du type de *ba, bal, bam, bar, bas,* etc.; exemple : le syllabaire sumérien), et les syllabaires *légers*, à syllabe ouverte (du type de : *ba, ca, da, fa,* etc.; exemple : le syllabaire japonais). Comme les syllabaires lourds ont un nombre de signes dépassant de loin la centaine, tandis que les syllabaires légers en comportent généralement entre une cinquantaine et une centaine, il est probable que les signes non idéographiques du LA sont des syllabogrammes légers, dont la structure phonétique a toute chance d'avoir été soit de type V et CV, soit du type V et C^1C^2V, soit enfin du type V, CV et C^1C^2V.

---

[15] Sur ce groupe d'idéogrammes, voir BENNETT 1989 (je remercie l'auteur de m'avoir communiqué le manuscrit de cet article).

[16] D'après RAISON-POPE 1977, 17-33 et 48-53, on a 110 signes non idéographiques (il faut y ajouter maintenant un signe supplémentaire, LA *113),* dont sept formes pourraient être des variantes. Ceci donne de 104 à 111 signes. GODART-OLIVIER 1976-1985, vol. 5, xviii-xix se refusent à préciser la fonction des signes LA.

Ces considérations sont facilement vérifiables. Le tableau de la fig. 6 donne le nombre de signes différents attestés dans des échantillons d'environ 245 signes écrits en écritures diverses : (1) texte français - alphabet de 26 signes[17]; (2) chypriote classique - syllabaire de 55 signes[18]; (3) sumérien - syllabaire de plusieurs centaines de signes[19]; (4) chinois - système idéographique de plusieurs milliers de signes[20]; (5) linéaire A[21].

Il est manifeste que les 57 signes différents du LA s'opposent nettement aux échantillons en écriture alphabétique et idéographique. Ils sont, en revanche, extrêmement proches des échantillons syllabiques et se situent, plus précisément, entre le chypriote et le sumérien.

Une confirmation de cette conclusion peut être fournie par une écriture apparentée au LA et qui est déchiffrée : le LB, attesté uniquement au IIe millénaire, est une adaptation assurée du LA. Or, il possède un syllabaire à syllabes ouvertes de 89 signes[22]. Un échantillon linéaire B de même longueur que nos échantillons de référence (244 signes) donne d'ailleurs 53 syllabogrammes différents, ce qui est remarquablement proche des 57 signes LA[23].

On peut se demander si le nombre de syllabogrammes linéaires A ne risque pas de s'accroître à mesure que l'on découvrira de nouveaux textes. En fait, ceci paraît hautement probable. Mais il semble aussi que l'augmentation ait peu de chances d'être considérable : d'après la formule mise au point par MACKAY 1965, qui permet d'estimer le nombre de signes probables d'une écriture dont on ne dispose que d'un échantillon limité, le nombre total des signes phonétiques du LA ne devrait très probablement pas dépasser environ 130 signes[24].

---

17 Dans le comptage des signes différents de l'échantillon, les majuscules et les lettres diacritées ont été conventionnellement assimilées aux minuscules non diacritées.

18 Références dans DUHOUX 1980, 131 (échantillon *A* du chypriote).

19 Références dans DUHOUX 1980, 130-131.

20 Échantillon extrait de HUANG-DAI 1979, 94. L'écriture chinoise est de type réformé, et donc simplifiée.

21 Échantillon constitué par : KN Z 6, 7, 11, 13, 31; KO ? Z 1 (§ 6 n° 7); PK Z 11 (§ 6 n° 2); PR Z 1 (§ 6 n° 8); ZA Z 3; GODART-OLIVIER 1976-1985 CR (?) Zf 1; KO (?) Zf 2.

22 L'écriture syllabique chypriote, attestée depuis les environs de l'an 1.000 jusqu'à la fin du IIIe siècle avant notre ère, est également un syllabaire à syllabes ouvertes de 55 signes. Sa parenté avec les LA et LB a parfois été contestée, mais à tort. Voir HEUBECK 1979, 54-73; MASSON 1983, 30-42; PALAIMA 1989.

23 Références dans DUHOUX 1980, 135-136 (échantillon *d* linéaire B).

24 Calculée sur un échantillon de 2.387 signes LA, la formule donne : nombre de signes différents : 98-105 (certains signes pourraient être des doublets); estimation du nombre total de signes du syllabaire : 102-110; total corrigé (de + 8 à + 19 %) : 110-131 signes (DUHOUX 1978, 119). La probabilité d'exactitude de la formule de Mackay dépend de divers facteurs, en particulier du nombre de signes différents du système graphique étudié et de la longueur de l'échantillon d'écriture. Il serait souhaitable qu'une formule meilleure soit mise au point pour les systèmes graphiques de plus de cinquante signes.

2.2.2.2. Lecture phonétique des syllabogrammes LA

Nous venons de voir que le LB est dérivé du LA; qu'il comporte un syllabaire; et qu'il a été déchiffré. Il faut ajouter qu'une septantaine de syllabogrammes linéaires B ont des correspondants formels exacts en LA (fig. 7)[25]. Il est extrêmement tentant de transférer les valeurs phonétiques du LB au LA, de manière à pouvoir lire ce qui, autrement, n'est qu'un amas de signes inintelligibles.

Avant de se lancer dans l'entreprise, il faut toutefois s'interroger sur ses chances de succès.

Il paraît certain que le LB n'a pas été créé par emprunt pur et simple du LA. Il résulte d'une adaptation[26]. Dans le secteur des syllabogrammes, deux signes syllabiques linéaires A sur dix paraissent ne pas avoir été repris par le LB[27], et le LB semble avoir introduit une vingtaine de syllabogrammes inconnus du LA[28] - l'un d'entre eux au moins est presque certainement une création (*dwo*, formé par l'accolement de deux signes *wo* dont le second est inversé :).

En ce qui concerne la valeur phonétique des syllabogrammes communs aux linéaires A et B, on ne peut, bien entendu, pas exclure que les créateurs du LB aient repris telles quelles les valeurs phonétiques des signes LA dont ils empruntaient le tracé. Mais il est tout aussi possible - et en fait, il semble bien plus probable, d'après les nombreux parallèles qu'offre l'histoire des écritures - qu'ils aient effectué une adaptation, partielle ou totale, des valeurs phonétiques linéaires A pour constituer le LB.

Avant, donc, de se lancer dans le remplacement systématique des syllabogrammes LA par les valeurs phonétiques de leurs correspondants LB, il y a lieu de s'assurer que des refontes importantes n'ont pas été opérées.

---

25 Le tableau 7 donne les correspondances formelles entre syllabogrammes LA et signes LB pour lesquelles il y a accord de RAISON-POPE 1977, 60 et de GODART-OLIVIER 1976-1985, vol. 5, 114-117. D'autres syllabogrammes ont fait l'objet d'interprétations différentes dans ces deux ouvrages. RAISON-POPE 1977 : LA *07* = LB *so;* LA *10* = LB *zo;* LA *43* = LB **64;* LA *66* = LB *twe;* LA *88* = LB *jo;* LA *94* = LB *we;* LA *99* = LB *wo;* LA *100b* = LB *no;* LA *101* = LB *do;* LA *114* = LB *nwa.* GODART-OLIVIER 1976-1985 : LA *43* = LB **164;* LA *88* = LB *twe;* LA *94* = LB *ri;* LA *101* = LB **79;* LA *667* = LB *zo.* Notez que RAISON-POPE 1977 et GODART-OLIVIER 1976-1985 reconnaissent l'identité des deux *idéogrammes* LA suivants avec deux syllabogrammes LB : LA *16* = LB *ze*; LA *140* = LB **22.*

26 DUHOUX 1985, 19-23; HOOKER 1988; PALAIMA 1988.

27 Sont sans correspondants LB connus, d'après RAISON-POPE 1977 et GODART-OLIVIER 1976-1985, vol. 5 : LA *03, 08, 09, 14, 33, 36, 37, 63, 67, 75b, 81b, 83a, 123, 129, 138, 150, 155, 161, 163a, 163b, 188, 201;* d'après RAISON-POPE 1977, les syllabogrammes LA suivants : *20, 41, 42, 48a, 65, 68, 79, 82a, 82b, 83b, 87, 109, 111, 135, 151, 154, 162, 202;* d'après GODART-OLIVIER 1976-1985, vol. 5 : *07, 10, 66, 88, 99, 100b, 114.*

28 Sont sans correspondants LA connus, d'après RAISON-POPE 1977, 60-61 et GODART-OLIVIER 1976-1985, vol. 5, 114-117, les syllabogrammes LB suivants : a_2, a_3, *dwe, dwo, mo, pe, pte, qo,* ra_3, ro_2, *two, *18, *19, *63, *83, *89.* Selon GODART-OLIVIER 1976-1985, seraient, en outre, sans correspondants LA les signes LB suivants : *do, jo, no, nwa, so, we, wo, *64.*

2.2.2.2.1. *Éléments favorables à une lecture phonétique LA > B*

Plusieurs arguments peuvent être avancés :

a) Position des signes LA répondant à des signes *V* du LB

Il semble que dans tout syllabaire, les signes débutant par voyelle aient normalement tendance à figurer plus souvent à l'initiale absolue des mots qu'en toute autre position, sauf lorsqu'ils notent un second élément de diphtongue. Ceci tient au fait qu'en milieu ou en fin de mot, la voyelle sera le plus souvent précédée d'une consonne, et sera donc notée par un signe de type $C^1(C^2)V$; à l'initiale absolue, elle sera soit seule et notée par V, soit précédée de consonne(s), et notée par $C^1(C^2)V$. Cette caractéristique paraît indépendante de la langue notée, puisqu'elle se retrouve aussi bien en accadien qu'en LB ou en chypriote[29].

La fig. 8 donne le pourcentage des emplois initiaux, médians et finaux des cinq signes vocaliques de base LB et des signes LA qui leur correspondent[30].

Conformément aux prévisions, LA *52* ~ LB *a*, LA *44* ~ LB *e*, LA *80* ~ LB *o* et même LA *100a* ~ LB *i* figurent le plus souvent à l'initiale des mots. C'est le cas également pour LA *97*, mais non pour son correspondant LB, *u*, qui figure surtout à la *finale* absolue (ceci est dû à son utilisation fréquente comme second élément de diphtongue). Résultats favorables, donc, pour les cinq signes LA.

Dans le détail de la répartition des emplois initiaux, médians et finaux, LA *52* ~ LB *a* sont remarquablement proches. Pour LA *44* ~ LB *e*, les pourcentages sont assez proches, mais il faut observer la très faible fréquence de LA *44* : un dixième de LA *52*, alors que LB *e* représente les huit dixièmes de LB *a*. Nous aurons à revenir sur ce point (§ 2.2.2.2.2.a). LA *100a* ~ LB *i* semblent avoir une répartition compatible - noter la haute fréquence de LA *100a* : 90 % de LA *52*, alors que LB *i* représente 40 % de LB *a*. Par contre, LA *80* ~ LB *o* et LA *97* ~ LB *u* ont des répartitions assez différentes.

Au total, l'examen des cinq signes se révèle particulièrement favorable pour LA *52* ~ LB *a*, LA *44* ~ LB *e* et LA *100a* ~ LB *i*. Il semble moins probant pour LA *80* ~ LB *o* et LA *97* ~ LB *u*. Bien entendu, il ne résulte pas nécessairement des résultats favorables que LA *52* et *100a* aient une identité absolue de timbre vocalique ou d'articulation avec LB *a* et *i* : il est *a priori* possible qu'au *a* du LB réponde un /a/ d'aperture différente en LA; que certaines voyelles LA puissent être des voyelles nasales; etc.

b) Alternances de signes LA > B possédant C ou V commune

Dans un syllabaire à syllabes ouvertes, des phénomènes morphologiques, phonétiques ou orthographiques peuvent entraîner l'alternance de signes ayant en

---

29 PACKARD 1974, 80-81.

30 Les données du LA proviennent de mes comptages personnels des séquences de GODART-OLIVIER 1976-1985, vol. 5 où la position des signes (initiale, médiane et finale) est assurée. Les nombres de la colonne LB donnent les occurrences de chaque signe dans les mots complets d'après OLIVIER 1965, 395-396.

commun une voyelle ou une consonne (alternances du type de LB : ***jo***- ~ ***o***- ou *ko-to-**na*** ~ *ko-to-**no***) - en LB, ce phénomène et ses implications avaient été détectés par A. Kober et furent systématiquement utilisés par M. Ventris dans son déchiffrement[31].

Si, donc, il était possible de découvrir des alternances LA > B mettant en jeu des signes ayant des voyelles ou des consonnes communes, on disposerait d'un indice favorisant l'idée de valeurs phonétiques fondamentalement semblables en LA et en LB.

Or, il existe un certain nombre de mots LA répondant à ces conditions. Ces termes suscitent toutefois une question importante : les alternances qu'ils nous montrent sont intéressantes. Mais sont-elles significatives ? Autrement dit, ne sont-elles pas, tout simplement, le fruit du hasard ? Jusqu'en 1974, il était impossible de répondre à cette question, de sorte que ces rapprochements étaient dénués de toute valeur probante. C'est le grand mérite de PACKARD 1974 d'avoir établi, grâce à une série de neuf déchiffrements fictifs réalisés par ordinateur, que le hasard devait très probablement être exclu dans une partie importante des cas[32].

PACKARD 1974, 67-84, 178-192 a montré, en effet, que les alternances internes du LA sont plus élevées en LA > B que dans ses pseudo-déchiffrements (18 couples, contre, respectivement, 7 - 9 - 10 - 5 - 4 - 7 - 12 - 6 - 9). Ceci implique que le seul hasard ne suffit pas à expliquer ces alternances, et qu'elles reflètent probablement des phénomènes phonétiques, morphologiques ou orthographiques.

Reste la question de savoir si *toutes* les alternances relevées mettent bien en jeu des formes différentes de mots identiques. La réponse est clairement négative. Comment, alors, juger si les alternances sont, ou non, correctes ? Cette question n'a pas été abordée par Packard, et il y aurait intérêt à y répondre. Il serait utile de constituer un *corpus* LB de même longueur et de même structure que le *corpus* LA, d'y analyser les alternances, de relever les rapprochements erronés, et de déterminer quels types de rapprochements sont les plus sûrs.

En attendant que ce travail soit réalisé, il est prudent de ne retenir que les alternances dont il est assuré qu'elles mettent en jeu des formes différentes de mots identiques. C'est ce qui a été fait dans la liste ci-dessous. Pour les couples n° 1-6, 8-9, voir § 3.2.1-3.2.2. Le couple n° 7 figure dans deux tablettes (HT 86a et 95a-b), écrites par deux scribes différents et réunissant cinq autres mots identiques; il est dès lors hautement probable qu'il s'agisse de graphies différentes d'un seul et même mot[33].

	Termes linéaires A	**Transcription LA > B**
1)	LA *32-31-31-53-**84a***	> *ja-sa-sa-ra-**me***
	LA *32-31-31-53-**95**-26*	> *ja-sa-sa-ra-**ma**-na*

---

31 POPE 1975, 159-163.

32 Le travail de Packard repose sur les données linéaires A et B disponibles vers 1974 - pour le LA, RAISON-POPE 1971. Il y aurait évidemment lieu de les remettre à jour pour tenir compte des nouveaux textes et des nouvelles lectures intervenues depuis lors, tant en LA qu'en LB. Je pense cependant que ces chiffres donnent des indications fondamentalement proches de ce que doit être la réalité actuelle.

33 Voir, en dernier lieu, OLIVIER 1975, 447 n.1. Sur ces deux mots, voir aussi § 4.1.6.

2)	LA *32-51-103-**92**-92*	>	*ja-di-ki-**te**-te*
	LA *32-51-103-**06***	>	*ja-di-ki-**tu***
3)	LA ***32**-74-1̣0̣0ạ-88-̣**97**-32*	>	***ja**-ta-ị-88-̣**u**-ja*
	LA ***52**-74-100a-88-**75a**-32*	>	***a**-ta-i-88-**wa**-ja*
4)	LA ***52**-31-31-53-84a*	>	***a**-sa-sa-ra-me*
	LA ***32**-31-31-53-84a*	>	***ja**-sa-sa-ra-me*
5)	LA ***52**-51-103-92-92*	>	***a**-di-ki-te-te*
	LA ***32**-51-103-92 -92*	>	***ja**-di-ki-te-te*
6)	LA *52-74-**100a**-88-75a-32*	>	*a-ta-**i**-88-wa-ja*
	LA *]5̣2̣-26-**78**-88-75a-32[*	>	*]ạ-na-**ti**-88-wa-ja[*
7)	LA ***91**-58-**97***	>	***qe**-ra$_2$-**u***
	LA ***62**-58-**75a***	>	***qa**-ra$_2$-**wa***
8)	LA *97-26-55-29-26-**7̣8̣***	>	*u-na-ru-ka-na-**ṭị***
	LA *97-26-29-26-**57***	>	*u-na-ka-na-**si***
9)	LA *100a-56a-26-**95***	>	*i-pi-na-**ma***
	LA *100a-56a-26-**76**-26*	>	*i-pi-na-**mi**-na*

c) Possibilités d'emprunts lexicaux du LB au LA

Le LA et le LB sont utilisés en Crète. D'un point de vue linguistique, on s'attend à ce que la langue du LA, qui est la plus anciennement attestée, ait exercé une influence sur celle du LB, qui est documentée à date plus récente. Dans cette hypothèse, il devrait exister un certain nombre de termes empruntés par le LB au LA. Si c'est le cas, si les déformations phonétiques infligées par les Mycéniens lors de l'emprunt ne sont pas trop grandes, et si les valeurs phonétiques des syllabogrammes LA ne sont pas trop différentes de celles du LB, on devrait trouver un certain nombre de séquences identiques en LA et en LB. Or, on en trouve.

Une question préjudicielle se pose toutefois : dans quelle mesure ces séquences LA et LB ne sont-elles pas le produit du pur hasard ? Ici encore, PACKARD 1974 a apporté une réponse intéressante, en montrant que les rapprochements étaient toujours de loin moins fréquents dans ses neuf pseudo-déchiffrements qu'en LA > B (25 rapprochements, contre, respectivement, 7 - 7 - 3 - 10 - 8 - 6 - 7 - 12 - 6).

Dans ce même examen, bon nombre de termes LB sont des anthroponymes ou des toponymes; telle semble aussi être la fonction d'une partie importante des mots LA mis en cause. Si les ressemblances LA ~ LB ne sont pas totalement fortuites, les anthroponymes ou toponymes suspectés d'avoir été empruntés au LA doivent être normalement plus fréquents en LB crétois qu'en LB continental, puisque ce dernier a moins subi l'influence du LA (§ 1.2). Or, en LA > B, le nombre de termes ressemblant à du LB et exclusivement crétois est de loin plus élevé que dans les pseudo-déchiffrements (19 termes exclusivement crétois, contre, respectivement, 6 - 3 - 2 - 4 - 2 - 3 - 3 - 6 - 2; 4 termes exclusivement continentaux, contre, respectivement, 0 - 3 - 0 - 6 - 6 - 3 - 4 - 3 - 2).

L'étude de PACKARD 1974 montre donc que, globalement, une bonne partie des couples LA ~ LB ont une chance raisonnable de constituer des emprunts. Mais il doit indubitablement s'y trouver des rapprochements erronés - il est, en effet, inévitable, surtout dans une écriture syllabique, que des séquences formellement identiques servent, en réalité, à noter des mots différents (comparer par exemple LB *pa-te,* qui note aussi bien πατήρ, «père», que πάντες, «tous»).

Comment détecter les rapprochements exacts ? Il existe un cas où l'on peut démontrer l'identité de signification des termes LA et LB - voir n° 3 ci-dessous. Dans les autres cas, on est, en réalité, extrêmement démuni, et l'on en est réduit à *parier* que chaque membre des couples comparés a la même signification. Pour éviter que ce pari ne soit perdu d'avance, il y a intérêt à limiter au maximum les risques.

Un des facteurs utilisables dans ce but est la longueur des mots rapprochés. En effet, un test effectué sur quatre échantillons linéaires B d'environ 2.400 signes chacun a permis de montrer que la probabilité d'exactitude de rapprochement de mots comportant des séquences identiques de signes consécutifs était directement liée à la longueur des séquences comparées[34] : des séquences ayant en commun au moins quatre signes consécutifs y ont une probabilité de 99 % de mettre en jeu des formes différentes de mêmes mots. Cette probabilité diminue et tombe à 81 % dans des séquences ayant trois signes consécutifs communs. Si l'on retient des séquences ayant seulement deux signes consécutifs communs, le risque d'erreurs croît de façon alarmante.

Il semble certain que l'on pourrait diminuer le risque d'erreur en ajoutant au critère de longueur des mots un critère contextuel. En l'état de notre connaissance du LA, ce dernier sera le plus souvent le suivant : que les termes LA et LB rapprochés appartiennent à la même catégorie sémantique : anthroponymes, toponymes, théonymes, mots du lexique, etc. Des recherches devraient être effectuées dans des échantillons LB de même longueur que le *corpus* LA pour déterminer dans quelle mesure cette méthode se révèle efficace.

En attendant de disposer des résultats de cette analyse, j'ai sélectionné les termes LB susceptibles d'être des emprunts au LA d'après les trois critères suivants[35] :

(i) les paires de termes LA ~ LB ayant au moins quatre signes consécutifs communs ont été retenues sans discussion, sauf en cas de trop grandes incertitudes de lecture;

---

34 DUHOUX 1978, 73-83, 93-95. Les critères de rapprochement utilisés étaient les suivants : (a) ne pas tenir compte du contexte; (b) ne retenir que des mots ayant en commun soit (i) une séquence de quatre signes consécutifs, soit (ii) une séquence de trois signes consécutifs et un «affixe» attesté dans les mots du groupe (i).

35 D'après l'avis que l'on a sur le caractère grec ou non hellénique de la langue du LA, on pourrait ajouter d'autres critères - par exemple, que les termes LB n'aient pas d'étymologie satisfaisante et soient suspectés d'être des emprunts.

(ii) les paires de termes de trois signes consécutifs communs n'ont été retenues que si chacun de leurs membres semble appartenir à la même catégorie sémantique;

(iii) les paires de termes comportant une séquence identique de moins de trois signes consécutifs n'ont été retenues que lorsque l'identité de chacun de leurs membres était démontrable. Je signalerai pour mémoire quelques termes éliminés d'après ce dernier principe, mais peut-être intéressants.

Les termes retenus sont les suivants :

1) Mots LA et LB comportant une **séquence identique d'au moins quatre syllabogrammes consécutifs**

α) LA *30-100a-56a-74* (ZA 9b.4-5 et 12.5; anthr.[36]) = LB *da-i-pi-ta* (toponyme ?; anthr. ?; hapax crétois)

β) LA *]59-103-72-74* (PH W 37; ?; hapax). = LB *su-ki-ri-ta* (top.; crétois). Si la petite lacune gauche du terme LA avait été inscrite, elle pourrait avoir contenu au maximum un signe. Il existe en HT Z 158a une séquence LA *59-103-72-92-100a-32* (= LA > B *su-ki-ri-te-i-ja),* qui pourrait être issue de notre LA > B *su-ki-ri-ta* (§ 2.2.2.2.3.c), mais son contexte n'est pas éclairant (le mot est inscrit sur un grand pithos).

Il existe un troisième couple de termes à séquence identique d'au moins quatre syllabogrammes consécutifs, mais dont la lecture est incertaine. Il n'en sera donc pas tenu compte ici. Il s'agit d'un mot attesté en PR Z 1b. Son début est extrêmement difficile à lire. RAISON-POPE 1980 lisent LA *52-02-100a-32,* tandis que GODART-OLIVIER 1976-1985 lisent LA *77-39-100a-32* - ce n'est que cette dernière lecture qui fournirait un correspondant à LB *se-to-i-ja.* Le terme mycénien est un toponyme; le mot LA pourrait être un anthroponyme (§ 3.2.1 : X^{14h}; voir § 3.2.3.2).

2) Mots LA et LB comportant une séquence identique de **trois signes consécutifs**

α) LA *52-53-26-54* (LA > B *a-ra-na-re)* (anthr. ?[37]; HT 1.4) ~ LB *a-ra-na-ro* (anthr.; hapax crétois)

β) LA *56a-74-24-57* (LA > B *pi-ta-ke-si)* (anthr. ?[38]; HT 87.2) ~ LB *pi-ta-ke-u* (anthr.; hapax continental)

---

36 Le mot est symétrique à une quinzaine d'hapax qui ont chance d'être des noms d'hommes.

37 Terme parallèle notamment à deux hapax et à LA *98-01-25* (= LA > B *ku-*56-nu),* qui est probablement un anthroponyme en HT 88.3 et 4 (noter la répétition du même mot, qui exclut, sauf homographies, que l'on ait affaire à un toponyme).

38 Parallèle notamment à trois hapax et à un terme attesté en HT 117, où il semble être un anthroponyme.

γ) LA *100a-74-32* (LA > B *i-ta-ja)* (anthr. ?[39]; HT 28b.6 : hapax) ~ LB *i-ta-ja* (anthr.; crétois)

3) Mots LA et LB comportant une séquence identique de **moins de trois signes consécutifs**

LB *NI* est l'idéogramme de la «figue». Il semble bien que nous connaissions la forme grecque du terme dont *NI* est l'abréviation : il s'agit de νικύλεον, qui est un nom crétois de la «figue»[40]. Ce terme est dépourvu d'étymologie et pourrait être un emprunt.

Or, il doit très probablement remonter au LA, puisque l'on a vu que l'abréviation LA *60* = LA > B *NI* paraissait avoir la même signification qu'en LB (§ 2.2.1). Si tout ceci est correct, nous disposerions d'un argument en faveur d'une lecture de LA *60* par LA > B *ni* ou, à tout le moins, par /n/ suivi de voyelle antérieure.

Il n'existe pas d'autre terme LA de moins de trois signes consécutifs dont l'identité de signification avec leur correspondant LA > B soit démontrable. Toutefois, on peut signaler des couples comme LA *51-102a-55* (anthr. ?; HT 86a.3, 95a.4, 95b.4; LA > B *di-de-ru)* ~ LB *di-de-ro* (anthr.; hapax crétois) ou LA *62-62-55* (anthr.?; HT 93a.4-5, 111a.3, 118.2-3; LA > B *qa-qa-ru)* ~ LB *qa-qa-ro* (anthr.; hapax crétois)[41].

Il s'agit de mots intéressants en raison de leur statut, qui paraît identique (anthroponymes assurés en LB; probables en LA). D'autre part, leur dernier signe comporterait la même consonne en LA et LB, et à un *-o* final LB semblerait répondre un LA > B*-u*. Enfin, en LB, ils sont inexplicables par le grec, ce qui répond à la condition énoncée note 35.

d) Parallèles LA ~ LB ~ LC

Dix syllabogrammes de forme identique ou très proche sont présents à la fois en LA, en LB et dans le syllabaire classique chypriote (fig. 9)[42].

Dans les cinq cas où les examens précédents avaient été favorables à une lecture phonétique LA > B, les valeurs du LC donnent trois fois les valeurs phonétiques suggérées; ils montrent deux fois de minimes différences phonétiques. Ces six signes fournissent donc une confirmation de la lecture LA >

---

39 Terme parallèle notamment à : (i) deux hapax; (ii) un mot attesté en HT 116a.2, lui-même parallèle à quatre hapax; (iii) LA *31-58* (= LA > B *sa-ra₂*), qui est l'un des mots les plus fréquents du LA.

40 NEUMANN 1957, 1962.

41 Voir LEJEUNE 1972, 203-209.

42 Voir le tableau de MASSON 1987, 370, groupe 1a-b - cet auteur mentionne encore LB *i* [= LA *100a*] ~ LC *i* et LB *ra* (= /la/ /ra/) [= LA *53*] ~ LC *la* (= /la/), mais les signes LC me paraissent présenter des différences trop grandes par rapport à leurs correspondants LA et LB pour pouvoir être retenus à ce stade. Sur la parenté entre LA ~ LB ~ LC, voir § 2.2.2.1 note 22.

B et font penser que les cinq autres signes LA répondant à des syllabogrammes LB et LC pourraient avoir des valeurs phonétiques identiques ou très proches de leurs homomorphes.

2.2.2.2.2. *Éléments défavorables à une lecture phonétique LB > A*

Tout ce qui précède parle en faveur d'une similitude fondamentale des valeurs phonétiques des signes syllabiques homomorphes LA ~ LB. On a toutefois avancé des raisons qui font penser qu'il pourrait ne pas y avoir eu nécessairement identité entre les deux.

a) Il est frappant de voir que, dans le syllabaire LA > B, la fréquence des signes comportant un /o/ est extraordinairement faible : j'en ai compté 5,64 % (contre 37,9 % pour les signes en /a/, 15,32 % pour ceux en /e/, 24,09 % pour ceux en /i/ et 17,03 % pour ceux en /u/[43]).

Par ailleurs, les correspondants de plusieurs signes LB en /o/ manquent en LA : LB *dwo, mo, qo* *ro₂*, et *two.* Les signes suivants pourraient, en outre, manquer : LB *do, jo, no, so, wo* et *zo* (§ 2.2.2.2).

On en a tiré la conclusion que la langue du LA (de même que son syllabaire) pourrait n'avoir comporté qu'une seule voyelle vélaire, et non pas deux, comme le mycénien[44]. Il résulterait de ces déductions que les signes LB hérités du LA et qui comportent /o/ seraient le produit d'une réaffectation de certains syllabogrammes LA.

Un raisonnement analogue a été tenu pour les signes LA > B en /e/[45] - les signes LB *dwe, pe* et *pte* sont sans correspondants connus en LA; les signes LB *twe* et *we* pourraient, en outre, manquer (voir § 2.2.2.2). Par ailleurs, les signes LA > B en /e/ n'ont qu'une fréquence de 15,32 % (voir aussi 2.2.2.2.1.a).

Que valent ces hypothèses ? Un premier élément à prendre en considération est que nous ne connaissons probablement pas tous les syllabogrammes LA (§ 2.2.2.1) : il n'est donc pas impossible que les signes LB en /o/ et en /e/ puissent se voir dotés un jour de certains des correspondants LA actuellement manquants.

Cela dit, la faible fréquence des signes en LA > B /e/ et /o/ est un fait incontournable. Il est parfaitement possible qu'elle soit due à l'existence d'une seule voyelle antérieure et d'une seule voyelle postérieure en LA. On ne peut toutefois complètement exclure qu'elle puisse s'expliquer par la basse fréquence de *plusieurs* voyelles antérieures et postérieures dans la langue du LA.

b) Des raisonnements similaires ont été tenus en se fondant sur la manière dont le LB rend phonétiquement le grec :

---

43 DUHOUX 1982, 254. Ces chiffres reposent sur un comptage personnel des syllabogrammes LA pour lesquels RAISON-POPE 1977 ont admis des correspondances en LB (§ 2.2.2.2 note 25). Chaque occurrence de chaque syllabogramme a été comptée.

44 LEJEUNE 1972, 387.

45 PACKARD 1974, 112-114.

(i) Le syllabaire LB rend de façon inadéquate un certain nombre de phonèmes du grec : il ne distingue pas /l/ de /r/ (sauf, peut-être, dans le signe **34/35*, s'il est bien à lire *lu*, ce qui n'est pas assuré); il ne distingue pas les occlusives sonores ~ sourdes ~ aspirées (seules exceptions : la dentale sonore /d/, rendue par les signes de la série *d-* ; de même, le syllabogramme pu_2, qui rend /bu/ ou /phu/; il se pourrait que **22* et **56* rendent respectivement /bi/ ou /phi/ et /ba/ ou /pha/).

(ii) Inversement, le LB comporte une série de signes qui sont superflus du point de vue du phonétisme grec : signes de type C+*w* (*dwe, dwo, nwa, twe, two);* signes notant l'aboutissement (discuté quant à ses réalisations phonétiques) de **C+y+V* (ra_2, ro_2, ta_2); signes ne faisant pas partie d'une série cohérente : *au*, a_2 (= /ha/), a_3 (= /(h)ai/), *pte*, pu_2 (= /bu/ ou /phu/), ra_3 (= /lay/ ou /ray/).

(iii) On a aussi relevé que pas moins de sept doublets et complexes[46] LB sur quatorze ont le vocalisme /a/ - il n'y en a que 3 en /o/, 3 en /e/ et 1 en /u/.

On a supposé que ces particularités pourraient peut-être s'expliquer par un héritage du LA, et que, par ricochet, il serait possible de reconstituer grâce à elles la structure phonétique de l'écriture et de la langue LA. De là est venue l'idée que le syllabaire LA pourrait avoir possédé des séries consonantiques *vélarisées* (de type C*w*), *palatalisées* (de type C*y*), et *simples* (de type C). Il n'aurait pas marqué de distinction de sonorité ni d'aspiration. Il n'aurait eu qu'une liquide (/r/ ?) à laquelle s'ajouterait un phonème intermédiaire entre /l/ et /d/.

Dans cette perspective, le LB se serait constitué, d'une part, en redistribuant une partie des syllabogrammes LA (par exemple : tous les signes LB notant labio-vélaire - *qa, qe*, etc. - pourraient être issus d'une série LA hypothétique notant occlusive vélarisée du type **kwa, *kwe*, etc.). D'autre part, le LB aurait altéré les valeurs phonétiques de certains signes LA (ainsi, le signe LB *pte* pourrait être issu d'un syllabogramme LA **pye* appartenant à l'hypothétique série occlusive palatalisée).

Dans le domaine vocalique, le LA aurait eu plusieurs voyelles de timbre /a/, qui auraient été affectées, en LB, à la notation d'une partie des doublets et complexes[47].

Que valent ces idées ? Elle paraissent séduisantes, dans la mesure où elles rendent compte de manière économique d'une série de bizarreries du système syllabique LB. Elles ont toutefois leurs limites, parce que huit des quatorze signes LB qui nous paraissent superflus du point de vue grec sont actuellement sans syllabogrammes LA connus qui leur correspondent : a_2, a_3, *dwe, dwo, pte*, ra_3, ro_2, *two* (cette situation pourrait peut-être changer à l'avenir : voir § 2.2.2.1). Il est toutefois remarquable que trois des sept doublets et complexes LB en /a/ *aient* des correspondants LA (*au*, ra_2, ta_2; *nwa* pourrait également en avoir un) : ici, on pourrait bien se trouver devant une particularité significative.

46 Sur ces termes, cf. LEJEUNE 1972, 91-104.

47 LEJEUNE 1958, 321-330; HEUBECK 1961, 23-30; PACKARD 1974, 112-117; CREVATIN 1975, 8-19; STEPHENS-JUSTESON 1978, 280-283.

On retiendra de ceci qu'il semble bien possible qu'il y ait eu, lors du passage du LA au LB, des modifications, apparemment légères, des valeurs phonétiques d'origine, mais que le sens de ces modifications n'est actuellement pas démontrable.

c) En LB, un certain nombre de corrections de syllabogrammes se font par substitution de signes possédant C ou V commune - ainsi, écriture de *au* sur ⟦*a*⟧; de *ja* sur ⟦*jo*⟧; etc. Ces corrections fournissent des alternances de signes du type de celles étudiées § 2.2.2.2.1.b. On peut donc s'attendre à ce que des phénomènes semblables s'observent en LA. Or, on a cru trouver des corrections qui s'opposeraient à la lecture LA > B d'un syllabogramme. À trois reprises[48], en effet, LA ⟦*91*⟧ a été corrigé en LA *95*, c'est-à-dire que LA > B ⟦*qe*⟧ est devenu *ma*. L'absence de tout élément consonantique ou vocalique commun à *ma* et à *qe* prouverait, a-t-on pensé[49], que ces signes devraient avoir des valeurs phonétiques différentes en LA et en LB.

En fait, ces exemples sont dépourvus de valeur probante. En ZA 11 et 20, ce qui est en cause, c'est une confusion purement formelle : dans ces textes, LA *91* et *95* ont la forme d'un cercle. Les scribes, voulant écrire LA *95*, ont d'abord tracé par erreur LA *91;* ensuite, sans effacer, ils ont ajouté chaque fois les traits supérieurs caractéristiques de LA *95* (fig. 10). En KH 61, ce facteur graphique n'a pas pu jouer, car LA *91* a la forme d'un cercle et ne peut être matériellement confondu avec LA *95*, qui est triangulaire. Mais dans ce texte, LA *91* et *95* fonctionnent comme abréviations, c'est-à-dire comme idéogrammes (§ 2.2 note 13), de sorte que la correction porte non pas sur des éléments phonétiques, mais sur des *notions* - comparer le remplacement de l'abréviation française F (= Franc) par L (= Livre).

2.2.2.2.3. *Conclusion*

Il ressort de ce qui précède que, selon toute vraisemblance, les créateurs du LB n'ont probablement pas bouleversé de fond en comble le phonétisme de tous les syllabogrammes linéaires A qu'ils ont empruntés, puisque trente syllabogrammes paraissent avoir des valeurs phonétiques compatibles avec celles du LB. Cette impression paraît particulièrement fondée dans le cas de douze signes (en grasses dans la liste ci-dessous), où l'homophonie est inférée par au moins deux examens différents :

Linéaire A	**Linéaire B**	**Examens**
02	*pa*	(d)
06	*tu*	(b2)
21	*po*	(d)
22	*ro*	(d)
24	*ke*	(c2β)
26	***na***	**(c2α)(d)**

[48] KH 61.3; GODART-OLIVIER 1976-1985 ZA 11a.2 et 20.3.
[49] GODART 1976, 41.

30	***da***	**(c1α)(d)**
32	***ja***	**(b3-4-5)(c2γ)**
39	*to*	(d)
44	*e*	(a)
52	***a***	**(a)(b3-4-5)(c2α)(d)**
53	*ra*	(c2α)
56a	***pi***	**(c1α-c2β)**
57	***si***	**(b8)(d)**
59	*su*	(c1β)
60	*ni*	(c3)
62	*qa*	(b7)
72	*ri*	(c1β)
74	***ta***	**(c1α-β-c2β-γ)**
75a	***wa***	**(b3-7)**
76	*mi*	(b9)
77	*se*	(d)
78	***ti***	**(b6-8)(d)**
84a	*me*	(b1)
91	*qe*	(b7)
92	*te*	(b2)
95	***ma***	**(b1-9)**
97	***u***	**(b3-7)**
100a	***i***	**(a)(b6)(c1α-c2γ)**
103	*ki*	(c1β)

De légères divergences de valeurs phonétiques entre signes LA et LB sont toutefois possibles (et même probables) en raison de la différence vraisemblable (mais non démontrable actuellement) de phonétisme entre les langues du LA et du LB.

La lecture LA > B peut donner quelques résultats intéressants, dont voici quelques exemples.

a) La tablette HT 88.2 comporte l'idéogramme de la «figue», LA *60* (§ 2.2.1), qui est suivi par un diviseur et par le mot (hapax) LA *103-103-26*, lui-même suivi du chiffre 7. L'interprétation la plus plausible de LA *103-103-26* est qu'il s'agit d'un terme en rapport étroit avec l'idéogramme (désignation des figues en question). Lu phonétiquement, LA *103-103-26* donne LA > B *ki-ki-na*. Or, on connaît en grec un nom de la «figue de sycomore», κεικύνη/κίκυνα - et Théophraste signale que les sycomores étaient connus en Crète. Ce terme grec n'a pas d'étymologie connue, et il est tentant de penser qu'il s'agit d'un emprunt. Comme le flottement entre /u/ et /i/ s'observe dans des emprunts assurés ou probables, il paraît vraisemblable que κεικύνη/κίκυνα puisse être un emprunt grec à LA > B *ki-ki-na* [50]. Pour la lecture phonétique de LA *103* et *26* par LA > B *ki* et *na*, voir ci-dessus.

---

[50] NEUMANN 1960.

b) La tablette HT 31 comporte cinq idéogrammes de vases au dessus desquels sont écrits cinq mots en petits caractères. Selon toute vraisemblance, il s'agit de termes en rapport direct avec les récipients - on a songé soit à une désignation de contenu, soit, plus probablement[51], au nom des vases eux-mêmes. Ces termes sont les suivants : LA *62-01, 59-64, 29-2̣2̣-01, 59-01-53* et *02-74-91,* c'est-à-dire LA > B *qa-*56, su-pu*[52], *ka-ṛọ-*56* et *su-*56-ra.* Ce qui est frappant, c'est la récurrence, à trois reprises, du signe LA *01,* répondant à LB **56.* Ceci pourrait suggérer un élément morphologique ou lexical typique d'un certain nombre de noms de récipients. Or, il existe en LB un terme cnossien qui est, de façon assurée, un nom de vase, et qui se termine par LB **56 : ku-ru-su-*56.* Il n'est pas impossible que ce mot mette en jeu le nom de l'«or»[53], χρυσός, mais sa deuxième partie nous échappe. On a supposé qu'il pourrait s'agir d'un emprunt minoen[54]. Si c'était le cas, on pourrait se trouver devant la réapparition, en grec, de l'élément morphologique ou lexical LA dont nous venons de supposer l'existence. Cette suggestion a pour elle plusieurs arguments qui semblent fortement limiter la possibilité d'une rencontre de hasard : (i) LB **56* est majoritairement attesté à Cnossos; (ii) en outre, il s'agit d'un signe rare (environ quatre-vingt occurrences en tout); (iii) LB *ku-ru-su-*56* est un hapax cnossien; (iv) LA > B **56* est également un signe rare (une quarantaine d'occurrences); (v) il est frappant qu'une séquence de deux signes consécutifs comportant LA > B/LB **56* soit commune à LA > B ***su-*56**-ra* (terme en rapport avec un récipient) et à LB *ku-ru-**su-*56*** (nom de vase assuré). Si tout ceci ne s'écarte pas trop de la réalité, il en découlerait que les valeurs phonétiques des deux signes LA et LB pourraient être identiques ou relativement proches.

c) Les emprunts possibles du LB au LA ne se limitent pas au lexique. On a observé que le mycénien utilise un suffixe -ειος dans des emplois inattendus du point de vue grec, puisqu'il peut servir à former non pas des adjectifs de matière, mais des possessifs. Or, ces emplois sont davantage documentés en Crète que sur le continent. Il se pourrait donc que l'on ait affaire à une influence morphologique de la (ou des) langue(s) préhellénique(s) crétoise(s). On a suggéré que -ειος pourrait être issu d'un suffixe préhellénique en **-eyyos*[55]. Or, ce morphème pourrait se retrouver dans le terme LA *59-103-72-92-1̣0̣0̣ạ-32* (= LA > B *su-ki-ri-te-ị-ja)*[56], qui pourrait (mais ce rapport n'est actuellement pas démontrable) être issu de LA *]59-103-7̣2̣-74* (= LA > B *]su-ki-ṛị-ta* : sur ce dernier mot, voir § 2.2.2.2.1.c). Observer que l'alternance LA *92 ~ 74* mettrait en jeu des signes dont la lecture phonétique, proposée par ailleurs, impliquerait une consonne commune : LA > B *te ~ ta.*

---

[51] Cf. CHADWICK 1975, 145.

[52] NEUMANN 1958 a rapproché LA > B *su-pu* de σιπύη, «huche à pain». L'identité des deux termes n'est toutefois pas assurée, voir CHANTRAINE 1968-1980, 1006.

[53] Le terme (hapax : KN K 740.4) est suivi d'un idéogramme représentant un récipient à trois pieds; il pourrait s'agir d'un vase métallique, car les objets qui lui sont parallèles dans la tablette sont en bronze.

[54] En dernier lieu, MELENA 1987, 208-209, 216, 229.

[55] RUIJGH 1967, 258-262.

[56] MORPURGO DAVIES 1969, 162; KILLEN 1983.

3. INTERPRÉTATION DES TEXTES

3.1. *TEXTES COMPTABLES*

Les textes comptables ont un grand avantage : leur structure est relativement aisée à analyser grâce aux idéogrammes et à l'une de leurs composantes, les chiffres.

C'est dans ces textes que l'on a réussi à découvrir les deux seuls mots de tout le LA dont le sens soit totalement assuré :

(i) LA *98-22* (= LA > B *ku-ro :* une quarantaine d'exemples; c'est le mot le plus fréquent de tout le *corpus* LA) sert à introduire le total d'une série de nombres, et doit donc signifier «somme, tant, etc.» (c'est l'équivalent du LB *to-so/to-sa,* τόσ(σ)ος/τόσ(σ)α, «tant»). Le sens ressort lumineusement de tablettes comme HT 117a (fig. 3), où le nombre introduit ligne 6 par LA > B *ku-ro* est égal à la somme des chiffres des lignes 2-5[57] :

HT 117a.1-6 (LA)		**HT 117a.1-6 (LA > B)**	
1. *95-29-72-92* , *103-22* ,		*ma-ka-ri-te* , *ki-ro* ,	
1.-2 *97-76-26-57* ,		*u-mi-na-si* ,	
2. *97-59*	1	*u-su*	1
2. *76-06*	1	*mi-tu*	1
2.-3. *98-53-27*	1	*ku-ra-mu*	1
3. *95-55*	1	*ma-ru*	1
3. *98-01-25*	1	*ku-*56-nu*	1
3.-4. *06-68-95*	1	*tu-68-ma*	1
4. *97-51-76*	1	*u-di-mi*	1
4.-5. *76-55-74-53-54*	1	*mi-ru-ta-ra-re*	1
5. *92-32-54*	1	*te-ja-re*	1
5. *26-30-54*	1	*na-da-re*	1
6. ***98-22***	**10**	***ku-ro***	**10**

(ii) LA *21-39-98-22* (= LA > B *po-to-ku-ro :* 2 exemples) sert à introduire le total général d'une série de nombres, et doit donc signifier «somme des totaux partiels, tant en tout, etc.» (c'est l'équivalent du LB *to-so-(ku-su)-pa,* τόσ(σ)ος (ξύμ)πανς, «tant en tout»). Le sens ressort clairement d'une tablette comme HT 122 : la ligne a8 a un LA > B *ku-ro* de 31; la ligne b5 a un LA > B *ku-ro* de 65; on a ensuite (b6) un LA > B *po-to-ku-ro* de 96[], égal à la somme des deux LA > B *ku-ro* précédents (31 + 65) :

[57] Il faut signaler, cependant, que certains totaux introduits par LA > B *ku-ro* font difficulté, les uns, à cause d'erreurs arithmétiques des scribes, les autres, en raison de facteurs qui nous échappent.

HT 122 (LA)			HT 122 (LA > B)	
a1.	*[. .]53-72 ,*		*[. .]ra-ri ,*	
a1.	*97-102a-23*	2	*u-de-za*	2
a2.	[	]2	[	]2
a2.	*30-57-85*	2	*da-si-*118*	2
a2-3.	*02-[.]-[.]* [	]	*pa-[.]-[.]* [	]
a3.	*]-51*	1	*]-di*	1
a3.	*92-103*	2	*te-ki*	2
a4.	*62-63-100a*	3	*qa-63-i*	3
a4.	*32-76-30-54*	1	*ja-mi-da-re*	1
a5.	*57-30-54*	1	*si-da-re*	1
a5.	*07-51-53*	1	*07-di-ra*	1
a5.	*02-102a*	1	*pa-de*	1
a6.	*98-01-25*	1	*ku-*56-nu*	1
a6.	*02-74-61*	1	*pa-ta-ne*	1
a6.	*83a-06*	1	*83a-tu*	1
a7.	*[.]-93*	1	*[.]-du*	1
a7.	*98-01-25*	1	*ku-*56-nu*	1
a7.	*30-94-30*	1	*da-94-da*	1
a8.	***98-22***	**31**	***ku-ro***	**31**
a8.	*98-30*	1	*ku-da*	1
b1.	*81a-51 , 11, 99[*	]	*je-di , 11,* VIR[	]
b2.	*83a-103-86*	7	*83a-ki-ta$_2$*	7
b2-3.	[	]	[	]
b3.	*52-53-68 97-102a-23*	2	*a-ra-68 u-de-za*	2
b3-4.	*62-62-55*	2	*qa-qa-ru*	2
b4.	*51*	2	*DI*	2
b4.	*30-54*	2	*da-re*	2
b4bis.	*vacat*		*vacat*	
b5.	***98-22***	**65**	***ku-ro***	**65**
b6.	***21-39-98-22***	**96[]**	***po-to-ku-ro***	**96[]**
b7.	*vacat*		*vacat*	

En dehors de ces deux termes, on ne se meut que sur le terrain mouvant du probable, du possible et de l'inconnu. Je me limite ici à deux exemples.

(iii) LA *103-22* (= LA > B *ki-ro)* est l'un des mots LA les plus fréquents. Ce terme est attesté une quinzaine de fois, uniquement dans des tablettes, et fait visiblement partie du vocabulaire économique. Dans son contexte le plus clair, HT 123a, il se comporte comme le mot LB *o-pe-ro*, ὄφελος, qui signifie «manque, déficit» : après une quantité de produit LA *90*, LA > B *ki-ro* introduit un nouveau nombre, toujours inférieur au précédent. Il semble donc s'agir de quantités manquantes :

HT 123a (LA)

1-2.*103-74-100a* ,	*49*	31	*90*	8E	***103-22***	1ẠẠ
3-4. *64-82a*	*49*	31J	*90*	8ẸJ̣	***103-22***	1Ạ
4-5.*31-55*	*49*	16	*90*	4AẠ	***103-22***	JE[[ ]]
6-7.*30-06*	*49*	15	*90*	4E	***103-22***	JE
7-9.*98-22*	*49*	93J	*90* , *98-22*	2̣5H	***103-22***	6̣[

HT 123a (LA > B)

1-2. *ki-ta-i*	*49*	31	*90*	8E	***ki-ro***	1ẠẠ
3-4. *pu-82a*	*49*	31J	*90*	8ẸJ̣	***ki-ro***	1Ạ
4-5. *sa-ru*	*49*	16	*90*	4AẠ	***ki-ro***	JE[[ ]]
6-7. *da-tu*	*49*	15	*90*	4E	***ki-ro***	JE
7-9. *ku-ro*	*49*	93J	*90* , *ku-ro*	2̣5H	***ki-ro***	6̣[

Il y a par ailleurs une abréviation LA *103* (= LA > B *ki)*, qui a chance de représenter LA *103-22* et qui paraît fonctionner exactement comme l'abréviation LB *o(-pe-ro)* (voir HT 118). Il existe toutefois certaines particularités qui pourraient faire penser que le parallèle de LB *o-pe-ro* ne rend pas compte de tous les emplois de LA > B *ki-ro,* et l'on peut se demander si l'on n'a pas affaire à deux mots homographes, mais de signification différente[58].

(iv) LA *98-60-59* (LA > B *ku-ni-su)* est compris par un certain nombre d'interprètes comme le nom LA du «froment». Il est vrai que, en HT 86a.1-2, b.1-2, le mot est suivi de l'idéogramme LA *511* (= LA > B GRA, «froment», ligaturé à deux autres signes), ce qui ne s'oppose pas à cette interprétation. Toutefois, LA > B *ku-ni-su* apparaît aussi en HT 95a.3, b.3, où il est symétrique à cinq noms. En HT 120.1-2, l'un de ces cinq noms (LA *30-84a* = LA > B *da-me)* est suivi de l'idéogramme LA *511* (= LA > B GRA, «froment», ligaturé). En HT 106.1, le deuxième de ces noms (LA *76-25-92* = LA > B *mi-nu-te)* est suivi de l'idéogramme LA *71* (sans correspondant LB assuré). En HT 123a.4, le troisième de ces noms (LA *31-55* = LA > B *sa-ru)* est suivi de l'idéogramme LA *49* (= LA > B OLIV, «olive»). La conclusion que doit tirer un esprit non prévenu est que ces trois mots, susceptibles d'être associés à des idéogrammes différents, doivent être non pas des noms de denrées, mais bien plutôt des désignations des individus (ou des groupes) qui fournissaient ou recevaient les fournitures symbolisées par les idéogrammes. Mais il en découle que LA > B *ku-ni-su,* puisqu'il leur est symétrique, a chance de faire partie de la même catégorie sémantique qu'eux, et a donc peu de chances d'être le nom du «froment».

---

[58] Cf. HOOKER 1975, 167-168.

3.2. *Textes non comptables*

Les textes non comptables se sont enrichis ces dernières années d'une remarquable collection d'inscriptions provenant des sanctuaires de Kato Symi (SY) et du mont Iouktas (IO). Ces nouveaux textes ont renouvelé dans une mesure non négligeable nos connaissances de ce secteur de l'épigraphie LA.

Bon nombre de documents non comptables offrent l'avantage de présenter des énoncés visiblement structurés, à variations probablement syntaxiques très visibles. Leurs difficultés principales sont les suivantes : (i) le sens des termes qui les constituent est presque toujours extrêmement difficile à établir, fût-ce approximativement; (ii) l'analyse morphologique et syntaxique est ardue, parce qu'il est malaisé d'isoler les morphèmes utilisés, et il est encore plus difficile de déterminer leurs fonctions.

3.2.1. Les mots-clés

Une série de textes comprennent tout ou partie d'un ensemble de dix termes, souvent de formes variables. Ils seront conventionnellement désignés ci-dessous par A-B-C D E F G H I J K X. En voici la liste (j'exclus ici les exemples trop mutilés; les variantes sont indiquées par un chiffre en exposant; la plupart des références renvoient à la liste des textes du § 3.2.2) :

A-B-C

A-B-C comporte un ensemble de trois éléments, constituant le début (A-), le milieu (-B-) et la fin (-C) d'une série de huit mots.

Ces éléments sont les suivants :

A-	A1- : LA > B *]ạ-na-t-* :	***]ạ-na-ti**-88-wa-ja[* (IO Za 8)
	A2- : LA > B *a-ta-* :	***a-ṭạ**-i-88-de-ka* (ZA Z 3)
		***[a-]ta**-i-88-wa-e* (n° 2)
		***a-ta**-i-88-wa-ja* (n° 1, 3, 5, 6, 7, 10, 23, 24)
		***a-ṭạ**-ị-8̣8̣-wa[* (n° 25)
	A3- : LA > B *ja-ta-* :	***ja-ta**-ị-88-u-ja* (AP Z 1)
	A4- : LA > B *ta-na-* :	***ta-na**-i-88-u-ti-nu* (n° 4)
		***ta-na**-ị-88-?ọ* (n° 9)
		***ta-na**-ra-te-u-ti-nu* (n° 1)
-B-	-B1- : LA > B *-i-88-* :	*]ạ-na-ti-**i-88**-wa-ja[* (IO Za 8)
		*a-ṭạ-**i-88**-de-ka* (ZA Z 3)
		*[a-]ta-**i-88**-wa-e* (n° 2)
		*a-ta-**i-88**-wa-ja* (n° 1, 3, 5, 6, 7, 10, 23, 24)
		*a-ṭạ-**ị-8̣8̣**-wa[* (n° 25)
		*ja-ta-**ị-88**-u-ja* (AP Z 1)
		*ta-na-**i-88**-u-ti-nu* (n° 4)
		*ta-na-**ị-88**-?ọ* (n° 9)

-B²- : LA > B *-ra-te- :* *ta-na-**ra-te**-u-ti-nu* (n° 1)

-C	-C¹ : LA > B	*-de-ka* :	*a-ṭa-i-88-**de-ka*** (ZA Z 3)
	-C² : LA > B	*⸗u-ja* :	*ja-ta-ị-88⸗**u-ja*** (AP Z 1)
	-C³ : LA > B	*-u-ti-nu* :	*ta-na-i-88-**u-ti-nu*** (n° 4)
			*ta-na-ra-te-**u-ti-nu*** (n° 1)
			]-ti-nu ou *]**ụ-ti-nu*** (n° 11)
	-C⁴ : LA > B	*⸗wa-e* :	*[a-]ta-i-88⸗**wa-e*** (n° 2); -C⁴ ou ⁵ figure en n° 25.
	-C⁵ : LA > B	*-wa-ja* :	*]ạ-na-ti-88-**wa-ja**[* (IO Za 8); -C⁴ ou ⁵ figure en n° 25.
			*a-ta-i-88-**wa-ja*** (n° 1, 3, 5, 6, 7, 10, 23, 24)
	-C⁶ : LA > B	*-2̣0̣* :	*ta-na-ị-88-**2̣0̣*** (n° 9)

Dans l'analyse ci-dessous, les huit formes d'A-B-C seront symbolisées comme suit :

A¹-B¹-C⁵ : LA > B *]ạ-na-ti-88-wa-ja[* (IO Za 8)
A²-B¹-C¹ : LA > B *a-ṭa-i-88-de-ka* (ZA Z 3)
A²-B¹⸗C⁴ : LA > B *[a-]ta-i-88⸗wa-e* (n° 2); A²-B¹-[C⁴ ou ⁵] figure en n° 25.
A²-B¹-C⁵ : LA > B *a-ta-i-88-wa-ja* (n° 1, 3, 5, 6, 7, 10, 23, 24; A²-B¹-[C⁴ ou ⁵] figure en n° 25)
A³-B¹⸗C² : LA > B *ja-ta-ị-88⸗u-ja* (AP Z 1)
A⁴-B¹-C³ : LA > B *ta-na-i-88-u-ti-nu* (n° 4)
A⁴-B¹-C⁶ : LA > B *ta-na-ị-88-2̣0̣* (n° 9)
A⁴-B²-C³ : LA > B *ta-na-ra-te-u-ti-nu* (n° 1)

D LA > B D¹ : *a-di-ki-te-te* (n° 2, [3])
D² : *ja-di-ki-te-te* (n° 12, 13, 18)
D³ : *ja-di-ki-tu* (n° 1)

E LA > B E¹ : *a-sa-sa-ra-me* (n° 2, 8; IO Zb 10; [E¹ ou ³] figure en n° 3)
E² : *ja-sa-sa-ra-ma-na* (n° 14; [E² ou ³] figure en n° 10, 13, 19, 20)
E³ : *ja-sa-sa-ra-me* (n° [1], 4, 5, 9, 15, 26; [E¹ ou ³] figure en n° 3; [E² ou ³] figure en n° 10, 13, 19, 20)

F LA > B F¹ : *u-na-ka-na-si* (n° [1], 5, 7, [13], [17]; [F¹ ou ³] figure en n° 16; [F¹ ou ²] figure en n° 20)
F² : *u-na-ka-na-si-89* (n° 6; [F¹ ou ²] figure en n° 20)
F³ : *u-na-ru-ḳạ-ṇạ⸗ịạ⸗ṣị* (n° 3; [F¹ ou ³] figure en n° 16)

F^{4} : *u-na-ru-ka-na-ṭị* (n° 2)

G LA > B G^{1} : *i-pi-na-ma* (n° 1, [5], 7, 17, 18, 22)
G^{2} : *i-pi-na-mi-na* (n° [2], 16)
]G[: (n° 9, 13)

H LA > B *si-ru-te* (n° 1, [2], [3], 5, 7, [16], 18, [21], [22], 25)

I LA > B *du-*pu_2*-re* (n° 2, [3], 12, 13)

J LA > B J^{1} : *ị-da-a* (n° 7)
J^{2} : *i-da-mi* (n° 10)
J^{3} : *i-na-i-da-[* (n° 11 ; *i-na-i-da-ṃị[* possible)
J[: *i-da-[* (n° 1)

K LA > B *tu-me-i* (n° 13[̣, 19)

X Termes attestés une seule fois dans le *corpus* votif de référence; un ^{h} en exposant signale que les mots sont des hapax LA assurés. En voici la liste en transcription LA > B :

X^{1h} : *p̣ị-te-ẓạ* (n° 2)
X^{2h} : *a-ko-̣ạ-ṇạ* (n° 2)
X^{3} : *i-na-ja-̣pa-ṛị* (n° 2; cf. X^{6}, X^{28} ?)
X^{4} : *[...]ṇẹ* (n° 3)
X^{5h} : *a-̣pa-̣du-̣pa-̣[* (n° 3)
X^{6} : *pa-̣ṛị* (n° 3 ; cf. X^{3} ?)
X^{7h} : *i-na-ta-i-*7̣9̣-di-si-ka* (n° 4)
X^{8h} : *o-su-qa-re* (n° 5)
X^{9h} : *ja-su-ma-tu-re* (n° 6)
X^{10} : *a-ja* (n° 6)
$X^{11h-12h}$: *tu-ru-sa-*ra_2*-̣163b-re* (n° 7)
X^{13h} : *ṭạ-̣ta-*56-du* (n° 8)
X^{14h} : *ạ-p̣ạ-ị-̣jạ* (n° 8)
X^{15} : *]-2̣0̣* (n° 9)
X^{16} : *]na-[.]-da-da[...][* [59] (n° 11)
X^{17h} : *[ ]-̣*56-2̣0̣* (n° 13)
X^{18h} : *]ta-nu-*$ṭạ_2$*-ti* (n° 14)
X^{19h} : *da-wa* (n° 14)
X^{20h} : *ạ-du-wa-ṇạ* (n° 14)
X^{21} : *i-ja[* (n° 14)
X^{22} : *]-[.]-̣te-ja-ṛẹ* (n° 15)
X^{23h} : *u-qe-ti* (n° 15)
X^{24} : *ṭạ-ṇụ-[...]* (n° 15)
X^{25h} : *ni-nu-ni-[.]-tu-i* (n° 15)
X^{26} : *]ị-̣ku-*56-na-tu-na-te[* (n°17)
X^{27h} : *]pi-mi-na-te* (n° 17)
X^{28} : *i-na-ja-re-ṇụ[* (n° 17 ; cf. X^{3} ?)
X^{29} : *]qa* (n° 17)
X^{30} : *i-di[* (n° 21)
X^{31} : *au[* (n° 23)
X^{32h} : *ja-ti-03[* (n° 24)
X^{33} : *i-ti[* (n° 26)

---

[59] Si le deuxième signe était bien à lire LA > B *ṃị* ou *p̣ị*, on pourrait songer à rapprocher cette séquence du terme J, et en particulier de *i-da-da* en KT ? Z 2 : § 3.2.3.7.

3.2.2. LE FORMULAIRE VOTIF

Le regroupement de ces dix termes constitue clairement des énoncés cohérents.

Leurs variantes peuvent, *a priori*, être de nature phonétique, morphologique, lexicale, graphique, ou provenir d'une combinaison de tout ou partie de ces quatre facteurs. Il semble toutefois que la plupart d'entre elles doivent être morphologiques. Ceci ressort du texte n° 1, où figurent à la fois les formes A^2-B^1-C^5 et A^4-B^2-C^3. De même, les variations concomitantes observables en -C D E F G dans les textes n° 1, 5, 7 ~ 2 font presque invinciblement penser à des phénomènes morphologiques du genre de ce que l'on aurait dans des phrases comme, par exemple, le français «il aime son chat» ~ «ils aime**nt leurs** chats»[60].

Le schéma suivant montre les principaux regroupements attestés dans les textes les mieux conservés :

1. Textes substantiellement complets (voir § 6)

Texte n° 1. A^2-B^1-C^5 D^3 [E^3] [F^1] G^1 H A^4-B^2-C^3 J[± 8 signes] (GODART-OLIVIER 1976-1985 IO Za 2)
Texte n° 2. A^2-B^1-C^4 D^1 I X^{1h} X^{2h} E^1 F^4 [G^2] [H] X^3 (PK Z 11 : texte virtuellement complet : trois signes manquants)
Texte n° 3. A^2-B^1-C^5 [D^1] [I] [H] [$E^{1 \text{ ou } 3}$] [X^4] F^3 X^{5h}[ ] X^6 (PK Z 12)
Texte n° 4. A^4-B^1-C^3 X^{7h} E^3 (GODART-OLIVIER 1976-1985 IO Za 6 - coupelle : texte complet)
Texte n° 5. A^2-B^1-C^5 X^{8h} E^3 F^1 [G^1] H (TL Z 1 - «louche» : texte virtuellement complet : un signe manquant)
Texte n° 6. A^2-B^1-C^5 X^{9h} F^2 X^{10} (GODART-OLIVIER 1976-1985 SY Za 2 : texte complet)
Texte n° 7. A^2-B^1-C^5 $X^{11h-12h}$ J^1 F^1 G^1 H (KO? Z 1 - socle de statuette : texte complet)
Texte n° 8. X^{13h} X^{14h} E^1 (PR Z 1 : texte complet)

2. Textes mutilés

Texte n° 9. A^4-B^1-C^6 [ ]X^{15} E^3[ ]G[(PS Z 2)
Texte n° 10.]A^2-B^1-C^5 J^2 $E^{2 \text{ ou } 3}$[(GODART-OLIVIER 1976-1985 SY Za 1)
Texte n° 11.]X^{16}[ ]-C^3 J^3[(KARETSOU-GODART-OLIVIER 1985 IO Za 11.2)
Texte n° 12.] D^2 I [(PK Z 15)
Texte n° 13.]X^{17h} D^2 I K[ ] $E^{2 \text{ ou } 3}$[ ]F^1[ ] G[(PK Z 8)
Texte n° 14.]X^{18h} E^2 X^{19h} X^{20h} X^{21}[(KN Z 10)
Texte n° 15.]X^{22} X^{23h} E^3 X^{24} X^{25h} (PL Z 1 - «épingle» en or)
Texte n° 16.]$F^{1 \text{ ou } 3}$ G^2 H[(PK Z 10)
Texte n° 17.]F^1 G^1[ ] X^{26}[ ]X^{27h} X^{28}[ ]X^{29} [(AP Z 2 - gobelet)
Texte n° 18.]G^1 H [(VR Z 1)
Texte n° 19.] K $E^{2 \text{ ou } 3}$[(PK Z 14)

---

60 Pour davantage de détails sur cette question, voir DUHOUX 1990.

Texte n° 20. $E^{2\text{ ou }3}$[$F^{1\text{ ou }2}$[(GODART-OLIVIER 1976-1985 IO Za 9; voir § 1.4 note 11)
Texte n° 21. [H] X^{30}[(KARETSOU 1987 IO Za 14)
Texte n° 22.]G^{1} [H][(KARETSOU 1987 IO Za 15)
Texte n° 23. A^{2}-B^{1}-C^{5} X^{31}[(GODART-OLIVIER 1976-1985 IO Za 3)
Texte n° 24. A^{2}-B^{1}-C^{5} X^{32h}[(GODART-OLIVIER 1976-1985 IO Za 7)
Texte n° 25. A^{2}-B^{1}-C[$^{4\text{ ou }5}$]H (GODART-OLIVIER 1976-1985 SY Za 3)
Texte n° 26.] E^{3} X^{33h}[(KARETSOU-GODART-OLIVIER 1985 IO Za 12)

L'immense majorité des phrases retenues ci-dessus (21/26) figurent sur une catégorie spécifique d'objets, conventionnellement appelés «tables à libation». Il s'agit de récipients qui ont été trouvés par centaines dans des lieux de culte (la plupart d'entre eux sont d'ailleurs anépigraphes).

Les phrases gravées sur d'autres supports sont les suivantes. N° 4 : inscrite sur une coupelle provenant du même sanctuaire que le n° 1; n° 15 : «épingle» trouvée dans ou à proximité d'un tombeau; n° 5, 7 et 17 : contexte archéologique précis inconnu; incisées sur, respectivement, «louche» de marbre, socle de statuette et gobelet.

Chaque fois que le contexte archéologique de nos textes est déterminable, il se situe dans une ambiance clairement religieuse (22 fois sur 26). Il n'existe qu'un seul texte à connotation funéraire possible (n° 15). Nos phrases doivent donc très probablement être des formules votives.

3.2.3. SIGNIFICATION DES TERMES DU FORMULAIRE VOTIF

3.2.3.1. A-B-C D E F G H I J K X

Puisque notre petit *corpus* a chance d'être votif, il semble raisonnable de supposer que trois éléments devaient y occuper une place centrale : (i) nom du dédicant; (ii) désignation de la divinité dédicataire; (iii) expression de l'acte réalisé par le dédicant («offrande, prière», etc.).

En outre, d'après les documents parallèles fournis par les civilisations antiques, on s'attend à ce que puissent figurer des mentions accessoires du type de : (iv) désignation générique («cadeau», etc.) ou spécifique («vase», etc.) de l'objet offert; (v) qualification du dédicant («fidèle, prêtre», etc.); (vi) qualification de la divinité («tout-puissant», etc.; pourraient s'y ajouter des désignations de lieux); (vii) expression des sentiments du dédicant ou du motif de son offrande («en reconnaissance», etc.); (viii) datation («lors de la fête de...», etc.)[61]; etc.

Si des éléments comme des démonstratifs, des possessifs, etc. étaient graphiquement soudés à certains mots (§ 4.1.6), il serait, bien entendu, difficile de les déceler.

La fréquence des termes symbolisés par A-B-C D E F G H I J K X est la suivante dans les textes votifs examinés :

---

61 Je remercie Denise Schmandt-Besserat pour cette dernière suggestion.

X : 33 ex.
A-B-C : 15 ex.
E : 15 ex.
F : 10 ex.
G : 10 ex.
H : 10 ex.
D : 6 ex.
I : 4 ex.
J : 4 ex.
K : 2 ex.

Trois termes émergent du lot par leur fréquence, X, A-B-C et E. Ce sont donc eux qui sont les meilleurs candidats pour rendre les trois notions cruciales évoquées à l'instant (§ 3.2.2).

Certaines associations sont si régulières qu'elles ont chance de former de véritables expressions. Leurs groupements sont les suivants :

A^2-B^1-C D (3 fois : n° 1, 2, 3)
A-B-C J (2 fois : n° 1, 10; en outre,]-C J en n° 11)
A-B^1-C X (6 fois : n° 4, 5, 6, 7, 23, 24)
D I (4 fois : n° 2, 3, 12, 13; I n'est pas attesté sans D; I est invariable)
E F (5 fois : n° 1, 2, 5, 13, 20)
E F G (4 fois : n° 1, 2, 5, 13)
F G (7 fois : n° 1, 2, 5, 7, 13, 16, 17 - dans les textes complets, on n'a aucun G sans F, mais on peut avoir F sans G : n° 3, 6; G^1 est toujours associé à F^1 : n° 1, 5, 7, 17; G^2 est associé à F^4 ou à $F^{1 \text{ ou } 3}$: n° 2, 16)
G H (7 fois : n° 1, 2, 5, 7, 16, 18, 22 - dans les textes complets, on n'a qu'un seul H sans G : n° 3; H est invariable)
F G H (5 fois : n° 1, 2, 5, 7, 16)
E F G H (3 fois : n° 1, 2, 5).

Trois termes de la série A-B-C D E F G H I J K peuvent apparaître dans des phrases brèves :

E (seul avec deux X^h : n° 8)
A^4-B^1-C^3 E (seul avec un X^h : n° 4)
A^2-B^1-C^5 F (seul avec un X^h et un X : n° 6)

3.2.3.2. X

Chacun des termes symbolisés par X n'est attesté qu'une seule fois dans nos documents, mais leur importance est considérable. En effet, ils figurent dans l'immense majorité des inscriptions bien conservées (seule exception : la première partie du n° 1, où X est absent - mais la seconde partie est mutilée après le deuxième mot, et il y a place pour environ 8 signes dans la lacune). Leur extrême fréquence et leur caractère d'hapax font qu'ils ont une bonne chance de représenter l'élément le plus variable de textes votifs, à savoir les noms des dédicants ou de leur famille. Cette conclusion semble virtuellement assurée dans les six textes où X figure en deuxième place du formulaire votif, juste après A-B-C (§ 3.2.3.3), ainsi que dans le texte n° 8, où X constitue l'initiale de la phrase. Dans ces sept textes, on ne trouve généralement qu'un seul

X (n° 4, 5) ou qu'un groupe de deux X consécutifs (n° 7 [?], 8) - dans un cas, on a X^{9h} F^{2} X^{10} (n° 6) - les textes n° 23-24 sont mutilés après X.

Dans le texte n° 17, X^{26} comporte une séquence LA > B *]ị-ku-*56-na-tu-na-te[* dont la partie centrale, LA > B *ku-*56-na-tu*, apparaît dans deux textes comptables, HT 47a.1-2 et 119.3. Dans cette dernière tablette, LA > B *ku-*56-na-tu* est parallèle à trois hapax et à LA *83-06*, attesté en HT 122a.6, qui semble être un anthroponyme. Si ce nom était bien l'une des composantes de X^{26} (où l'on aurait alors une *scriptio continua* partielle), on aurait un exemple (unique jusqu'ici) d'anthroponyme attesté à la fois dans les textes votifs et administratifs LA.

Les groupes de X consécutifs pourraient *a priori* constituer soit une formule onomastique complexe («Un Tel, fils de Un Tel»; «Un Tel, de la famille Une Telle»; etc.), soit une désignation de plusieurs dédicants. Observer que les X figurant ailleurs qu'en première ou deuxième place du formulaire apparaissent cinq fois en groupes (deux X : n° 2, 15 [2 ex..], 17; trois X : n° 14). Cette proportion est plus élevée que dans les X de début de phrase, ce qui pourrait être significatif.

Dans deux groupes de X (n° 2, 14), le second X commence par LA > B *a-* et finit par LA > B *...a-na*. Aurait-on là des marques de dérivation ou de coordination ? Les autres termes LA > B en *a-...a-na* (LA > B *a-du-ni-ṭa-na* [ARKH 5.1] et *a-re-sa-na* [TE Z 2]) ne paraissent pas incompatibles avec la première hypothèse, puisqu'ils pourraient être des anthroponymes. D'autre part, en n° 14, on a l'intéressante assonance *-d-w-* de LA > B *da-wa ạ-du-wa-ṇạ* qui évoque une formule onomastique complexe, du type du latin *Lucius Lucilius*. Il faut toutefois observer que la lecture de plusieurs signes cruciaux des mots de n° 2 et 14 est douteuse, ce qui réduit la portée des hypothèses qui viennent d'être formulées - GODART-OLIVIER 1976-1985 lisent, en n° 2, LA > B *a-ko-ạ-ṇẹ* (et non *-ṇạ*), et en n° 14, *da-wa-[.]-ḍụ-wa-ṭọ*.

Cela dit, il ne faut pas se dissimuler que certains termes ont pu être rangés ici à tort parmi les X. Ainsi, X^{3} (dernier mot du texte n° 2) se termine par LA > B *-pa-ṛị*; or, X^{6} (dernier mot du texte n° 3) se lit LA > B *pa-ṛị*. Si les lectures sont correctes, l'identité de signes, de contexte et de place de cette séquence suggère que LA > B *pa-ṛị* pourrait constituer un terme spécifique du formulaire votif.

Le début de X^{3} (texte n° 2) LA > B *i-na-ja-* rappelle X^{28} (texte n° 17), commençant par LA > B *i-na-ja-*. Comme ces séquences occupent des places très différentes dans leurs textes, il semble peut-être imprudent d'en faire des mots autonomes, mais si leur ressemblance n'est pas fortuite, elle pourrait s'expliquer par un élément morphologique commun à X^{3} et X^{28}. Observer aussi que X^{7h} commence par *i-na-*.

3.2.3.3. A-B-C (= LA > B *a-ṭạ-i-88-de-ka* et ses variantes)

Puisque X a été identifié comme constituant le nom du dédicant (§ 3.2.3.2), A-B-C et E, les deux mots les plus fréquents après X, sont d'excellents candidats pour les deux autres éléments cruciaux des formules votives, le nom de la «divinité» dédicataire et l'acte réalisé par le dédicant (§ 3.2.2). Comme A-B-C figure dans un texte qui n'a, selon toute apparence, rien de cultuel, puisqu'il s'agit d'un énorme pithos trouvé dans une remise de «ferme» minoenne (ZA Z

3), le mot peut malaisément se prêter à signifier «divinité». Cette objection ne vaut pas pour le terme E, à qui on conférera donc ce sens (§ 3.2.3.7). Par élimination, A-B-C doit alors vraisemblablement désigner l'acte du dédicant. Cet acte ne peut être spécifiquement religieux («prier» etc.) en raison de l'emploi apparemment profane d'A-B-C en ZA Z 3, mais une signification plus neutre du type de «donner» conviendrait bien à tous les contextes.

A-B-C possède douze composantes, ce qui est sans parallèle dans les mots analysés.

A- : Les quatre variantes de A- mettent en jeu quatre syllabogrammes (LA > B *a, ja, na, ta;* sur leur lecture phonétique, voir § 2.2.2.2.3) qui se combinent entre eux (LA > B *a-na-t-; a-ta-; ja-ta-; ta-na-)*. Observer que LA > B *-t-* est constant.

-B- : Les variations de -B- sont rarissimes : -B^{1}- est la forme utilisée dans presque tous les cas. La seule exception figure en n° 1, où l'on a à la fois -B^{1}- et -B^{2}-. La position de l'unique terme comportant -B^{2}- est remarquable. A^{4}-B^{2}-C^{3} (LA > B *ta-na-ra-te-u-ti-nu*) apparaît après A^{2}-B^{1}-C^{5} D E F G H, c'est-à-dire après la fin du formulaire votif habituel. Il semble donc constituer le début d'une nouvelle phrase. Cette dernière caractéristique est l'un des traits les plus frappants d'A-B-C dans tous ses autres emplois votifs. Le texte n° 1 serait donc constitué par deux propositions (ou phrases) symétriques, la première débutant par A^{2}-B^{1}-C^{5}, la seconde par A^{4}-B^{2}-C^{3}. Telle semble aussi être la structure du texte n° 11, avec, après la première ligne, une séquence]-C^{3} J^{3}[[62].

Comme -B- est l'élément le plus stable de l'ensemble A-B-C, on sera tenté de lui reconnaître le statut de lexème.

En n° 1, après la phrase introduite par -B^{1}- («don» ?), la deuxième phrase débuterait par un autre lexème, -B^{2}-. En contexte votif, on peut songer à des sens du type d'«écouter, accorder, demander», etc.

-C : Parmi les variantes de -C, il en est deux que l'on peut soupçonner d'être purement orthographiques : -C^{2} (LA > B *-u-ja*) et -C^{5} (LA > B *-wa-ja*). En effet, il existe une alternance orthographique LA assurée entre LA > B *wa* et *u* (§ 4.1.6). Si -B- est bien le lexème d'A-B-C, -C devrait être constitué, comme A-, de morphèmes et/ou de mots additionnels.

Observer que -C^{3} (LA > B *-u-ti-nu*) n'apparaît qu'avec A^{4}- (LA > B *ta-na-)*, de sorte que l'on a deux séquences à consonnes identiques : LA > B *t-n*. Il se peut qu'il ne s'agisse que d'une simple coïncidence, mais on ne peut exclure que l'on ait affaire à une sorte de redoublement ou à la récurrence d'éléments morphologiques apparentés[63].

Quelle peut être la fonction des variantes d'A-, -B- et -C ? Il est probable qu'elles puissent avoir un rapport avec le nombre ou le sexe des dédicants mentionnés dans les phrases.

---

[62] D'après tout ceci, il est tentant d'analyser ZA Z 3 comme comportant, à la ligne 2, une phrase qui commencerait par A^{2}-B^{1}-C^{1}.

[63] La troisième attestation d'A^{4}- s'observe avec -C^{6} (LA > B *-20*, signe que GODART-OLIVIER 1976-1985 identifient avec LB *ti*.

Si -B- était un verbe (à supposer que la langue du LA oppose verbes et noms), on pourrait avoir des variations de temps, mode, voix, personne, position sociale du dédicant, etc. On ne peut toutefois exclure qu'A-B-C puisse comprendre plus d'un seul mot. Si les usages LA étaient, sur ce point, comparables à ceux du LB, des mots additionnels, tels que particule initiale de phrase, pronom, démonstratif, article, possessif, etc., pourraient, en théorie, parfaitement y figurer (§ 4.1.6).

Quoi qu'il en soit de ces questions, la fig. 11 illustre les diverses formes possibles des variantes d'A-B-C. La fig. 12 donne, à titre de comparaison, les composantes des formes LB *di-do-si, do-ke, do-se, jo-do-so-si, o-di-do-si, o-do-ke, o-u-di-do-si, o-u-di-do-to* du verbe δίδωμι, «donner».

3.2.3.4. D (= LA > B *a-di-ki-te-te* et ses variantes)

L'alternance A^2-B^1-C D (3 ex.) ~ A-B^1-C X (6 ex.) suggère que D pourrait remplir la même fonction que X. Cette analyse semble trouver appui dans les textes n° 1 et 5, où l'on trouve exactement le même formulaire (A^2-B^1-C^5 E^3 F^1 G^1 H), mais où entre A^2-B^1-C^5 et E^3 figure tantôt D^3, tantôt X^{8h}. L'identité des formes de A-B-C E F G H semble montrer que, dans ces textes, la substitution de D^3 à X^{8h} n'est pas due à des raisons syntaxiques. Va dans le même sens le fait que X et D sont presque toujours incompatibles (seule exception : n° 13). Si X était bien un nom de dédicant, il serait tentant de penser que D puisse remplir la même fonction et être un terme générique («dévôt, serviteur, prêtre», etc.). En ce cas, la ressemblance que D semble présenter avec le nom du «Dicté» serait purement fortuite.

3.2.3.5. D I (= LA > B *a-di-ki-te-te du-pu₂-re* et ses variantes)

L'expression D I (4 exemples) pourrait s'interpréter comme le nom générique du dédicant (§ 3.2.3.4), suivi d'une détermination. Comme I ne semble pas avoir de variantes, il serait séduisant d'y voir une forme adverbiale (bien que des graphies homographes puissent, en théorie, camoufler des formes différentes cf. § 2.2.2.2.1.c) : - on peut songer à un mot signifiant «pour toujours», etc. Sur la séquence [I][H] en n° 3, voir § 3.2.3.7.

3.2.3.6. H (= LA > B *si-ru-te*)

H est l'un de nos rares termes qui soit dépourvu de variante. Comme il constitue avec G l'une des associations les plus fréquentes, on peut se demander si H ne serait pas l'équivalent d'une expression adverbiale, tout comme on l'a supposé pour I (§ 3.2.3.5)[64]. Sur G, voir § 3.2.3.7.

---

[64] Observer (mais il peut s'agir d'une simple coïncidence) que H et I se terminent tous deux par un syllabogramme à vocalisme LA > B *-e* (*du-pu$_2$-re* ~ *si-ru-te*) - *te* fait partie des syllabogrammes pour lesquels une lecture LA > B paraît plausible (§ 2.2.2.2.3); ce n'est pas le cas de *re*.

3.2.3.7. E F G H J

D'après ce qui a été dit plus haut, E F G H J pourraient constituer des désignations de : «divinité»; qualificatif de divinité; expression des sentiments du dédicant; «offrande»; etc.

E (= LA > B *a-sa-sa-ra-me* et ses variantes) : La haute fréquence de E (quinze exemples) le désigne comme un terme important du formulaire votif. On a déjà vu qu'il s'agit d'un excellent candidat au nom de la «divinité» (§ 3.2.3.3) - cette identification a d'ailleurs été fréquemment suggérée. Ceci s'harmonise bien avec la structure de textes comme n° 4, avec A-B-C X E, c'est-à-dire, selon nos hypothèses, «Don/ d'Un Tel/ pour la divinité (?)», ou comme n° 8, avec X X E, «Un Tel/ d'Un Tel/ à la divinité (?)». Voir aussi § 5.3.

J (= LA > B *i-da-a* et ses variantes) : Il est curieux que, en n° 7, E manque, mais que, apparemment à sa place, juste avant F, figure J. Ceci suggère que E et J pourraient avoir des significations similaires. Il est vrai que le texte n° 10 montre une séquence]A^2-B^1-C^5 J^2 E[, où J^2 (= LA > B *i-da-mi)* précède E, mais on pourrait assez facilement imaginer une expression où un terme générique (E) pourrait être associé à une désignation spécifique (J).

Il se fait que J est relativement fréquent dans les textes non comptables. Outre ses emplois dans les textes n° 1, 7, 10 et 11 de notre *corpus*, on l'y trouve sept fois sous les formes suivantes : LA > B *i-da-88* (PK Z 9), *]i-da* (PK Za 17), *i-da* (PK Za 18), *i-da-ma-te* (AR Z 1-2), *i-da-da* (KT? Z 2). La mention d'un nom de divinité serait assez indiquée sur les haches votives AR Z 1-2, où LA > B *i-da-ma-te* est le seul terme qui figure[65].

La transcription LA > B évoque inévitablement le nom de l'«Ida», la célèbre montagne crétoise connue pour être un centre de culte à l'époque minoenne. Se pourrait-il que cette assonance recouvre une identité véritable et que J désigne «la divinité de l'Ida» ? Un élément non défavorable à cette vue est fourni par le fait que LA > B *i* et *da* font partie des syllabogrammes en faveur de la lecture phonétique desquels il existe une présomption favorable (§ 2.2.2.2.3). Il est toutefois dommage que J soit presque toujours attesté dans des textes fragmentaires. D'autre part, LA > B *i-da* figure dans deux tablettes administratives (ZA 21b.1, 27a.1), où il pourrait, entre autres choses, être compris comme anthroponyme. L'interprétation est certainement attrayante, par conséquent; elle est toutefois loin d'être assurée.

F G H (= LA > B *u-na-ka-na-si i-pi-na-ma si-ru-te* et leurs variantes) : Si tout ce qui vient d'être supposé ne s'écarte pas trop de la réalité, le groupe F G pourrait rendre l'expression de l'«offrande» et des sentiments du dédicant («reconnaissant», etc.).

L'association de G avec H, constituant peut-être une expression adverbiale (§ 3.2.3.6), suggérerait pour G H une expression du type de «reconnaissant à

---

[65] Sur une interprétation possible de ce terme (sa finale pourrait avoir un rapport avec le second élément, sans doute préhellénique, du qualificatif divin crétois Βριτό-μαρπις/-μαρτις), voir CREVATIN 1975, 32-33. Sur la lecture des syllabogrammes LA > B *ma* et *te*, voir § 2.2.2.2.3.

jamais», etc., ce qui ferait attribuer à F le sens d'«offrande». Observer que, dans cette hypothèse, le texte n° 3 aurait une séquence du type de «dévôt pour toujours, à jamais à la divinité...» ([D[1]][I][H][E]...), avec une succession d'adverbes en asyndète, ce qui pourrait faire difficulté.

3.2.4. CONCLUSION

J'arrête ici mon analyse du formulaire des textes votifs[66]. Jusqu'ici, elle a abouti aux identifications hypothétiques suivantes :

-B¹- (= LA > B *-i-88-*) : «cadeau», «donner», etc. ? (§ 3.2.3.3)
-B²- (= LA > B *-ra-te-*) : autre lexème («écouter, accorder, demander», etc.) ? (§ 3.2.3.3)
D (= LA > B *a-di-ki-te-te* et ses variantes) : désignation du dédicant : «serviteur», etc. ? (§ 3.2.3.4)
E (= LA > B *a-sa-sa-ra-me* et ses variantes) : désignation du dédicataire : «divinité» ? (§ 3.2.3.7)
F (= LA > B *u-na-ka-na-si* et ses variantes) : «offrande» ? (§ 3.2.3.7)
G (= LA > B *i-pi-na-ma* et ses variantes) : «reconnaissant» ? (§ 3.2.3.7)
H (= LA > B *si-ru-te*) : expression adverbiale qualifiant généralement G ? : «à jamais» ? (§ 3.2.3.3, 3.2.3.7)
I (= LA > B *du-pu$_2$-re)* : expression adverbiale qualifiant D ? : «pour toujours» ? (§ 3.2.3.5)
J (= LA > B *i-da-a* et ses variantes) : «la divinité de l'Ida» ? (§ 3.2.3.7)
X : en tout cas en début de formule, nom propre du dédicant (§ 3.2.3.2)

Quelle valeur peut-on accorder à ces propositions ? La plupart d'entre elles sont, j'espère, raisonnables, peut-être séduisantes, et donnent des résultats globalement plausibles. Par exemple, le texte n° 4 pourrait signifier quelque chose comme «Un Tel a offert à la déesse» (?); le n° 5 : «Un Tel a offert à la déesse une offrande en reconnaissance à jamais» (?) - (autres exemples de traductions possibles : § 3.2.3.7).

La plupart de ces interprétations ont cependant un gros défaut : elles sont trop hypothétiques, parce qu'invérifiables. L'interprétation la plus solide me paraît celle de X. Viennent ensuite celles d'A-B-C et E. À partir de là, plus la chaîne des suppositions s'allonge, plus elle devient fragile.

Une autre remarque doit inciter à la modestie : bon nombre de faits ont été laissés sans aucune explication - le cas le plus flagrant est l'impressionnant groupe des douze composantes d'A-B-C, mais il y a aussi l'ensemble des variantes de D E F G J. Il faudrait essayer de les analyser, de comprendre les fonctions de leurs composantes et de rendre compte de leurs particularités.

---

66 Pour d'autres interprétations combinatoires des textes non comptables, voir MERIGGI 1975, 86-94; CREVATIN 1975, 35-42; BRICE 1983.

4. IDENTIFICATION DE LA LANGUE

Analyser les emplois des signes, essayer de comprendre des textes, c'est ennuyeux et difficile. Mais identifier la langue du LA, voilà qui est passionnant. Ce n'est pas seulement fascinant, c'est aussi facile. La preuve, c'est qu'on l'a fait souvent ! Le LA a été compris comme identique ou apparenté à une série impressionnante de parlers : hittite, louvite, lycien, sanskrit, grec, sémitique, indo-européen, carien, basque, etc[67].

4.1. *DIFFICULTÉS DE L'IDENTIFICATION*

En fait, la question de l'identification de la langue est peut-être la plus difficile de toutes celles que met en jeu le LA. Ceci tient à plusieurs causes.

4.1.1. LONGUEUR RÉDUITE DES TEXTES

Tout le *corpus* LA tient en une dizaine de pages dactylographiées (§ 2.1.3). C'est probablement plus qu'assez pour pouvoir faire des progrès significatifs dans la lecture phonétique des syllabogrammes. Est-ce suffisant pour pouvoir en identifier la langue ? Je ne sais pas s'il est possible de répondre à cette question[68]. Mais je voudrais rappeler que, entre janvier 1951, date de la première *Work Note* de M. Ventris, et juin 1952, date de la *Work Note* n° 20, cruciale pour le déchiffrement du LB, avaient été publiés successivement deux groupes capitaux de textes linéaires B : les tablettes de Pylos (environ 600) trouvées en 1939[69] et plus de 1.500 tablettes cnossiennes[70]. Le LA comporte actuellement un peu moins de 1.500 documents, c'est-à-dire environ un quart de moins que les ± 2.000 textes LB de Ventris.

En outre, les textes LA et LB ont des longueurs très différentes : tout le *corpus* LA actuellement édité totalise seulement 7.396 signes (§ 2.1.3), c'est-à-dire *quatre fois moins* que le seul *corpus* LB de Cnossos (présentement : 26.088 signes), et *huit fois moins* que tout le *corpus* LB actuel (57.398 signes). En fait, le nombre moyen de signes par texte s'élève actuellement à 5,16 en LA, mais à 12,04 en LB[71].

---

67 Références par exemple dans CREVATIN 1975, 45-52; HEUBECK 1979, 22-23; HILLER 1978-1979; JUCQUOIS 1969; POPE 1964, 5-6; POPE-RAISON 1978, 41-46.

68 En 1956, l'avis de M. Ventris était négatif sur ce point (VENTRIS 1956). Il est vrai que, selon les comptages de DOW 1954, 113, il n'existait à cette époque que moins de 300 textes LA édités.

69 BENNETT 1951 (mais Ventris avait reçu un exemplaire du manuscrit de l'édition en juillet 1950 : BENNETT 1989a). D'après DOW 1954, 87, ce volume comportait 566 tablettes.

70 EVANS-MYRES 1952. D'après DOW 1954, 82, le livre est sorti de presse en janvier 1952.

71 Sur les chiffres du LB, voir OLIVIER 1984, 13 et 1987, 237.

4.1.2. Pauvreté syntaxique et lexicale de la majorité des textes

Plus de 70 % des textes linéaires A (1.020/1.432) sont des nodules, scellés ou rondelles. L'immense majorité d'entre eux (plus de 900, d'après mes comptages) ne comporte qu'un seul signe par face. Ce matériel est, bien entendu, déplorable du point de vue linguistique.

Que valent les 30 % de textes restants ? Les cinq sixièmes de ces documents (318 textes) sont des tablettes comptables, consistant généralement en simples listes de mots. C'est un terrain moins défavorable que le groupe précédent, mais il n'est certainement pas optimal : dans des listes d'inventaire, il y a toutes raisons de penser que l'on doit avoir une syntaxe pauvre - or, ce qui est crucial pour l'identification d'une langue, c'est sa morphologie; et les faits morphologiques ne peuvent ressortir que d'une syntaxe riche.

Ce n'est pas tout. Le parallèle de documents similaires fait penser que la majorité des mots des tablettes comptables doivent être des noms propres (de personnes ou de lieux). Un fait semble confirmer cette hypothèse : les tablettes linéaires A comportent un grand nombre d'hapax[72]; or, il paraît hautement probable que ces termes ne sont si rares que parce qu'ils sont des anthroponymes (des toponymes ou des termes du lexique seraient attestés bien plus fréquemment). Ici aussi, le terrain est éminemment hostile à une étude linguistique, puisque l'on n'a vraisemblablement que peu de termes du vocabulaire.

Heureusement, les 94 textes non comptables ont toute chance d'échapper à ces deux défauts, puisque les plus longs d'entre eux doivent très probablement comporter une syntaxe élaborée et une grande proportion de termes du lexique. L'ennui est que ces documents ne représentent que 817 signes - l'équivalent d'une page dactylographiée environ. C'est peu.

4.1.3. Une ou deux langues ?

Il existe peu de mots communs aux textes comptables et non comptables linéaires A. Certains en ont tiré la conclusion que l'on pourrait se trouver devant deux langues différentes, notées par une seule écriture. Cette possibilité n'est pas à exclure *a priori* : en Crète même, au premier millénaire, l'alphabet grec sert à transcrire aussi bien le grec qu'une langue non hellénique, l'étéocrétois.

En fait, cependant, la différence de vocabulaire entre les deux groupes de documents pourrait peut-être s'expliquer par leur différence de sujets. D'autre part, l'analyse morphologique des deux groupes de textes semble montrer qu'ils ont des particularités identiques[73].

Jusqu'à preuve du contraire, il paraît donc plus sage de considérer que le LA ne note vraisemblablement qu'une seule langue.

---

72 À titre d'exemple, les textes comptables de Zakro comportent six hapax sur dix (57/92) - ce calcul se fonde sur un dépouillement personnel de tous les mots complets et des mots mutilés d'au moins trois signes.

73 DUHOUX 1978, 103-106.

4.1.4. EXISTENCE DE LANGUE(S) APPARENTÉE(S) AU LINÉAIRE A

Tous ceux qui identifient la langue du LA font le pari qu'elle serait identique ou apparentée à d'autres langues connues. C'est, incontestablement, une possibilité réelle, et il faut souhaiter vivement, pour notre confort scientifique, qu'elle se trouve un jour démontrée. On aurait, en effet, l'avantage inestimable de pouvoir recourir au connu pour expliquer l'inconnu. Sur la possibilité d'une parenté possible entre langues du linéaire A et du disque de Phaestos, voir § 5.3.

Toutefois, la situation peut être très différente. Le LA pourrait être, à nos yeux, une langue isolée, sans correspondants connus - soit parce qu'il n'existerait actuellement aucune langue connue qui lui serait apparentée; soit parce que des langues apparentées existeraient, mais auraient à ce point évolué qu'une ressemblance avec le LA ne nous serait plus perceptible. Cette possibilité ne peut pas plus être exclue que la précédente. Si elle devait malheureusement se révéler exacte, nous en serions réduits à la seule analyse combinatoire et à la recherche d'emprunts faits par le grec au LA ou par le LA à d'autres langues (§ 4.2.10) pour élucider la structure linguistique du LA.

4.1.5. DIFFICULTÉS CAUSÉES PAR L'ÉCRITURE

Le LA comporte des syllabogrammes (§ 2.2.2.1). Comment les lire ? On a vu que la question n'est pas élucidée, même si les valeurs phonétiques approximatives d'une trentaine de signes paraissent probables (§ 2.2.2.2.3).

Une deuxième difficulté est la suivante. Il se peut que les syllabogrammes notent adéquatement la langue qu'ils transcrivent. Mais on ne peut exclure que le LA ne soit pas parfaitement adapté à la langue qu'il note - en fait, et contrairement à ce qui est souvent écrit, il s'agit de l'hypothèse la plus plausible : aucune écriture naturelle n'atteint le niveau de l'alphabet phonétique international. Dans cette hypothèse, il faudrait admettre que, même si on lisait tous les signes LA, une série de particularités phonétiques des mots pourraient nous être dissimulées par les infirmités de leur système graphique.

4.1.6. DIFFICULTÉS CAUSÉES PAR LES CONVENTIONS ORTHOGRAPHIQUES

Un premier point, extrêmement favorable, vient de ce que le LA sépare généralement les mots par des blancs ou des diviseurs. Il existe quelques exemples de *scriptio continua* intégrale, et il est des cas où l'on peut soupçonner une absence de diviseurs entre deux mots, mais ils constituent l'exception. Il faut toutefois observer que ceci ne nous garantit pas que *tous* les mots LA soient séparés les uns des autres. On ne peut exclure, en effet, des phénomènes du type de ceux qui s'observent en LB : graphie en continu des mots monosyllabiques (à supposer que la langue du LA les ait connus), des mots dépourvus d'accent, etc. (§ 3.2.3.3 - voir aussi § 5.3).

Une autre question orthographique est la suivante : si la langue du LA connaissait des séquences /C^1C^2/, /$C^1C^2C^3$/, et /VC #/, comment les notait-on, puisque le syllabaire LA est probablement du type V, $C^1(C^2)V$ (§ 2.2.2.1) ? Il est possible de répondre en partie à ces questions. On a pu montrer, en effet, en étudiant la fréquence du dernier signe des mots LA, qu'il existait une répartition similaire à celle du LB[74]. Autrement dit, le LA ne connaîtrait pas de notation des consonnes finales de mots par un signe syllabique à voyelle «morte» constante, comme en chypriote classique.

D'autre part, une analyse des associations des syllabogrammes LA a mis en évidence qu'il ne semble pas y exister d'associations privilégiées, du type de ce que montre le LB dans les sons de liaison (...*i-j*-...), ou dans la notation de groupes consonantiques (C^1V^1-C^2V^1 notant /$C^1C^2V^1$/)[75].

Ces deux recherches indiquent que le LA note ses *glides* et voyelles «mortes» de manière non strictement codifiée - notation sporadique de *glides;* voyelles «mortes» inexistantes ou de timbre variable. Cette conclusion, si elle est correcte, témoigne de ce que le LA aurait des usages orthographiques (au moins) partiellement différents de ceux du LB.

Une confirmation de cette dernière vue est fournie par les formes LA *91-58-97* (HT 1a.1, 95a.4-5, b.4-5) = LA > B *qe-*ra_2*-u* ~ LA *62-58-75a* (HT 86a.3) = LA > B *qa-*ra_2*-wa*. Rappelons qu'il s'agit de deux graphies différentes d'un seul et même mot (§ 2.2.2.2.1.b). Comme ce mot figure au milieu de plusieurs autres termes, écrits, eux, de la même manière, il est probable que la différence de graphie ne recouvre pas une différence morphologique. Il doit bien plutôt s'agir de variations phonétiques ou purement orthographiques, puisque les deux formes ont été écrites par des scribes différents. L'alternance LA > B *u* ~ *wa* a des parallèles en LB (cf. LB *ra-**u**-ra-ti-jo* ~ *ra-**wa**-ra-ti-jo*), où elle traduit une graphie de /wC/, *mais jamais en position finale* et uniquement dans des conditions d'environnement phonétique bien déterminées. La forme LA donne l'impression d'une graphie /w/ (ou /wC/ ?) *en finale absolue.* Il semble donc probable, au moins sur ce point, que les conventions orthographiques LA diffèrent de celles du LB.

Cette conclusion est entièrement confirmée par une pratique matérielle comme la répartition des mots dans les tablettes : le LB n'écrit jamais de mots qui chevauchent deux lignes - il préfère modifier le format des signes, les serrer, ou les écrire au dessus de la ligne d'écriture. Le LA, lui, n'hésite pas à répartir un même mot sur deux lignes différentes.

4.1.7. ABSENCE DE BILINGUE

À ce jour, on ne connaît aucun texte bilingue LA ~ autre langue (en écriture LA ou autre).

4.1.8. DIVERSITÉ DES SYSTÈMES DE TRANSNUMÉRATION DES SIGNES LA

Ce qui précède a montré que le LA n'est pas simple. Il est d'autant plus regrettable qu'aux difficultés propres à cette écriture s'ajoutent des complications modernes. En effet, depuis peu (parution du dernier volume de GODART-

74 DUHOUX 1978, 68-70.
75 CONSANI-FEDERIGHI 1986.

OLIVIER 1976-1985), celui qui étudie le LA est confronté à deux systèmes radicalement différents de transnumération des signes. Ainsi, le terme LA > B *u-na-ka-na-si,* qui était transnuméré précédemment LA *97-26-29-26-57* par la plupart des savants, est désormais transcrit *10-06-77-06-41* par GODART-OLIVIER 1976-1985, vol. 5). Je trouve incompréhensible que dans un secteur déjà si ardu, des complications parfaitement évitables alourdissent à ce point la tâche des chercheurs. Il serait hautement souhaitable qu'un accord international règle les questions de transcription du LA, comme cela s'est fait, avec succès, pour le LB.

4.2. *CRITÈRES DE VALIDITÉ DES DÉCHIFFREMENTS*

À quelles conditions doit répondre un déchiffrement de la langue du LA pour avoir une chance d'être considéré comme convaincant ? Les lignes qui suivent tentent de donner des éléments de réponse, en énumérant onze conditions *nécessaires.* Je ne pense pas qu'elles soient suffisantes.

Les quatre premières ne sont pas linguistiques, mais la nécessité de leur respect paraît si importante pour la validité de tout déchiffrement que je les rappelle ici.

4.2.1. Utilisation de **textes correctement édités** (§ 2.1.1) : il va de soi que l'emploi de textes erronés vicie tout essai à la base. Rappelons aussi qu'il convient de tenir compte du degré de certitude des lectures : un texte pointé est toujours de lecture douteuse et il est dangereux de s'y fier pour des points cruciaux.

4.2.2. Reconnaissance de **la composante syllabique** de l'écriture (§ 2.2.2) : tout déchiffrement qui refuserait d'admettre l'existence de cette caractéristique est à rejeter sans appel.

4.2.3. Valeurs phonétiques linéaires A méthodologiquement justifiées (§ 2.2.2.2) : il est évident que des lectures phonétiques créées *ad hoc* sont dépourvues de toute valeur.

Les justifications de type acrophonique[76] doivent attirer la plus grande méfiance, étant donné le caractère presque nécessairement aléatoire des résultats[77].

Je voudrais attirer l'attention sur le fait que la présentation d'une «grille», donnant le classement des syllabogrammes par rangées de consonnes et par colonnes de voyelles *ne fournit en aucune manière la preuve qu'un déchiffrement du LA a suivi les mêmes méthodes que celui du LB.* Il ne suffit

---

[76] Dans ce type de démarche, un signe ayant la forme de, par exemple, une «main» sera censé avoir la valeur phonétique de la première syllabe du ou de l'un des mots signifiant «main» dans la langue rapprochée du LA.

[77] Ceci tient à plusieurs causes : (i) il arrive souvent que l'interprétation du graphisme d'un signe soit discutable; (ii) même en cas d'interprétation évidente, l'existence de synonymes ou de formes différentes variant avec le temps réduit considérablement la rigueur du raisonnement.

pas d'imiter la *présentation* de M. Ventris; il faut d'abord s'inspirer de sa *méthode*.

Par ailleurs, ce qui a été dit plus haut de la probabilité d'une série d'altérations mineures des valeurs phonétiques LA lors de la création du LB (§ 2.2.2.2.3) fait attendre d'un déchiffrement réussi qu'il découvre ces modifications et en rende compte de façon cohérente (ou qu'il établisse leur absence, dans le cas contraire).

4.2.4. Règles orthographiques explicites, permettant une interprétation rigoureuse des mots lus. Plus grandes sont les latitudes orthographiques que s'autorise un déchiffrement, plus petit est, en principe, le crédit que l'on peut lui donner - ainsi, si l'on ne tient pas compte des voyelles, on peut rapprocher (et considérer, si l'on veut, comme variantes d'un même mot) des formes aussi différentes que français «marteau» ~ «mérite» ~ «mort» ~ «myrte»; etc. Chacun sait, bien entendu, que ces rapprochements seraient irrecevables.

4.2.5. Mise en évidence du **système morphologique** de la langue : il ne suffit pas d'épingler quelques morphèmes isolés; il faut impérativement réussir à décrire la *structure linguistique* en cause, de manière à rendre compte d'une partie importante de la morphologie de nos textes. Ce point est crucial, car il touche à la nature même de la langue. En outre, comme les morphèmes sont moins sujets à l'emprunt que le lexique et l'onomastique, ils constituent un élément probant particulièrement valable.

Il se fait que la morphologie du LA met en jeu un ensemble d'éléments parfois très complexes - on en a un excellent exemple avec le terme A-B-C des textes votifs (§ 3.2.3.3). Un déchiffrement réussi doit être capable de rendre compte de l'intégralité des alternances observables.

4.2.6. Reconstitution de la structure phonétique de la langue, de manière à pouvoir effectuer une comparaison systématique avec la ou les langues que l'on suppose apparentées. On attend une élucidation du vocalisme (combien de voyelles et de quel type ?) et du consonantisme (quel type de consonnes ?) LA.

Une des voies d'approche qui a été employée dans la description du phonétisme LA a utilisé les particularités du syllabaire LA, tel qu'on croit pouvoir le reconstituer - entre autres, sa caractéristique la plus assurée, qui est de ne posséder sans doute que des signes à syllabe ouverte (§ 2.2.2.1). Se fondant sur une adéquation supposée entre graphie et phonétisme, on a été tenté d'en inférer que la langue du LA n'aurait possédé que ce type de syllabes.

En fait, cette conclusion semble éminemment hypothétique. Elle suppose que le syllabaire LA serait parfaitement adapté au système phonétique de la langue qu'il note. Or, il s'agit là d'un *a priori* dont l'histoire des écritures montre la fausseté quasiment générale. Il est d'ailleurs frappant de voir qu'un certain nombre de toponymes LB crétois non explicables par le grec, et qui ont donc chance d'être des emprunts préhelléniques, comportent des syllabes fermées - ainsi, 'Αμνισός, ῎Απταρα, Δίκτα, Φαιστός, etc.[78].

4.2.7. Établissement des **usages syntaxiques** propres à la langue du LA et comparaison systématique avec la ou les langues que l'on suppose apparentées.

[78] HEUBECK 1983, 157-159.

Ici encore, le terme A-B-C des textes votifs fournit un bon exemple de ce que doit fournir un déchiffrement réussi. A-B-C figure toujours en tête de proposition ou de phrase. On attend donc que la langue rapprochée du LA permette d'expliquer les raisons de cette position initiale.

4.2.8. Élucidation d'un nombre maximal de **termes du lexique**. Ce point est le moins probant, à cause de la possibilité constante d'emprunts à des langues diverses[79].

Il va toutefois de soi qu'à partir d'un certain pourcentage de *l'ensemble* des termes du *corpus* LA, la masse des concordances lexicales avec une langue donnée devrait constituer un argument en faveur de la parenté entre les deux idiomes.

4.2.9. Interprétation intégrale d'un nombre maximal de documents. Il ne suffit pas de prendre quelques textes sélectionnés et de les interpréter. Le même traitement doit être appliqué à l'ensemble du *corpus*, et spécialement à ses textes les plus révélateurs du point de vue linguistique, les textes non comptables (§ 3.2).

4.2.10. Compatibilité maximale avec les éléments LB suspectés d'être des emprunts aux créateurs du LA.

Le LB utilise une série d'abréviations non expliquées par le grec et qui se retrouvent en LA.

L'idéogramme du «tissu», LB TELA, peut être ligaturé avec les syllabogrammes LB *ku* ou *zo;* or, le même idéogramme se retrouve en LA, où il peut être ligaturé aux mêmes signes (LA *98* et *36).*

L'idéogramme LB du «boeuf» (BOS : emploi idéographique de LB *mu*), de la «chèvre» (CAP : emploi idéographique de LB **22*), du «mouton» (OVIS : emploi idéographique de LB *qi*) et du «porc» (SUS : emploi idéographique de LB *au*), se retrouvent avec la même signification en LA (respectivement LA *27, 140, 48b, 113* - LA *27, 48b* et *113* fonctionnent également comme syllabogramme).

L'indication du sexe mâle des animaux semble faite par la ligature du signe LB *pa*, et on la retrouve en LA, avec le signe *02* = LA > B *pa*, ligaturé aux mêmes idéogrammes.

On a déjà vu plus haut le cas de LB *NI*, «figue», qui semble reposer sur νικύλεον (§ 2.2.2.2.1.c.3), et qui se retrouve lui aussi en LA.

L'idéogramme LB de la «laine», LANA, est très clairement hérité de l'idéogramme LA *546*, lui-même formé par la ligature des deux syllabogrammes LA *95+55*. Il est donc possible que «laine» ait eu, en LA, une forme ressemblant à LA > B *ma-ru* ou *ru-ma*. On a suposé que telle serait la source du nom grec de la «touffe de laine», μαλλός, d'étymologie inconnue.

---

[79] Ainsi, la petite tablette LB MY Ge 605 (6 lignes) ne contient pas moins de quatre emprunts assurés ou probables : deux au sémitique («cumin», «sésame»); un à une langue préhellénique («menthe»); un au fond «méditerranéen» («coriandre»); plus un cinquième terme susceptible d'être un emprunt («fenouil»).

Une série de mots linéaires B semblent inexplicables par le grec et pourraient peut-être avoir été hérités de la langue LA. C'est le cas de termes techniques relatifs aux textiles, comme LB *ko-u-ra*, *te-pa* et *tu-na-no* dont on est sûr qu'ils désignent chacun une sorte particulière de tissus, mais qui semblent ininterprétables par le grec.

Dans aucun des cas cités ci-dessus, on n'est assuré que ces termes, s'ils sont bien des emprunts, soient issus du LA[80]. Mais ils peuvent théoriquement l'être, en tout ou en partie. Et en ce cas, un déchiffrement réussi devrait être capable de les expliquer.

4.2.11. Respect constant du **principe d'économie**

L'identification linguistique du LA doit mettre en jeu le moins d'hypothèses possible, et ces hypothèses devraient être à tous égards les plus simples possible.

Ainsi, du point de vue historico-géographique, recourir, par exemple, au chinois est théoriquement concevable, mais est moins économique que de supposer une parenté de la langue LA avec un parler du bassin méditerranéen.

Du point de vue sémantique, les interprétations proposées doivent être compatibles avec le contexte immédiat des inscriptions - type de l'objet et environnement archéologique direct - de même qu'avec leur contexte général - type de textes trouvés dans l'Antiquité méditerranéenne.

Du point de vue linguistique, tout déchiffrement devra postuler la régularité des usages orthographiques, des changements phonétiques et la récurrence des traits morphologiques et syntaxiques. En outre, il sera contre-indiqué de devoir faire appel, en dehors des emprunts lexicaux, à plusieurs langues différentes.

4.3. *VALEUR DES DÉCHIFFREMENTS PROPOSÉS À CE JOUR*

Y a-t-il un déchiffrement qui satisfasse aux critères qui viennent d'être indiqués ?

Malheureusement pour les déchiffreurs (et pour nous), la réponse est : non. Il ne suffit pas, en effet, de sélectionner quelques textes linéaires A choisis, d'expliquer (plus ou moins bien) une petite partie de leur vocabulaire, d'en justifier un peu de morphologie, et d'ajouter pour finir une pincée de phonétique. Ce que l'on obtient, avec cette procédure, c'est tout simplement une possibilité. Ce qu'un déchiffrement réussi offre, c'est tout autre chose : une nécessité impérieuse, qui fait que l'on se rend compte qu'il n'est pas possible d'échapper à la solution proposée.

Le jugement que je viens de formuler est évidemment pessimiste, mais il faut bien en préciser la valeur. Il ne signifie nullement que le LA ne puisse pas être apparenté à la famille sémitique, indo-européenne, ou à une quelconque autre langue de la Méditerranée ancienne. Il implique simplement que les essais

---

80 Rien ne permet de penser qu'il n'y ait eu qu'une seule langue non hellénique parlée en Crète au IIe millénaire. Au contraire, il existe des présomptions en faveur de l'existence de plusieurs idiomes non helléniques dans la Crète de l'âge du bronze (DUHOUX 1982, 14-16). D'autre part, si le LA a fourni certains termes au LB, il a pu lui-même les emprunter à d'autres langues.

actuels de déchiffrement par le sémitique, l'indo-européen, etc. ne sont pas convaincants - que l'on se souvienne des nombreuses tentatives de déchiffrement du LB par le grec avant 1952. Elles étaient toutes fausses, comme l'a montré le déchiffrement, réussi, de Ventris. Et pourtant, le LB est bien du grec - seulement, ce n'est pas le même que celui des déchiffrements incorrects.

Bien entendu, chaque déchiffreur est fermement et sincèrement convaincu qu'il a raison, et c'est cela qui fait difficulté. Car, pour citer un texte que j'aime bien, "no more than one decipherment could be true." Il est vrai que son auteur ajoute ce qui suit : "Further thought convinces me that they probably are all right-each in its own of those simultaneous universes, to which the science fiction writers have introduced us, and with which we have communication only through a fourth dimension[81]".

5. PERSPECTIVES D'AVENIR

Si l'on admet ce qui précède, on conclura que la langue du LA n'a pas encore été identifiée, que l'interprétation de ses textes n'est pas très avancée, et que la lecture phonétique de ses signes n'en est actuellement qu'au niveau des probabilités. Que peut-on faire pour améliorer les choses ?

5.1. *DÉCOUVERTE DE NOUVEAUX TEXTES*

Il faut d'abord mentionner un facteur qui échappe en grande partie au contrôle : la mise à jour de nouveaux textes. Très régulièrement, les archéologues - bénis soient-ils à tout jamais ! - trouvent de nouvelles inscriptions en LA. S'ils pouvaient mettre à jour un nouvel Haghia Triada (§ 1.2) ou un nouveau Iouktas (§ 3.2), les études minoennes feraient sans aucun doute des progrès substantiels. Ces trouvailles, et leur publication rapide, sont vitales pour le progrès de nos études, parce qu'elles permettent d'augmenter un *corpus* dont nous avons vu le caractère limité.

Indépendamment de ce facteur, il y aurait un intérêt considérable à intensifier l'étude interne, combinatoire, et externe, comparative, du LA.

5.2. *ÉTUDE INTERNE DU LA*

Il y aurait lieu d'étudier systématiquement, de façon purement combinatoire, les textes LA (et spécialement ses documents non comptables), de manière à en perfectionner la compréhension.

Ainsi, il faudrait : (i) reconstituer les ensembles d'archives écrits par un même scribe[82], de manière à replacer les tablettes dans leur contexte originel; (ii) déterminer le statut probable de tous les mots LA (anthroponymes, toponymes,

---

81 BENNETT 1968, 117.

82 Voir RAISON-POPE 1971, xx-xxi et GODART-OLIVIER 1976-1985, vol. 5, 83-113.

théonymes, termes du lexique; type de sphère lexicale : économique, religieuse, etc.); (iii) isoler les morphèmes du LA et tenter de découvrir leur fonction; (iv) mettre au point des modèles morphologiques et syntaxiques, et essayer de les appliquer au plus grand nombre de textes possible, de manière à en vérifier le pouvoir explicatif; (v) effectuer des comparaisons systématiques en vue de déceler d'éventuelles particularités linguistiques personnelles, locales ou chronologiques; (vi) étudier systématiquement la fréquence des signes et leurs associations, de manière à déceler les groupements vocaliques et/ou consonantiques; (vii) tester la valeur des rapprochements de termes LA ~ LA et LA ~ LB comportant des séquences communes de signes consécutifs (§ 2.2.2.2.1.b-c); etc.

5.3. *ÉTUDE EXTERNE DU LA*

Il serait intéressant d'éclairer le LA par les enseignements que peuvent apporter les textes écrits en d'autres écritures. Cette étude devrait s'opérer dans deux directions : la Crète et le reste de la Méditerranée ancienne.

En Crète, la langue de l'un des textes non linéaires de l'île, le disque de Phaestos (non déchiffré à ce jour, mais il est hautement probable que son écriture est un syllabaire à syllabes ouvertes[83]), semble présenter des similitudes de structure avec la langue linéaire A. Ceci a fait supposer que ces deux idiomes pourraient être apparentés ou même identiques[84]. Il y a sans doute peu de profit immédiat à tirer de cette hypothèse (à supposer qu'elle soit exacte), mais le rapprochement ne devrait pas être perdu de vue.

D'autres textes crétois qui pourraient se révéler intéressants sont ceux que note l'écriture «hiéroglyphique» crétoise (§ 1.1; en abrégé ci-dessous : H). Cette écriture a une composante phonétique qui note très probablement un syllabaire à syllabes ouvertes (POPE 1968). Bien entendu, le *corpus* «hiéroglyphique» actuel est déplorablement restreint[85], de sorte que la comparaison avec le LA risque d'être plus profitable à l'«hiéroglyphique» qu'au LA. D'autre part, cette comparaison risque de poser plus de problèmes qu'elle n'en résoudra. Elle vaut toutefois la peine d'être tentée. Je me limite à un exemple (fig. 13).

Il existe un terme «hiéroglyphique» qui apparaît à plusieurs reprises sur des sceaux : H *36-60-60-80-40.* Or, H *36* est formellement identique à LA *52* (= LA > B *a*), et H *60* à LA *31* (= LA > B *sa*). Si l'on suppose que ces signes H ont la même valeur phonétique que les signes LA > B[86], on aurait donc un terme débutant par H > LA > B *a-sa-sa-*.

On a depuis longtemps suggéré qu'il s'agirait du même mot que le terme LA *52-31-31-53-84a* (= LA > B *a-sa-sa-ra-me*), si fréquent dans les textes votifs[87]. Or, il existe une attestation du mot «hiéroglyphique» qui est spécialement digne

83 DUHOUX 1980, 117-119.

84 DUHOUX 1983.

85 270 documents, totalisant 1.537 signes (OLIVIER 1989) : c'est cinq fois moins que le *corpus* LA, et *plus de trente fois moins* que le *corpus* LB.

86 Cette question demanderait des développements qu'il n'est évidemment pas possible de donner ici.

87 Sur l'historique de ce rapprochement, voir GRUMACH 1958, 178.

d'intérêt. Dans le sceau P 41b[88], on a le texte suivant[89] : H *+36+ 60-60-80-40 +*, (= H > LA > B *+a+ sa-sa-80-ne +*, avec, très clairement, séparation du mot en deux éléments. Cette graphie suggère que LA > B *a-* (de même que sa variante : LA > B *ja-)*, pourrait peut-être constituer un mot accessoire dans LA > B *(j)a-sa-sa-ra-me.*

Tout ceci est extrêmement séduisant, mais il convient de voir que le fondement de toutes ces hypothèses est fragile, car l'identité des mots H et LA n'est actuellement pas démontrable. Il est vrai que le sens de «divinité» attribué hypothétiquement à LA > B *a-sa-sa-ra-me* (§ 3.2.3.7) serait compatible avec l'apparition de H *36-60-60-80-40* uniquement sur des scellés, mais il faut observer que le quatrième signe du mot «hiéroglyphique» comporterait une consonne /n/, alors que les trois formes du terme LA ont à cet endroit un signe en /m/ (§ 3.2.1, terme E).

Les langues de la Méditerranée ancienne pourraient, elles aussi, jeter une lumière intéressante sur le LA - ne fût-ce que par leur onomastique. Ainsi, le terme LA *75a-93-60-76* (= LA > B *wa-du-ni-mi)*, est attesté en HT 6b.1 et 85b.4-5, où il a chance d'être un anthroponyme. On a relevé depuis longtemps une similitude frappante avec le nom propre lycien *βadunimi*[90].

Parmi ces langues, les familles indo-européenne et sémitique constituent, bien entendu, un secteur extrêmement important. Il me semble qu'il y aurait toutefois intérêt à pousser l'enquête dans les zones, moins connues, mais peut-être plus prometteuses, des langues non indo-européennes et non sémitiques de la Méditerrannée : ce secteur pourrait probablement jeter des lumières nouvelles sur le LA.

5.4. *CONCLUSION*

Le linéaire A demande donc encore un travail considérable avant d'être déchiffré. Toutefois, les outils de travail sont désormais sous la main : éditions de qualité, *indices* bien au point. Si l'on a la patience de les utiliser dans un esprit désintéressé, sans vouloir déchiffrer à tout prix, mais, simplement, dans le but de mieux connaître, peut-être, quelqu'un, un jour, quelque part, aura-t-il la divine surprise de se dire : «Mais c'est du... ![91]»

---

[88] EVANS 1909, 157.

[89] Dans la transcription qui suit, le signe H + représente une marque de ponctuation.

[90] Cf. MERIGGI 1956, 6.

[91] Compléter les pointillés. Sur les questions évoquées ici, on consultera, outre les travaux déjà cités ci-dessus, les publications suivantes : SCHACHERMEYR 1964, 229-267; WARREN *et alii* 1969.

6. Annexe : Textes votifs subtantiellement complets examinés § 3.2.

Sauf indication contraire, l'édition suivie est celle de RAISON-POPE 1980. La référence de chaque texte est suivie d'une brève description de l'objet et de sa datation.

Texte n° 1

GODART-OLIVIER 1976-1985, vol. 5 IO Za 2 («table à libations»; datation : MM III ?)

LA 1. *52-74-100a-88-75a-32 , 32-51-103-06 , 32-31-31-53[-*
84a 97-26-29-26-]57[92] ⌞,⌟ *100a-56a-26-95 ,*
2. *57-55-92 , 74-26-53-92-97-78-25 , 100a-30*-[± 8 signes]

LA > B 1. *a-ta-i-88-wa-ja , ja-di-ki-tu , ja-sa-sa-ra[-me u-na-ka-na-]si*
⌞,⌟ *i-pi-na-ma ,*
2. *si-ru-te , ta-na-ra-te-u-ti-nu , i-da*-[± 8 signes]

Texte n° 2

PK Z 11 («table à libations»; datation : ?)

LA a. *[52*[93]*-]74-100a-88-̣75a-44 , 52-51-103-92-92 9̣3̣-*
b. *3̣4̣-54 , 56ạ-92-2̣3̣ , 52-45-̣5̣2̣-2̣6̣ 5̣2̣-*
c. *3̣1̣-31-53-84a , 97-26-55-29-26-7̣8̣*
d. *100ạ-5̣6̣ạ-2̣6̣-7̣6̣[-26-]57-55-[.] , 100a-26-32-̣02-7̣2̣*

GODART-OLIVIER 1976-1985, vol. 4 PK Za 11 :
a. *5̣2̣-74-100a-88-75a-44 , 52-51-103-92-92-[.]*
dernier signe : *9̣8̣, 9̣7̣,* ou *9̣3̣*
b. *[.]-3̣0̣ , 56a-92-7̣2̣ , 52-45-5̣2̣-6̣1̣ ,*

---

[92] L'inscription figure sur une «table à libations» carrée à cannelures externes. Il existe cinq cannelures par face, plus une cannelure à chaque coin. Le texte est gravé sur le côté externe du récipient, en deux lignes parallèles : (1) dans les cannelures constituant la décoration supérieure, à raison d'un signe par cannelure, sur tout le pourtour; (2) dans la zone inférieure, sur les faces a-c. L'inscription a été mutilée sur les deux tiers finaux de la face c et sur le premier tiers de la face d. Le nombre de cannelures permet d'évaluer avec exactitude le nombre de signes manquants à la ligne (1), qui doit se monter à cinq. Le parallèle du texte n° 5 impose la restitution.

[93] Premier signe : l'espace vacant exclut LA *32,* mais admet *52.*

c. *...97-26-55-29-26-78 ,*
d. *100a-56a-2̣6̣-7̣6̣-2̣6̣* ⌞ ⌟ *57-55-[.] , 100a-26-32-02-72*

LA > B a. *[a-]ta-i-88-̣wa-e , a-di-ki-te-te ḍụ-*
b. *pụ$_2$-re , p̣ị-te-ẓạ , a-ko-̣ạ-ṇạ ạ-*
c. *ṣạ-sa-ra-me , u-na-ru-ka-na-ṭị*
d. *ị-p̣ị-ṇạ-ṃị[-na-]si-ru-[.] , i-na-ja-̣pa-ṛị*

GODART-OLIVIER 1976-1985, vol. 4 PK Za 11 :
a. *ạ-ta-i-88-wa-e , a-di-ki-te-te-[.]*
dernier signe : *ḳụ*, *ụ*, ou *ḍụ*
b. *[.]-ḍạ , pi-te-ṛị , a-ko-ạ-ṇẹ ,*
c. *...u-na-ru-ka-na-ti ,*
d. *i-pi-ṇạ-ṃị-ṇạ* ⌞ ⌟ *si-ru-[.] , i-na-ja-pa-ri*

Texte n° 3

PK Z 12 («table à libations»; datation : ?)

LA a.1. *52-74-100a-88-75a-32 , 52-51-103-9̣2̣[-92 93-]*
b.1. *[34-]5̣4̣ 57-5̣5̣[-92 32/52-31-31-]53-84a*
c.1. *[...]6̣1̣ 97-26-55-2̣9̣-2̣6̣-̣3̣2̣-̣5̣7̣-̣*
d.1. *52-̣02-̣93-̣02-̣[ ]*
d.2. *vacat* *02-̣*
a.2. *7̣2̣ vacat*
b-c.2. *vacant*

d.1 : *...-̣[* compatible avec *...-̣3̣2̣[.*

GODART-OLIVIER 1976-1985, vol. 4 PK Za 12 :
b.1. *[ ]57-[* (*[ ]57-5̣5̣[* possible)
c.1. *52[ ]-61* (ou *]5̣2̣-61)* , *97-26-55-29[ ]32-57* ou *97-26-55-29-2̣6̣-32-57*
d.1. *52-0̣2-93-0̣2̣-[ ]32[ ]32-02-62*

LA > B a.1. *a-ta-i-88-wa-ja , a-di-ki-ṭẹ[-te du-]*
b.1. *[pu$_2$-]ṛẹ si-ṛụ[-te ja/a-sa-sa-]ra-me*
c.1. *[...]ṇẹ u-na-ru-ḳạ-ṇạ-̣ja-̣ṣị-̣*
d.1. *a-̣pa-̣du-̣p̣ạ-̣[ ]*
d.2. *vacat* *pa-̣*
a.2. *ṛị vacat*
b-c.2. *vacant*

d.1 : *...-̣[* compatible avec *...-̣jạ[.*

GODART-OLIVIER 1976-1985, vol. 4 PK Za 12 :
b.1. *[ ]si-[* (*[ ]si-ṛụ[* possible)

c.1. *a[ ]-ne* (ou *]ạ-ne)* , *u-na-ru-ka[ ]ja-si* (ou *u-na-ru-ka-ṇạ-ja-si)*
d.1. *a-pa-du-pạ-[ ]ja[ ]ja-pa-qa*

Texte n° 4

GODART-OLIVIER 1976-1985, vol. 5 IO Za 6 (coupelle onyx; datation : ?)

LA *74-26-100a-88-97-78-25* , *100a-26-74-100a-1̣0̣1̣-51-57-29* , *32-31-31-53-84a* ,

RAISON-POPE 1980 IO Z 3 : *100a-26-3̣2̣-...*

LA > B *ta-na-i-88-u-ti-nu* , *i-na-ta-i-*7̣9̣-di-si-ka* , *ja-sa-sa-ra-me* ,

RAISON-POPE 1980 IO Z 3 : *i-na-jạ-...*

Texte n° 5

TL Z 1 («louche» de marbre; datation : MM III ?)

LA a. *52-74-100a-88-75a-32* , *80-59-62-54*
b. , *32-31-31-53-8̣4̣ạ* *97-26-29-2̣6̣-5̣7̣*
c. *[100a-]5̣6̣ạ-26-95* , *57-5̣5̣-9̣2̣* *vacat*

GODART-OLIVIER 1976-1985, vol. 4 TL Za 1: c. *]-26-95* *57-5̣5̣[*

LA > B a. *a-ta-i-88-wa-ja* , *o-su-qa-re*
b. , *ja-sa-sa-ra-ṃẹ* *u-na-ka-ṇạ-ṣị*
c. *[i-]pị-na-ma* , *si-ṛụ-ṭẹ* *vacat*

GODART-OLIVIER 1976-1985, vol. 4 TL Za 1 : c. *]-na-ma si-ṛụ[*

Texte n° 6

RAISON-POPE 1990 SY Z 2 («table à libations»; datation : MM IIIb-MRIa)

LA a. *52-74-100a-88-75a-32* , *32-59-95-06-54* ,
b. *97-26-29-26-57-89* *vacat*
c. *vacat*
d. *52-32* *vacat*

GODART-OLIVIER 1976-1985, vol. 5 SY Za 2 :

a. *...32-59-95-06 49 ,*
b. *97-26-29-26-57 89*

LA > B a. *a-ta-i-88-wa-ja , ja-su-ma-tu-re ,*
b. *u-na-ka-na-si-89 vacat*
c. *vacat*
d. *a-ja vacat*

GODART-OLIVIER 1976-1985, vol. 5 SY Za 2 :
a. *...ja-su-ma-tu 49 ,*
b. *u-na-ka-na-si 89*

Texte n° 7

KO? Z 1 (base de statuette; datation : ?)

LA a. *52-74-100a-88-75a-32*
b. *06-55-31-58-163b-54 , 1ọọạ-30-*
c. *52 , 97-26-29-26-57 , 100ạ-*
d. *56a-26-95-57-55-92 vacat*

RAISON-POPE 1980 : b. *...1ọọ-30-*

GODART-OLIVIER 1976-1985, vol. 4 KO Za 1 :
b. *06-55-31 , 9̣3-163b-5̣4̣ , 100a-30-*
d. *56a-26-95 , 57-55-92*

LA > B a. *a-ta-i-88-wa-ja*
b. *tu-ru-sa-ra$_2$-163b-re , ị-da-*
c. *a , u-na-ka-na-si , ị-*
d. *pi-na-ma-si-ru-te vacat*

RAISON-POPE 1980 : b. *...ị/1ọọḅ-30-*

GODART-OLIVIER 1976-1985, vol. 4 KO Za 1 :
b. *tu ru sa , ḍụ-163b-ṛẹ , i-da-*
d. *pi-na-ma , si-ru-te*

Texte n° 8

PR Z 1 («table à libations»; datation : MR I ?)

LA a. *7̣4-74-01-93*
b. *5̣2-0̣2-100ạ-3̣2*
c. *52-31-31-53-84a*
d. *vacat*

GODART-OLIVIER 1976-1985, vol. 4 PR Za 1 :
a. *74-26-59-9̣2̣[ ]-̣2̣4̣*
b. *77-3̣9̣-100a-3̣2̣*

LA > B a. *ṭạ-̣ṭa-*56-du*
b. *ạ-p̣ạ-ị-̣j̣ạ*
c. *a-sa-sa-ra-me*
d. *vacat*

GODART-OLIVIER 1976-1985, vol. 4 PR Za 1 :
a. *ta-na-su-tẹ[ ]-̣ḳẹ*
b. *se-ṭọ-i-j̣ạ*

7. Abréviations bibliographiques

BARBER, E.J.W.
1974 *Archaeological Decipherment,* Princeton.

BENNETT, E.L.
1950 *American Journal of Archaeology* 54, 204-222.
1951 *The Pylos Tablets. A Preliminary Transcription,* Princeton.
1963 *Kadmos* 2 , 98-123.
1968 *Language* 44, 110-118.
1980 *Kadmos* 19, 12-23.
1985 *Πεπραγμένα τοῦ Ε' Διεθνοῦς Κρητολογικοῦ Συνεδρίου* I, Iraklion, 47-56.
1989a *Problems in Decipherment,* 9-23.
1989b *The Ideograms Common to the Minoan Scripts and to Mycenaean Linear B* (à paraître).

BRICE, W.C.
1961 *Inscriptions in the Minoan Linear Script of Class A,* Oxford.
1983 *Res Mycenaeae,* 55-62.

CHADWICK, J.
1975 *Journal of the Royal Asiatic Society* 1975, 143-147.

CHANTRAINE, P.
1968-1980 *Dictionnaire étymologique de la langue grecque. Histoire des mots,* Paris.

CONSANI, C. - FEDERIGHI, M.
1986 *Studi Classici e Orientali* 36, 17-34.

CREVATIN, F.
1975 *Studi Triestini di Antichità in onore di Luigia Achillea Stella*, Trieste, 1-63.

DOW, S.
1954 *American Journal of Archaeology* 58, 77-129.

DUHOUX, Y.
1978 *Études minoennes I*, 65-129.
1980 *Πεπραγμένα τοῦ Δ' Διεθνοῦς Κρητολογικοῦ Συνεδρίου*, Athènes, 112-136.
1982 *L'étéocrétois*, Amsterdam.
1983 *Minos* 18, 33-68.
1985 *Linear B*, 7-74.
1990 *Variations syntaxiques dans les textes votifs linéaires A* (à paraître).

Études minoennes I: Le linéaire A (Y. DUHOUX éd.), Louvain,1978.

EVANS, A.J.
1902-1903 *ABSA* 9, 1-153.
1909 *Scripta Minoa* I, Oxford.

EVANS, A.J. - MYRES, J.L.
1952 *Scripta Minoa* II, Oxford.

GELB, I.J.
1963 *A Study of Writing*[2], Chicago - Londres.

GODART, L.
1976 *La Parola del Passato* 166, 30-47.

GODART, L. - OLIVIER, J.-P.
1976-1985 *Recueil des Inscriptions en Linéaire A*, Paris.

GRUMACH, E.
1958 *Minoica. Festschrift zum 80. Geburtstag von Johannes Sundwall*, Berlin, 162-190.

HEUBECK, A.
1961 *Praegraeca*, Erlangen.
1979 *Archaeologia Homerica* X. *Schrift*, Göttingen.
1983 *Res Mycenaeae*, 155-169.

HILLER, S.
1978-1979 *Archiv für Orientforschung* 26, 221-235.

HOOKER, J.T.
1975 *Journal of the Royal Asiatic Society* 1975, 164-172.
1988 *Cretan Studies* 1, 169-189.

HUANG, Xin-Chuan - DAI, Kang-Shen
1979 *Shi Jiè Sān dà Zōng Jiao,* Pékin.

JUCQUOIS, G.
1969 *Le Muséon* 82, 507-516.

KAHN, D.
1967 *The Codebreakers,* New York.

KARETSOU, A.
1987 Εἰλαπίνη, Τόμος τιμητικὸς γιὰ τὸν Καθηγητὴ Ν. Πλάτωνα, Iraklion, 85-91.

KARETSOU, A. - GODART, L. - OLIVIER, J.-P.
1985 *Kadmos* 24, 89-147.

KILLEN, J.T.
1983 *Transactions of the Philological Society* 1983, 66-99.

LEJEUNE, M.
1958 *Mémoires de Philologie Mycénienne,* Première série, Paris.
1972 *Mémoires de Philologie Mycénienne,* Troisième série, Rome.

Linear B : A 1984 Survey (A. MORPURGO DAVIES - Y. DUHOUX éd.), Louvain-la-Neuve, 1985.

MACKAY, A.
1965 *Statistical Methods in Linguistics* 4, 15-25.

MASSON, O.
1983 *Les Inscriptions chypriotes syllabiques*[2], Paris.

MASSON, É.
1987 *Minos* 20-22, 367-381.

MELENA, J.L.
1987 *Tractata Mycenaea,* 203-232.

MERIGGI, P.
1956 *Primi elementi di Minoico A,* Salamanque.
1975 *Kadmos* 13, 85-94.

MORPURGO DAVIES, A.
1969 *Bulletin of the Institute of Classical Studies of the University of London* 16, 161-162.

NEUMANN, G.
1957 *Glotta* 36, 156-158.
1958 *Glotta* 37, 106-112.
1960 *Glotta* 38, 181-186.

1962 *Glotta* 40, 51-54.

OLIVIER, J.-P.
1965 *L'Antiquité Classique* 34, 387-397.
1975 *Le Monde grec*, Bruxelles, 441-449.
1984 *Pylos Comes Alive* (Th. PALAIMA - C. SHELMERDINE éd.), New York, 11-18.
1987 *Tractata Mycenaea*, 237-240.
1988 *Archäologischer Anzeiger* 1988, 253-268.
1989 *Problems in Decipherment*, 39-58.

PACKARD, D.W.
1974 *Minoan Linear A*, Berkeley - Los Angeles - Londres.

PALAIMA, Th. G.
1988 *Texts, Tablets and Scribes. Studies in Mycenaean Epigraphy and Economy offered to E. L. BENNETT, Jr.* (J.-P. OLIVIER - Th. G. PALAIMA éd.), Salamanque, 269-342.
1989 *Problems in Decipherment*, 121-187.

POPE, M.
1964 *Aegean Writing and Linear A*, Lund.
1968 *Atti e Memorie del 1° Congresso Internazionale di Micenologia* 1, Rome, 438-446.
1975 *The Story of Decipherment*, Londres.

POPE, M. - RAISON, J.
1978 *Études minoennes I*, 5-64.

Problems in Decipherment (Y. DUHOUX - Th. G. PALAIMA - J. BENNET éd.), Louvain-la-Neuve, 1989.

RAISON, J. - POPE, M.
1971 *Index du linéaire A*, Rome.
1977 *Index transnuméré du Linéaire A*, Louvain.
1980 *Corpus transnuméré du Linéaire A*, Louvain-la-Neuve.
1990 *Corpus transnuméré du Linéaire A²*, Louvain-la-Neuve (à paraître).

Res Mycenaeae (A. HEUBECK - G. NEUMANN éd.), Göttingen, 1983.

RUIJGH, C.J.
1967 *Études sur la grammaire et le vocabulaire du grec mycénien*, Amsterdam.

SCHACHERMEYR, F.
1964 *Die minoische Kultur des alten Kreta*, Stuttgart.

STEPHENS, L. - JUSTESON, J.S.
1978 *Transactions of the American Philological Association* 108, 271-284.

Tractata Mycenaea (P.H. ILIEVSKI - L. CREPAJAC éd.), Skopje, 1987.

VENTRIS, M.
1956 *Études mycéniennes* (M. LEJEUNE éd.), Paris, 267.

WARREN, P., CADOGAN, G., HAINSWORTH, J.B., CHADWICK, J., KILLEN, J.T., HUXLEY, G., LAMBERT, W.G., HART, G.R., STUBBINGS, F.H.
1969 *Bulletin of the Institute of Classical Studies of the University of London* 16, 155-169.

WEINGARTEN, J.
1983 *Kadmos* 22, 8-13.
1986 *Kadmos* 25, 1-21.

8. Sigles et abréviations

C	Consonne.
H	«Hiéroglyphique» crétois (numérotation des signes d'après EVANS 1909).
h	Hapax.
LA	Linéaire A (numérotation des signes d'après RAISON-POPE 1977).
LA > B	Linéaire A lu d'après les valeurs de ses correspondants LB.
LB	Linéaire B.
LC	Syllabaire chypriote classique.
V	Voyelle.
*	Devant un nombre : signe linéaire B non encore déchiffré.
#	Limite de mot.
//	Prononciation phonologique.
~	Alterne avec ou est associé à.
] [	Début et fin de lacune.
⟦ ⟧	Texte délibérément effacé dans l'Antiquité.
⌞ ⌟	Diviseur de mots probablement disparu.
3̣1̣ ou *ṣạ*	Signe de lecture non assurée.
,	Dans les textes LA : diviseur de mots.

9. Illustrations

H	LA	LB
23	16	ze
44	32	ja
74	95	ma

1. Signes identiques en «hiéroglyphique» crétois, linéaire A et linéaire B (§ 1.1)

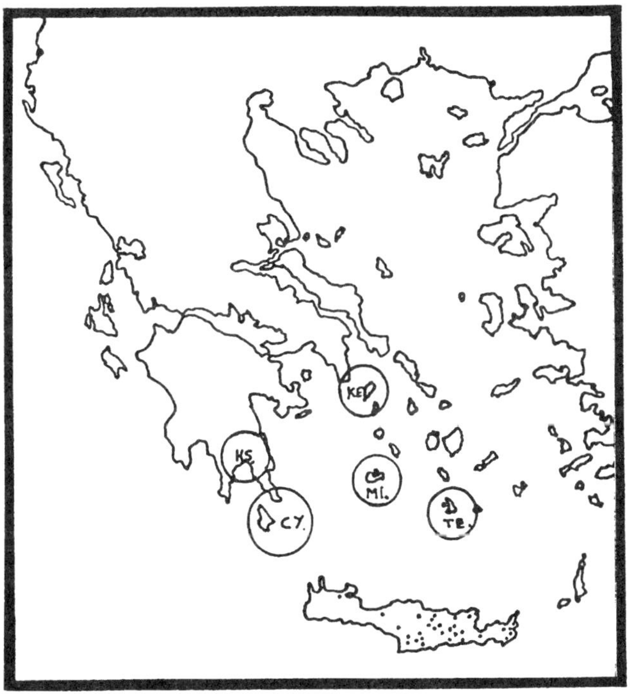

2. Lieux de trouvaille du linéaire A (§ 1.2)

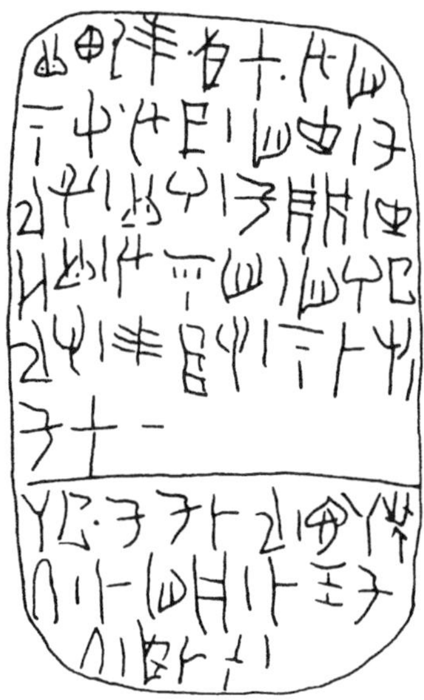

3. Tablette comptable linéaire A HT 117a
(en réduction) - texte : § 3.1.

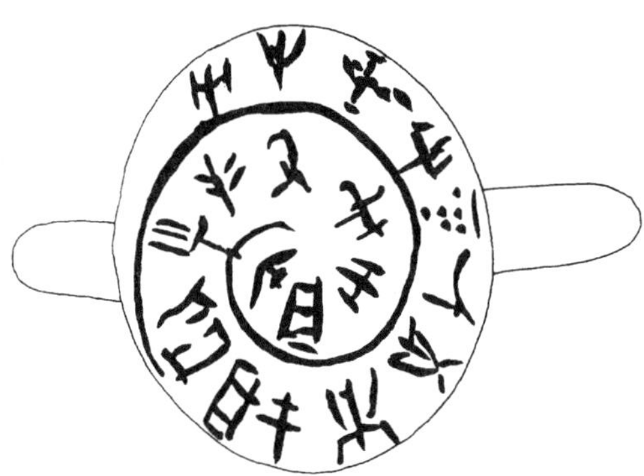

4. Bague en or KN Z 13 avec inscription linéaire A
(diamètre du chaton : 0,85-1 cm)

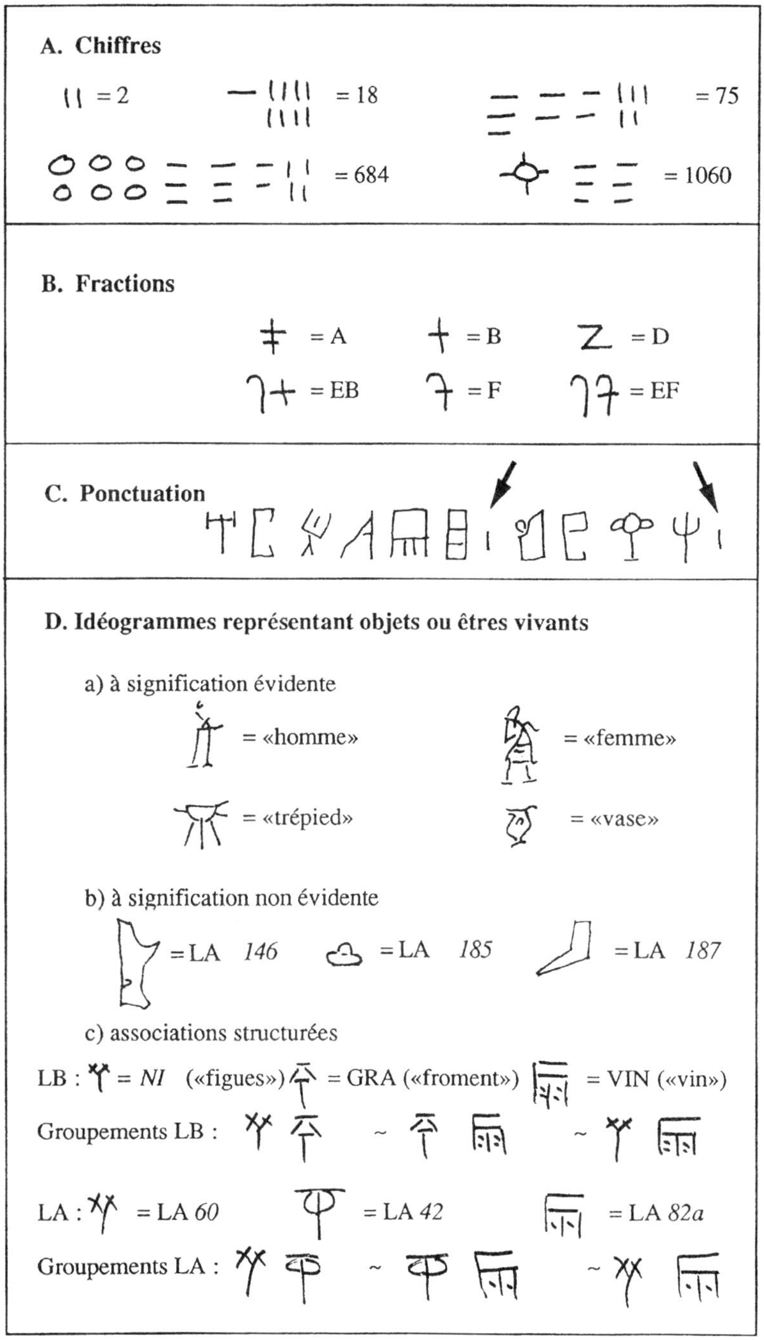

A. Chiffres

= 2 = 18 = 75

= 684 = 1060

B. Fractions

= A = B = D

= EB = F = EF

C. Ponctuation

D. Idéogrammes représentant objets ou êtres vivants

a) à signification évidente

= «homme» = «femme»

= «trépied» = «vase»

b) à signification non évidente

= LA *146* = LA *185* = LA *187*

c) associations structurées

LB : = *NI* («figues») = GRA («froment») = VIN («vin»)

Groupements LB : ~ ~

LA : = LA *60* = LA *42* = LA *82a*

Groupements LA : ~ ~

5. Signes idéographiques LA (§ 2.2.1)

	Longueur du texte	**Nombre de signes différents**
Alphabet français	242	26
Syllabaire chypriote	243	42
Syllabaire sumérien	242	64
Idéogrammes chinois	250	144
Linéaire A	**242**	**57**

6. Nombre de signes différents dans diverses écritures (§ 2.2.2.1)

LA	LB	LA	LB
01	**56*	*61*	*ne*
02	*pa*	*62*	*qa*
06	*tu*	*64*	*pu*
21	*po*	*69*	**34*
22	*ro*	*72*	*ri*
23	*za*	*74*	*ta*
24	*ke*	*75a*	*wa*
25	*nu*	*76*	*mi*
26	*na*	*77*	*se*
27	*mu*	*78*	*ti*
28	*wi*	*80*	*o*
29	*ka*	*81a*	*je*
30	*da*	*84a*	*me*
31	*sa*	*84b*	*mu*
32	*ja*	*85*	**118*
34	pu_2	*86*	ta_2
35	**86*	*91*	*qe*
39	*to*	*92*	*te*
44	*e*	*93*	*du*
45	*ko*	*95*	*ma*
48b	*qi*	*96*	**65*
51	*di*	*97*	*u*
52	*a*	*98*	*ku*
53	*ra*	*100a*	*i*
54	*re*	*101*	**79*
55	*ru*	*102a*	*de*
56a	*pi*	*102b*	**47*
57	*si*	*103*	*ki*
58	ra_2	*113*	*au*
59	*su*	*120*	**49*
60	*ni*	*208*	**82*

7. Correspondances formelles entre syllabogrammes LA et signes LB (§ 2.2.2.2)

Signes	Initiale	Médiane	Finale
LA *52*	89,74 % (140)	5,12 % (8)	5,12 % (8)
LB *a*	93,50 % (1.296)	2,81 % (39)	3,67 % (51)
LA *44*	64 % (16)	8 % (2)	28 % (7)
LB *e*	77,67 % (863)	11,25 % (125)	11,07 % (123)
LA *100a*	55,06 % (87)	31,01 % (49)	13,92 % 22
LB *i*	42,21 % (233)	28,44 % (157)	29,34 % (162)
LA *80*	85,18 % (23)	7,40 % (2)	7,40 % (2)
LB *o*	55,47 % (522)	7,86 % (74)	36,66 % (345)
LA *97*	56,36 % (31)	25,45 % (14)	18,18 % (10)
LB *u*	14,54 % (113)	37,19 % (289)	48,26 % (375)

8. Fréquence des signes vocaliques LB
et de leurs correspondants LA (§ 2.2.2.2.1.a)

Linéaire B	Syllabaire chypriote	Linéaire A
a	*a*	*52*
da (/d/)	*ta* (/t- th- d-/)	*30*
na	*na*	*26*
pa (/p- ph- b-/)	*pa* (/p- ph- b-/)	*02*
po (/p- ph- b-/)	*po* (/p- ph- b-/)	*21*
ro (/r- l-/)	*lo* (/l-/)	*22*
se	*se*	*77*
si	*si*	*57*
ti (/t- th-/)	*ti* (/t- th- d-/)	*78*
to (/t- th-/)	*to* (/t- th- d-/)	*39*

9. Syllabogrammes de forme identique en LB ~ LC ~ LA (§ 2.2.2.2.1.d)

	état initial	**correction**
	LA *91* = LA > B *qe*	LA *95* = LA > B *ma*
ZA 11a.2		
ZA 20.3		

10. Corrections de LA *91* en LA *95* (§ 2.2.2.2.2.c)

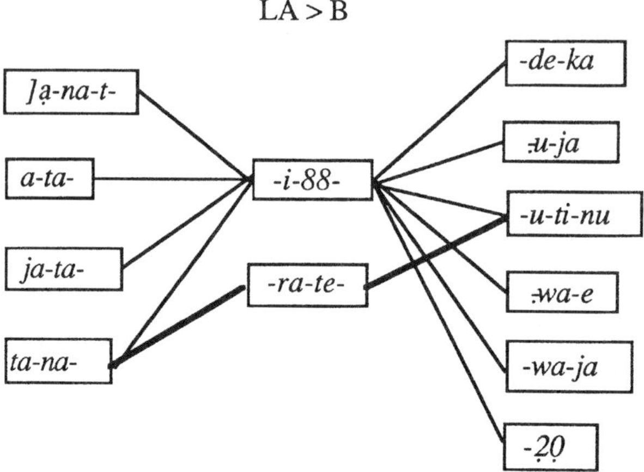

11. Structure du terme LA A-B-C (§ 3.2.3.3)

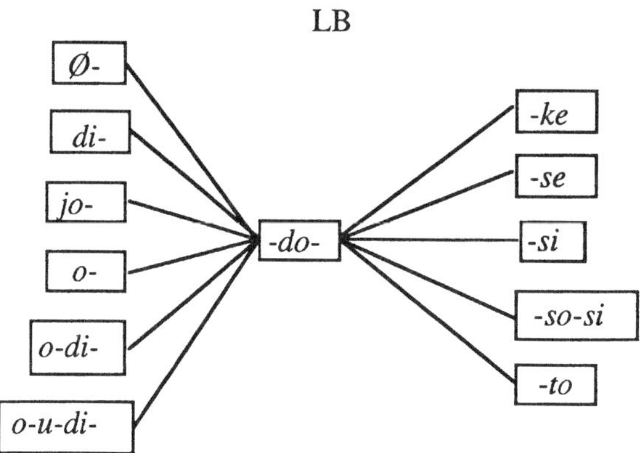

12. Structure de huit formes du verbe LB δίδωμι, «donner» (§ 3.2.3.3)

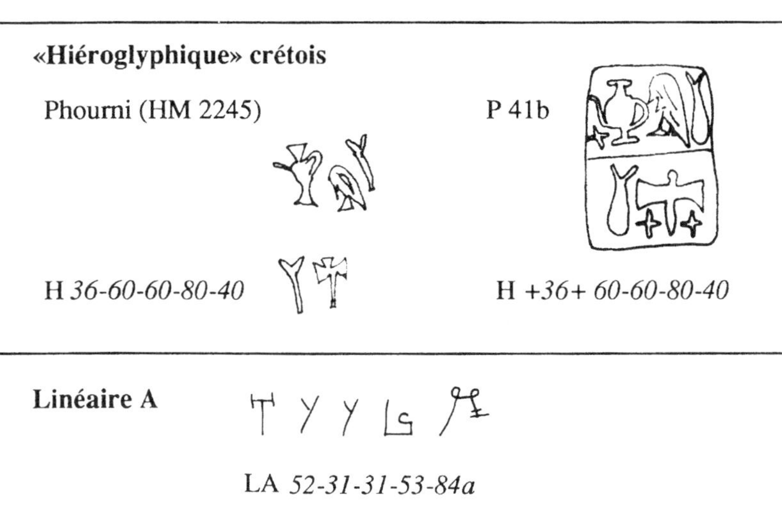

LA > B *a-sa-sa-ra-me*

13. Mots peut-être identiques en LA
et en «hiéroglyphique» crétois (§ 5.3)

Place Pascal 1
B-1348 Louvain-la-Neuve
Belgique

BCILL 49 : *Problems in Decipherment,* 121-187.

CYPRO-MINOAN SCRIPTS: PROBLEMS OF HISTORICAL CONTEXT

Thomas G. PALAIMA
Program in Aegean Scripts and Prehistory
University of Texas at Austin

"Every branch of knowledge is entertaining and the longest life is too short for the pursuit of it."

Lady Mary Wortley Montagu 1689-1762

Abstract: This paper presents a critical historical survey of problems in research on Cypriote Bronze Age writing (Cypro-Minoan = CM) and draws the following conclusions: (1) the current classification of the epigraphical data into 4 general subdivisions of writing (archaic CM, CM 1, CM 2 and CM 3) is invalid, being based on faulty palaeographical assumptions, unwarranted geographical clustering, and *contaminatio* of inscriptions of distinct typological classes; (2) the palaeographical connection between archaic CM and Minoan Linear A is far closer than has heretofore been acknowledged; (3) the creation of Cypro-Minoan under the strong influence of Cretan linear writing is understandable in terms of the historical development of Cypriote contacts with the Aegean and in terms of the relative simplicity and adaptability of Linear A in comparison with contemporary Near Eastern cuneiform scripts; (4) Cypro-Minoan retains a remarkable independence and integrity throughout its 500 year history, despite the Near Eastern milieu in which it existed; (5) *all* past and current schemes of decipherment of Cypro-Minoan are improbable; (6) there is a pressing need for a critical corpus raisonné which will present the epigraphical material (8 clay tablets, 83 clay balls, 6 clay cylinders, and numerous inscribed artefacts such as cylinder seals, gold rings, ivory objects, and especially pottery) with due attention to typological classes, dates and circumstances of discovery, and palaeographical analysis; (7) the number of signs now attested in formal Cypro-Minoan inscriptions (ca. 2500) compares unfavorably with the number known from the undeciphered Minoan Linear A documents (over 7000) and the number available in Mycenaean Linear B at the time of its decipherment (ca. 30,000); (8) but properly analyzed, Cypro-Minoan has advantages as a script for decipherment: diversity and length of texts, discernible word-divisions, well-studied archaeological and historical contexts, and the reasonable prospect of continuing significant discoveries.

This paper will not offer a full analysis of the particular problems associated with each of the partial decipherments which have been advanced for the Bronze Age writing of the island of Cyprus, Cypro-Minoan.[1] Nothing would be gained thereby. None of the proposed decipherments is systematic or comprehensive. None establishes anywhere near an acceptable percentage of confirmable values for the signs that are so far attested on texts of the various subsystems of Cypro-Minoan. None produces, and, to be fair, most do not claim to produce, more than limited results applicable to isolated lexical items on a few specific texts. In short, none is capable of proof; and some are not even deserving of the expenditure of mental energy that skeptical criticism would entail. Most of these schemes of decipherment receive clear and remarkably impartial summaries in HILLER 1985, 79-93; and the weaknesses, linguistic and historical, of several of the more prominent tentative decipherments are severely, albeit justly, critiqued in KNAPP and MARCHANT 1982. I shall offer much later in this paper a critique of one specific recent study: FAUCOUNAU 1988. This will illustrate directly some of the weaknesses of the current approaches to decipherment.

The most recently proposed decipherment deals with the small group of tablets now classified as CM 2. It is a good example of the "universality principle" of decipherment, whereby scholars, during the course of research, decide that it is just as easy, while deciphering one script and language, to decipher others as well. In this case the Phaistos Disk[2] and a limited cross-section of Cypro-Minoan are simultaneously "deciphered." Fortunately CHADWICK 1989, has written a restrained and gentlemanly review, the subtext of which should serve as an adequate warning, to scholars and those librarians who have a choice, not to waste precious book-purchasing funds (ca. $32.50 US) on a volume which should not have progressed past the the stage of manuscript review. Chadwick sounds his clearest warning simply by quoting and analyzing the preposterous results yielded in the first sentence of the proposed translation of the Phaistos Disk. It remains to express dismay that, through a reputable publisher, such a work is spreading the contagion of pseudo-decipherment to unsuspecting prehistorians and linguists and to libraries with standing series orders the world over.

---

[1] I would like to thank Dr. Vassos Karageorghis, Dr. Ino Nicolaou, and the staff of the archaeological museums in Nicosia and Larnaca for making it possible for Ms. Nicolle Hirschfeld and me to examine many Cypro-Minoan documents during the week of March 13, 1989. They have also graciously supported this year the work of Ms. Hirschfeld on pottery incised with Cypro-Minoan marks. Dr. Alison South also kindly permitted us to examine the inscribed material from Kalavassos-Ayios Dhimitrios and provided us with a copy of the publication of this material listed in the bibliography as E. MASSON forthcoming. The library of the Cyprus Museum in Nicosia permitted me to read the rare and impressive early study of Cypro-Minoan: MARKIDES 1916. I thank also Dr. Stuart Swiny and the staff of the Cyprus American Archaeological Research Institute for providing fine facilities with which to conduct research. In this paper I shall use the word "figure" to refer to my own text figures. I shall use the abbreviated form "fig." to refer to figures in other published works. For full clarity, this paper should be read with reference to the provisional Cypro-Minoan sign charts in MASSON 1974, 12-15, and HILLER 1985, 62-65.

[2] For sober information about the Phaistos Disk, see OLIVIER 1975.

Convenient discussions of earlier theories of Cypro-Minoan decipherment can be found in J. KARAGEORGHIS 1961, 43-51, and O. MASSON 1956a, 201-204. E. MASSON 1985a and 1987a, furnish good overviews incorporating work with more recently discovered material. HEUBECK 1979, 54-60, offers the most succinct summary overview of the Cypro-Minoan epigraphical data now available. Readers may consult these studies and HEUBECK 1979, 60-64, to learn about the attempts to identify Hittite, Luwian, Hurrian, Hurrianoid, Greek, Semito-Cypriote, and an unknown language group,[3] along with some Semitic personal names and phrases, in Cypro-Minoan texts.

However, the judgment expressed by Olivier Masson, the first great researcher in Cypro-Minoan during the generation following Ventris's brilliant and conclusive decipherment of the Mycenaean Linear B script as Greek, still holds true. We may elaborate upon it and apply it as follows: without the discovery of a bilingual–perhaps even bilinguals, since different languages may be represented by certain of the Cypro-Minoan subsystems–or many more texts in each subsystem, the complex circumstances surrounding Cypro-Minoan are such that one is reduced to mere suppositions. In fact, the unknowns connected with Cypro-Minoan are still far greater than those which were associated with Linear B before its decipherment (O. MASSON 1956a, 201; 1956b, 246). The published material is extremely limited in terms of the numbers of formal texts (8 clay tablets, 2 very fragmentary, 1 complete; 83 completely published and at least partially legible clay balls;[4] 6 clay cylinders, 4 very fragmentary)[5] and the total number of

---

[3] On the clay cylinders from Kalavassos-Ayios Dhimitrios, E. Masson claims to be able to read vocabulary items which are paralleled in Ugaritic and on other Cypro-Minoan texts from Enkomi (tablet and clay ball) and Ras Shamra (tablet): a term for a divine title or determinative, which is then followed by an emphatic or adverbial termination and a toponym, the whole structure again being based on an earlier unprovable hypothesis about the formulaic structure of the Enkomi tablet (E. MASSON 1986, 187-188 and n. 18, 200). For a valid criticism of such piecemeal readings of the three times fuller Minoan Linear A material as a step toward decipherment, see OLIVIER 1985, 383. Even if such readings prove to be correct, one must always be careful about loan words and foreign anthroponyms and toponyms, which can be misleading for the identification of the language represented by the script.

[4] E. MASSON 1972, 102, 110, mentions that there are about 80 such inscribed balls total. In addition, there were, in 1972, some 4 uninscribed balls, all irregular, perhaps discards deemed unsuitable for inscription. E. MASSON 1973, 92, cites 82 clay balls from Enkomi and 1 from Hala Sultan Tekké. We now, too, have 2 inscribed clay balls from Kition: KARAGEORGHIS 1976a, 238-239, fig. 8; KARAGEORGHIS 1985, 114, n. 4995 (plate CXVIII); and 1 additional clay ball from Hala Sultan Tekké. General reference to the find contexts of the Enkomi balls can be found in Karageorghis's yearly reports on Cypriote archaeology in *BCH* 84 (1960) 283; 86 (1962) 395; 88 (1964) 355; 94 (1970) 249. The full publication of the 83 legibly inscribed clay balls is found in E. MASSON 1971a (25 from Enkomi, 1 from Hala Sultan Tekké); E. MASSON1971c (53 from Enkomi plus 2 [nos. 33 and 44] damaged so as to be illegible); DIKAIOS 1971 (from Enkomi; 1 partially legible: no. 1140 = plate 316/83; 1 damaged and illegible: no. 1302 = plate 319/88; 1 blank: no. 1548 = plate 132/60); ÖBRINK 1979, 46, 88-89, N 6035; E. MASSON 1985a, 281-282 (2 from Kition: II/4215 and II/4995).

[5] See HILLER 1985, 66-74; E. MASSON 1971a; E. MASSON 1983, 131-135; E. MASSON 1987a, 189-190 and fig. 1. KARAGEORGHIS 1981, 83, figs. 53-55, provides color

occurrences of the signs represented. For example, the earliest and only so-called archaic Cypro-Minoan tablet, Enkomi 1885, contains 23 total signs. The fullest CM 1 text, a clay cylinder from Enkomi (Enkomi 19.10), contains ca. 179 inscribed signs, from which one can deduce about 36 different characters in a standard signary. The 5 CM 1 clay cylinders from Kalavassos-Ayios Dhimitrios have on them ca. 112, 5, 10, 10 and 27 signs respectively. The other major source for the formal CM 1 signary is the peculiarly Cypriote inscribed clay balls. 83 legible inscriptions of this kind are now known. These normally have 3-5 signs (8 signs maximum on, e.g., boules 1 and 7 in E. MASSON 1971a, 10-18, and boule 41 in E. MASSON 1971c, 495). All together these balls contain ca. 359 signs; cautiously restoring fragmentary of damaged texts yields ca. 370 signs. This gives an average of ca. 4.5 signs per ball; and indeed the majority of balls (ca. 55%) closely brackets this average (out of 83 legible balls, 22 [26.5%] contain 5 signs and 24 [29%] contain 4 signs). From the whole set one can deduce ca. 70 different standard signs. From the 26 examples published in E. MASSON 1971a, fig. 27a, ca. 46 characters have been identified; from the 53 legible balls in E. MASSON 1971c, 58 characters and 5 possible alternates. The full CM 1 signary of ca. 85 signs has been established by supplementing these formal inscriptions with single marks or groups of signs on all sorts of other objects (E. MASSON 1974, 12). In addition, two tablets from Ugarit, RS 19.01 and RS 19.02, are classified as CM 1 (mistakenly termed CM 3 in both HILLER 1985, 72, and KNAPP and MARCHANT 1982, 22) and contain 8 and 24 preserved signs respectively. The four fragments of tablets now classified CM 2 have about 1310 legible signs total, from which a signary of 59 standard characters has been deduced. The CM 3 tablet fragments (RS 17.06 and RS 20.25) have ca. 60 and 159 non-numerical, non-punctuational signs on their recto and verso surfaces. From these signs a repertory of ca. 44 standard characters has been identified.

It is clear from such statistics that signs are frequently repeated in CM 1, 2 and 3. It is also clear that the the standard sign repertories which have been established for each sub-system are based on extremely limited and imbalanced groups of formal written texts: archaic = 23 signs; CM 1 = 713 signs (745 signs with RS 19.01 and 19.02); CM 2 = 1310 signs; CM 3 = 219 signs. Thus all the signs on formal inscriptions in all the supposed sub-systems of Cypro-Minoan add up to slightly less than 2300. Signs on all the other objects listed in the next paragraph, except pottery, total ca. 150. An additional 50 signs might be found in sequences of two or more characters on pottery. Thus we are dealing with a total repertory of some 2500 signs found in actual sign-sequences, i.e., about one third the total number of signs attested in the still undeciphered Linear A script, and less than 10% of the number of signs (ca. 30,000) attested on Linear B documents at the time of its decipherment. We might even contrast the lexical and syntactical variety furnished by the 2,000 Linear B texts available at the time of the decipherment and the 318 tablets and bars now thoroughly published in Linear A

---

photographs of the archaic Enkomi tablet, the large clay cylinder from Enkomi, and CM 2 tablet fragment Enkomi 1953 no. 1687.

with the meager 97 clay Cypro-Minoan documents now published.[6] Moreover, this formal Cypro-Minoan material is spread thin geographically and chronologically: from ca. 1500 to 1150 B.C. and from a variety of sites (Enkomi, Hala Sultan Tekké, Kition, Kalavassos-Ayios Dhimitrios, Ras Shamra: see figures 1-3).

Nonetheless the Cypro-Minoan picture is not completely bleak. Cypro-Minoan, as a script for decipherment, has certain partial advantages, even over Linear A. These are:

(a) the broad range of applications of the script. Besides the formal inscriptions mentioned above, sign-sequences are found on a wide variety of objects such as: inscribed and painted marked pottery,[7] a carved ivory plaque of the Egyptian god Bes, an ivory bar, an ivory pipe, a perforated clay weight (?),[8] metal weights,[9] cylinder seals, gold rings, bronze and silver bowls, a jeweler's anvil, gypsum pithos lids,[10] a bronze votive liver (?) and other votive objects including a terracotta animal figurine from Famagousta, large and small copper ingots, various bronze tools, support rings for bronze tripods, and even lead sling bullets.[11]

(b) the relative fullness of a few of the formal texts now attributed to each of Cypro-Minoan classes 1, 2 and 3;[12]

---

[6] For statistics about Linear A and B currently and at the time of the decipherment, see OLIVIER 1985, 382-384. In Linear A we also have rather full inscriptions on pottery and objects like libation tables and gold pins. The case of Cretan hieroglyphic, for which we have data preserving approximately 1500 signs, is discussed by OLIVIER in this volume.

[7] In particular see the extensive painted inscription on a fragment of a clay offering roaster: E. MASSON 1979, 210-213, pl. XX.

[8] BAURAIN 1980, 566-567, 580, and esp. 570, casts doubt on the identification of this singular inscribed object from so early a period (LC I A = 1575-1525 B.C.) as a weight, proposing as possible alternative identifications a talisman or label. See Baurain, 1984, 155, fig. 22 for a drawing. However, the object does resemble the perforated clay weights from many Cypriote Late Bronze Age sites.

[9] E. MASSON forthcoming, 40.

[10] E. MASSON forthcoming, 40.

[11] O. MASSON 1957 a; O. MASSON 1957b, especially figs. 2-30, for a photographic survey of such material; O. MASSON 1968, plates I and II, for the bronze bowls; E. MASSON 1987a, 194-195, fig. 4, 201, fig. 8, for inscriptions on the gold rings from Kalavassos–Ayios Dhimitrios and the jeweler's anvil from Enkomi; KARAGEORGHIS 1976a, 232-234, for the Kition ivory finds, and fig. 3 for an illustration of the carved plaque with inscriptions on the upper part of its attachment tenons; E. MASSON 1985a, plates A and B, for the plaque (II/4252), the bar (II/4250), and the pipe (II/4267); ÅSTRÖM and NICOLAOU 1980, nos. 5 and 7 for the two lead sling bullets from Hala Sultan Tekké inscribed in Cypro-Minoan; E. MASSON 1973, 94-96 with references, for votive objects, tripod rings and other bronze objects. KARAGEORGHIS 1976b, 82, color plates V and X, illustrate a gold finger ring and the bronze votive liver with incised Cypro-Minoan marks. See also CAUBET and COURTOIS 1986, 74-75, fig. 6, pl. XIX, 3.

[12] For example, as we have mentioned, in CM 1 the best preserved clay cylinders from Enkomi and Kalavassos-Ayios Dhimitrios have some 179 and 116 non-numerical, non-punctuational signs respectively. The longest CM 2 text from Enkomi is the fragmented, but joined tablet Enkomi 1193 (1952) + Enkomi 20.01 (1969) which preserves over 225 signs on the 26 lines

(c) the use of obvious word-separators on full texts of all classes, except the archaic Enkomi tablet, which enables one to work with well-defined sign-groups.[13] Thus E. MASSON 1976, 67-70, 82-85, is able to identify 78 and 110 lexical units on the fullest CM 2 tablets fragments (CM 53.5 and CM 20.01).

I shall content myself with applying to the conclusions of the widely differing proposals for the decipherment of Cypro-Minoan the opinion which Emmett L. Bennett, Jr. once expressed in regard to the many proposed decipherments of Minoan Linear A. Even though he at first believed that "no more than one decipherment could be true," further thought convinced him that "they probably all are right–each in its own of those simultaneous universes, to which the science fiction writers have introduced us, and with which we have communication only through a fourth dimension" (BENNETT 1968, 117). The same applies to the results of "readings" of parts of Cypro-Minoan texts, based on incomplete series of assignments of values to signs and on interdependent arguments derived from hypothetical readings and assumptions about the contents of undeciphered texts and about the possible differences in languages behind the subsystems of Cypro-Minoan. E. MASSON 1986, 200, stresses that her own "lectures sporadiques n'annoncent pas un déchiffrement."[14] One should add the further caution that, since every link in the elaborate supporting structures of hypotheses for such readings or decipherments is a critical stress point, each such system is in constant danger of collapse and only stands by virtue of the generally arbitrary principles used by the scholars who devise these linguistic universes. Thus the metaphor "houses of cards" has been aptly applied to such decipherment schemes. Appropriately enough, I shall use some contemporary science fiction in discussing the other sorts of problems which I think have complicated, or are impeding progress in, the study of Cypro-Minoan scripts.

I have to confess to thinking at one time that I had a distinct advantage over other speakers at the symposium held in Madison, Wisconsin in April, 1988, from which this volume arose, because I was among the *aliis* to whom *E L Bennett salutem dat* [now *dedit*] in a MEMORANDUM of 10 September 1987 and because the section pertaining to my proposed involvement in that event read as follows:

---

of the left column of face A alone. For the join see MICHAELIDOU-NICOLAOU 1980, 13-16, figs. 1-4. The fullest CM 3 text from Ras Shamra RS 20.25 bears ca. 159 such signs on its two faces.

13 Although even here an unnoticed problem exists, because two forms of "word-dividers" are used with one another on, for example, the CM 1 clay cylinder from Enkomi and the CM 3 text RS 20.25, often occurring next to each other. This phenomenon has not been explained. In fact, the "word-dividers" are not even listed as signs in the standard signaries or noted in what pass as "transcriptions" of this material, e.g., E. MASSON 1974, 35-37; E. MASSON 1983, 138. For something approximating a proper epigraphical transcription of RS 20.25, produced entirely for secondary reasons–in order to compare the "readings" of the three principal "decipherers"–see HILLER 1985, 79-82. Even here the peculiarity of the double "word-dividers" is not noted.

14 Cf. Ventris's similar disclaimer about his early 'Etruscan reading' of Linear B: BENNETT, this volume. Masson expresses proper caution about the procedure of sign-matching in order to arrive at values for the characters of an unknown script like Cypro-Minoan (E. MASSON 1972, 111).

However particularly I wish Thomas Palaima to participate, for other reasons and for his present interest in the Cypriote and Cypro-Minoan scripts. The first was deciphered rather quickly about a century ago, the second, in some degree and some fashion probably related to the Linear A script, is currently the subject of investigation.

The advantages I then thought I saw in my topic were these:

(1) Cypro-Minoan presents us with a complicated picture of its development and applications, so that there were many problems suitable to the theme of the Burdick-Vary symposium to discuss;

(2) Cypro-Minoan functions "in some degree and some fashion" as a bridge between the Minoan-Mycenaean scripts and the later Classical Cypriote syllabary, i.e., between termini which have been deciphered, or, in the case of Linear A, can at least be studied in relation to a closely related deciphered writing system;[15]

(3) at an advanced stage of its development Cypro-Minoan also is generally thought to provide a link, in terms of certain of its purely formal elements, to the Near Eastern cuneiform systems of writing;

(4) Emmett Bennett, in these sentences, had provided me with an explanatory introduction and, I then thought, a gently humorous point of departure. For, if I wanted to be a strict constructionist, that is, a pedant, I could have faulted him for referring, however obliquely, to a single Cypro-Minoan scrip**t**.

It is certainly nothing but an acquired *vitium magistri* if I now claim to see none of these points as an advantage and if I now wonder whether his use of a singular verb form with an understood Cypro-Minoan scrip**t** may not have been intentional and wise. In any event, I am forced to use a different and then unforeseen opening to the following discussion of problems associated with the decipherment of Cypro-Minoan, but one which will no less honor the distinguished honoree of that occasion.

Among many other things in Mycenaean studies–I have in mind here the procedures and principles of palaeographical analysis, the careful study of joins, the standard conventions for editing and transcribing Linear B texts, and even the theoretical vocabulary for categories of signs and their functio–the monthly bibliographical newsletter, which has long united, in its special way, researchers in Aegean scripts and prehistory, was Emmett Bennett's doing.[16] First it was simply called a *Mycenaean Bibliography* and then, when it had grown garrulous, it was named *Nestor* and published at the Institute for Research in the Humanities

---

15 Progress in understanding Linear A has been made chiefly by analyzing its overall structure, sign repertory, and applications in comparison to Linear B. See particularly PACKARD 1976; DUHOUX 1978; PALAIMA 1988b; HEUBECK 1983 with references.

16 See the section entitled Bibliography of Emmett L. Bennett, Jr. in *Studies Bennett*, adding BENNETT 1963.

of the University of Wisconsin–Madison from 1959 to 1978. It continues, still in the American Midwest at the University of Indiana; and, from time to time, some of us try to inject into it a small portion of the spirit, the gentle whimsy, which had filled its pages during Emmett's tenure as editor. So it was that a note appeared, substantially as follows, in *Nestor* 15:2 (February 1988) 2184 under the heading, as requested by its submitter, which was seen much more regularly in the pages of *Nestor* during the first two decades of its existence: *...qu'il est permis de rire entre mycénologues*:

A graduate student, Frederick Schwink, in my Mycenaean Script seminar today provided me with startling evidence of the use of Linear B in ways previously unattested and at a date much later than the material known at present. As often happens with significant new information, the evidence was published as a minor part of a full article on LH III C Troy in an out-of-the-way, but well-established journal: S. Sucharitkul, "The Shattered Horse," *Amazing* 58:1 (May 1984) 26-49, a copy of which I enclose. The author even provides a new theory on the development of the Mycenaean Linear B script. Here are the pertinent passages:

–p. 34 (describing fresco remains from the palace area of LH III B Troy) "There were scrawls in strident red paint, in the Mycenaean characters: 𐀲𐀙𐀵 *Ta-na-to—Thanatos*. There were names too, all written in the script that the Akhaian nations borrowed from somewhere east, in the lands of barbarous tongues."

–p. 41 (describing a sword discovered in an altar area at Troy) "...I recognized the sword, with the syllabic signs 𐀁𐀒𐀵 —*E-ko-to*—etched into the bronze blade."

What is particularly startling about these discoveries is the use of Linear B on a wall painting and as a mark of ownership (or manufacturer's mark?) on the bronze sword. We only have one remotely possible instance of a painted fresco sign in a linear script, from Knossos (cf. my article in *Kadmos* 20 [1981] 79-82), and so far no hint of full Linear B used on anything other than clay records and painted vase inscriptions. The signs are few and simple in form, thus preventing us from drawing any firm conclusions about palaeographical affiliations. Of course, this assumes that the author's drawings and transcriptions are accurate, which the sword inscription gives us cause to doubt. One would think more likely that the author has failed to note a fourth and final sign on the sword blade, perhaps worn away through at least ten years of use. I would suggest restoring *e-ko-to*[*-ro* cons. stem liquid gen. sing. "of Hektor", thus denoting the owner of the sword. Since, however, the sword may be

Achaean, of the sort MacDonald (*BSA* 79 [1984] 68, citing Sandars) describes as 12th century *sui generis*, a more speculative restoration, and the one I prefer as being more "Homeric," would be *e-ko-to*[*-re* cons. stem liquid dat. sing. "for Hektor," i.e., a sword marked out by an Achaean warrior, perhaps the *a-ki-re-u* attested on our Linear B tablets, as intended to have Hektor as corporeal recipient. This would be a form of Mycenaean slang: "Take this, Hektor!" and a rare discovery indeed.

I am much less confident about the author's proposal that Linear B derived from literally barbarous eastern scripts. We may see some eastern influence in Cypro-Minoan, but by and large the Minoan-Mycenaean scripts seem to be, to use Sandars again, *sui generis*. I would welcome further thoughts on this subject.

Sincerely,

Thomas G. Palaima

UT Austin

This is the entire text of my archaeological and palaeographical spoof inspired by a genuine short story in a first-rate journal of science fiction. The story intrigued me since it contained accurately drawn, or at least recognizably standardized, Linear B characters and equally accurate transcriptions and translations. A complete novel by the same author, using a different *nom de plume*, has now appeared. The author has incorporated additional Linear B characters, words, and phrases into his fuller story of events in post-destruction Troy, undoubtedly as a curiosity for his readers, but also to lend an air of exotic authenticity to his fiction. The Linear B appears almost as a recurrent leitmotif along with a bit of Egyptian hieroglyphic and Homeric Greek. Again carefully drawn conventionalized signs are used for all the Linear B; and the phonetic transcriptions make up a mini-onomasticon/lexicon of mythologically important names (Orestes and Astyanax, Achilles and Patroclus) and vocabulary (*wa-na-ka*, *e-re-ta*) (SOMTOW, 1986, 89, 104, 231, 243, 255, 273, 308-09, 315). Of course, in my version, sent camera-ready to Indiana, I used, as I have here, Jean-Pierre Olivier's Macintosh Linear B font "Mycenae" to print the characters.

What concerns us here in discussing Cypro-Minoan is an ironic twist on the Horatian motto about critical observations: *ridentem dicere verum*. I had been warned by one of the co-editors to this volume that some scholar or other was bound to mistake my innocuous bit of fun for an announcement of, and a serious commentary on, genuine epigraphical discoveries at Troy. I dismissed this prophecy then, little thinking that John Bennet was capable of playing Mycenological Cassandra. But within days of my receiving the February 1988 *Nestor*, I also received a letter (dated March 9, 1988) from one of the leading researchers intent upon the decipherment of Cypro-Minoan, J. Faucounau.

Monsieur Faucounau somehow had missed the French heading to *Nestor*'s humor section and took both the original Linear B texts and my fuller "scholarly" discussion at face value. Having at times been gullible or unobservant myself, I can hardly find fault with such a harmless oversight. What disturbed me, however, was the further speculation about the relationships of Aegean, Cypriote and Near Eastern scripts, one to another, prompted by this misunderstanding. Monsieur Faucounau and I have subsequently been in correspondence, and he has kindly granted me permission to quote from his initial letter. The question he raised in regard to Somtow's "discoveries" was intriguing: "Is it possible to find Linear B (or [a] similar) script in LH III Troy?" Faucounau's answer was positive, based on the idea that "'Lukki' Cilician kings *knew about* [the] *Cypro-Minoan script*"; and, since they are linked to western Anatolia, "there is a good possibility [of] find[ing] a kind of Cypro-Minoan script (not Linear B stricto sensu) in this area." This script may have been transmitted "from Cret[e] to the Cyclades and/or Miletus, then to Cilicia and Cyprus (and eventually to Troy). The alternative is the [at] present unproven theory of a direct transmission from Cret[e] to Cyprus and/or Ugarit or Byblos." The hypothesizing concluded with a postscript declaring that the signs from the engraved sword, i.e., 𐀴𐀫𐀲, looked like Cypro-Minoan, rather than Linear B characters.

Thus did a fictitious account of Troy and a further bit of playful fiction circulated *entre mycénologues* reemphasize to me an Achilles heel of Cypro-Minoan studies, namely a carelessness about the necessary epigraphical and palaeographical features of Cypro-Minoan inscriptions coupled with a neglect of archaeological data associated with the Cypro-Minoan texts.[17] Since these inscriptions form a sizable body of chronologically, contextually and typologically diverse texts, some of which might not even be formal inscriptions *per se*, a systematic and thorough epigraphical and palaeographical analysis of the entire corpus constitutes the essential first step for any attempt at decipherment. Texts found in secure stratigraphical contexts must also be securely dated, and scholars must pay attention to those dates. Otherwise one can construct rather wild hypotheses about the historical path taken by writing to and from the island of Cyprus and about the historical development of writing on the island itself. Further troubles arise when such historical speculation is then used to validate the results of a given "decipherment."

In the present instance, Jean-Pierre Olivier should be as astonished as I am that anyone seriously interested in deciphering the Cypro-Minoan script would be inattentive of palaeographical details to such an extent as to mistake characters of the perfectly regular Linear B font "Mycenae" for those belonging to the Cypro-

---

[17] I am speaking here, of course, of the studies of Cypro-Minoan *per se*. Many of the individual publications of excavations and excavated materials are near models of precise information about the contexts of inscribed objects, e.g., ÅSTRÖM and NICOLAOU 1980; DIKAIOS 1963, 1967, 1969a, 1971; KARAGEORGHIS 1985. Yet this carefully assembled information is often not assimilated into epigraphical discussions , e.g., E. MASSON 1985b. A clear example of contextual data put to good use is furnished by E. MASSON 1971a, 28-29.

Minoan repertories. This is a particularly serious fault in attacking Cypro-Minoan because, as we shall see, two major problems rest primarily on epigraphical-palaeographical-typological considerations: (1) the possible division of Cypro-Minoan into separate subsystems with discrete signaries; and (2) the affiliation of Cypro-Minoan and its possible independent subsystems with other Aegean or Near Eastern scripts.[18] The first problem, which has two parts, obviously affects our approach to decipherment: to what degree should the already limited Cypro-Minoan data be (a) pooled together as a relatively homogeneous system capable of a single decipherment or (b) separated into smaller bodies of data in self-sufficient systems representing either the same language(s) in different ways or different languages altogether? The second problem affects what we might call the next stage of current attempts at decipherment: how do the individual signs of the Cypro-Minoan signary(-ies) match up with those of deciphered scripts, which are then used to suggest tentative values for the Cypro-Minoan characters? Both these problems are also tied up with the historical and archaeological contexts of the inscriptions, which will be one major focus of this paper.

Maurice Pope may also acknowledge in my tale of humor in *Nestor* and its rather disturbing consequences one more illustration of the words he wrote in Oxford or Paris just about ten years ago (May 15, 1978): "...there are many to whom the prospect of decipherment is like a lamp to a moth or the name of a race-horse to an addicted gambler." (RAISON and POPE 1978, 45) This is, I think, another of the major problems besetting current work in Cypro-Minoan studies. I stress the word "current," because full-scale research on Cypro-Minoan got off to a fairly good start in the 1930's-50's, continuing into the 60's and early 70's, although some obstacles were inadvertently laid even then by virtue of the chronological sequence in which, and the contemporary scholarly ideas by which, Cypro-Minoan texts were discovered, published and studied. Now many of the preconditions necessary for decipherment are being overlooked, or at least given less than full consideration and attention, because of the eagerness of the few scholars seriously working in this area to attain a decipherment. Here ironically it is the fullness of the few formal texts in CM 1, 2 and 3 that has inspired a kind of cart-before-the-horse impulse to "read" and "decipher" instead of properly analyzing the entire repertory of inscriptions and incised material. I would go so far as to say that it is virtually impossible, given the present state of publication of the Cypro-Minoan material, for any scholar–perhaps even those primarily concerned with the decipherment of the script–to obtain a critical view of this epigraphical material sufficient for evaluating independently–no, even proposing–what the general scholarly community would consider a valid decipherment. Lady Mary's remark is apt in this instance. The study of Cypro-Minoan texts and the problems associated with them is fascinating and entertaining. But the current state of scholarship is such that too large a share of one's life is required just to get a grasp of the almost inaccessible data and to

[18] BAURAIN 1980, 569-570, raises this question most recently in regard to the two earliest Cypro-Minoan inscriptions: the clay "weight" and archaic tablet from Enkomi.

understand the contexts in which they are to be interpreted. I write from experience.

Perhaps it is the relative ease, noted by Emmett Bennett, with which the descendant of some form of Cypro-Minoan, the Cypriote syllabary, was deciphered in 1871, that is seductive, even if one acknowledges that this feat was accomplished with the help of a Phoenician-Greek Cypriote Syllabic bilingual from Idalion (O. MASSON 1983, 48-51, 246-248, §220). Perhaps it is the degree of similarity Cypro-Minoan displays to the Mycenaean-Minoan scripts and to the later Cypriote syllabary (in terms of both the size of the proposed Cypro-Minoan signaries and the forms of their characters) which has seduced researchers into transferring values, too arbitrarily and with little agreement among themselves (HILLER 1985, 62-65), from known to unknown systems and afterwards proceeding with identification and interpretation. Perhaps it is the number and variety of Cypro-Minoan texts and their relatively well-known, albeit complicated, cultural-historical environments that suggest that we ought to know what they say. As another problem of historical context, I shall review how we have reached our present impasse in the study of Cypro-Minoan. These are the peculiar problems of decipherment confronting researchers of Cypro-Minoan.

Let us begin by asking two questions. What elements are necessary to make decipherment of an unknown script possible? How then should a decipherer present his or her results in order to convince a generally skeptical scholarly audience? The skeleton of an answer to the first question can be found in E.J.W. Barber's *Archaeological Decipherment: A Handbook* (Princeton 1974), and needs only minimal fleshing out by means of examples which can be drawn easily from a work such as M. Pope's *The Story of Archaeological Decipherment* (New York 1975) or from the other contributions to this volume. One needs a large enough corpus of texts to establish a reasonably complete set of characters used by the script. The texts must offer enough syntactical and grammatical variety to make analysis of the underlying linguistic structure of the language possible (this is lacking in Etruscan). If these two conditions are fulfilled, one must then either have the benefit of a bilingual text to suggest possible meanings for words and test-values for a first group of signs (e.g., the Cypriote syllabary and Egyptian hieroglyphs) or be able to do this by some other means such as isolating formulaic expressions with historical parallels (the titles of kings in Old Persian cuneiform) or by identifying common vocabulary items (as in Ugaritic cuneiform). This then will lead, in the case of a known language, to a chain reaction of value assignments based on the careful preliminary structural analysis that was undertaken, one would hope, without preconceptions.

If a decipherment were attained by these procedures, the decipherer ideally would then demonstrate to a critical audience that she or he:

(1) had made use of a carefully established corpus of texts;

(2) had determined the essential characters used by the script;

(3) had identified as many structural clues as possible to the nature of the language represented by the script;

(4) had, in the case of scripts like Linear A or Cypro-Minoan which do not offer bilingual texts, intelligently selected the first test-values;

(5) had then been able to assign values to all essential and sufficiently represented characters of the script; and

(6) could support the historical likelihood of the script representing the language attained by the decipherment.

Such a convincing demonstration has not been offered by those who claim to read, in greater or lesser part, texts written in Cypro-Minoan. The currently proposed decipherments or "readings" fail to convince on one, several or all of points 1, 3, 4, 5 and 6. Even point 2 is troublesome. Moreover, none of the "decipherments" is anything but partial even within the uncertain and often not altogether clear subsets of Cypro-Minoan writing devised by its students. The wide variation in these approaches and solutions does not inspire confidence. Rather it underscores, and stems from, the problems I have already isolated.

As far as historical context is concerned, a major complicating factor is that the island of Cyprus, particularly in the late Bronze Age (1600-1050 B.C.), had a spread of many settlements which were exposed, in varying degrees, to external cultural influences (figure 1). It is therefore a mistake to view the island, from a later Helleno-centric, or at least Aegeanist, perspective, as solidly part of the Greek-speaking sphere of the eastern Mediterranean (figure 2). A more realistic perspective reveals just how precariously the island lay on the extreme limit of that sphere, even in the historical period (figure 3). The process of Hellenization was a long time in being fully completed. No doubt part of the explanation is to be found in the political and cultural history of the island during the archaic and classical periods, when a strong and continuous Phoenician trade presence and first Assyrian domination (ca. 709-669 B.C.) followed by Egyptian (570/60-545 B.C.) and then Persian (ca. 545 B.C. onwards) control affected much that is distinctive in Cypriote culture, although in some ways it also heightened a distinctive sense of Greekness among elements of the population (V. KARAGEORGHIS 1982, 57-60, 64-68).[19]

In the late fourth century B.C. in the district of Amathous, the Classical Cypriote syllabary was still being employed for inscriptions in the indigenous language of the island, eteo-Cypriote (O. MASSON 1953 and 1957c). Four eteo-Cypriote texts from this site run 4 to 6 lines (O. MASSON 1983, 203-206, §192-195) while one digraphic-bilingual text in Cypriote Syllabic-Greek alphabetic offers further testimony about the mixed population of the area (O. MASSON

[19] MEIGGS 1972, 477-486, presents a condensed account of Greek and non-Greek foreign influence on Cyprus in the sixth and fifth centuries B.C. See also the essay by POUILLOUX 1976.

1983, 206-209, §196).[20] Eteo-Cypriote mercenaries of the fourth century B.C. carved at least one of their full names in Cypriote Syllabic along with Greek graffiti in the sanctuary of Seti I at Abydos in Egypt (O. MASSON 1983, 356-57, 362, §388). Phoenician texts also were not uncommon as late as the fourth century, including reasonably lengthy (7-10 lines) digraphic-bilinguals (e.g., O. MASSON 1983, 226-228 and 246-248, §216 and §220).[21] More to the point is the fact that in this late period even the Hellenic population of the island persisted in standing apart in one crucial regard from the rest of the greater Greek world. A syllabary was still being used, alongside the Greek alphabet, to write Greek on Cyprus until well into the third century B.C. (MITFORD and MASSON 1982, 80-82; MITFORD 1980; J. KARAGEORGHIS 1961, 58-60). This is odd, in a characteristically Cypriote way, from *both* an Aegean *and* a Levantine perspective.

For the Late Bronze Age we must imagine a similar, if not greater, diversity within the population of the island of Cyprus which was subject to the same sorts of external influences as in historical times. A. B. Knapp, in a study of "Alashiyan" names mentioned in Late Bronze Age Akkadian, Ugaritic, Hittite and Egyptian documents, demonstrated a decided Semitic bias: perhaps as many as 24 of 33 names are Semitic, with the remainder being Hurrian or Anatolian (KNAPP 1983, 40). Although we must keep in mind the distortion associated with the provenience and perspective of such evidence,[22] it does suggest, when taken together with other archaeological evidence for Near Eastern and Egyptian influence (for example, finds of imported Canaanite pottery, the prevalent use of Near Eastern seal types and practices, the vital involvement of Cyprus in the well-documented Near Eastern-Aegean-Egyptian-Anatolian trade in tin, copper, spices, oil, ivory, lapis lazuli, cloth, vessels and various luxury items during the period 1700-1200 B.C.) that the island had considerable ethnic and cultural diversity and that any Aegean affinities discernible in the Bronze Age archaeological record must have been hard won (BAURAIN 1984, 135-164; CATLING 1975, 192-209; GEORGIOU 1979; KNAPP 1985, 241-243, 245-250, n. 112; PORTUGALI and KNAPP 1985, esp. 44-45, 60-67; KNAPP 1986, 42-44; PORADA 1986, 289; PALAIMA forthcoming).[23] It is thought that Cypriotes

---

[20] There is now, too, a recently rediscovered yellowish limestone tablet inscription in eteo-Cypriote, probably from Amathous. See O. MASSON 1988.

[21] See MASSON and SZNYCER 1972, for a full study of the earliest Phoenician inscription in Cyprus (9th century) and other assorted minor Phoenician texts. For the history of Phoenician presence in Cyprus from the 9th century B.C. onward, see GJERSTAD 1979, esp. 249-254.

[22] For example, SCHAEFFER-FORRER 1978a, 97-104, argues that several 13th century Ugaritic documents list princely persons and their households (some 100 individuals, mostly Hurrite) installed in Alasia (Cyprus) during a time of political crisis. Tablet RS 11.857 preserves a record of 28 households. Of the 16 names of proprietors listed, only 3 are Semitic, while 13 are Hurrian.

[23] BAURAIN 1984, 27-103, documents the changes in the island of Cyprus, during the transition to LC I A (ca. 1620-1520 B.C.), brought about by increased Hittite influence in northern Syria and the intensified maritime activities suggested by discoveries at Minet-el-Beida (Ras Shamra). He goes so far as to speak of a "Syro-Palestinian infiltration" seeking

were installed at Minet-el-Beida by the 16th century B.C., and Cypriote objects and artifacts begin to be spread significantly throughout Syro-Palestine and Egypt in MC III-LC I and after. Although the conclusions to be drawn from the evidence are debatable in detail, one cannot deny a reverse flow of goods and people, if initially only craftsmen and traders, into the various natural geographical zones of Cyprus during this same time (E. MASSON 1976a, esp. 162-164 and n. 136).

Various sites on the island of Cyprus show definite signs of Aegean influence in this period. Because of recent excavation and study of excavated material, Minoan contact in Cyprus, quite reasonable on general grounds, has been confirmed for the beginning of the Late Bronze Age (1600-1450 B.C.) at the sites of Ayia Irini, Toumba tou Skourou, Kouklia, Limassol, and Enkomi (counter-clockwise NW to NE in figure 1: see appendix on Aegean objects in Cyprus in PORTUGALI and KNAPP 1985, 71-73). Clear evidence of Cypriote trade contacts with the Aegean world is provided by the coastal *emporion* of Kommos in southern Crete, where imported Cypriote pottery is found in Middle Minoan to Late Minoan I levels and greatly increases in LM III A:1-2 (WATROUS 1985) when the site and island were undoubtedly under Mycenaean control. Some of the imports from Cyprus and the Levant bear marks in the Cypro-Minoan tradition (BENNET forthcoming). BAURAIN 1984, 146-147, soberly discusses the likelihood that ox-hide copper ingots from the LM I period on the island of Keos and at Zakro and Hagia Triada on Crete are Cypriote in origin, thus attesting to the important trade item which led first to Cretan and then to Mycenaean interest in the island of Cyprus. This first period of Minoan contact is followed by periods of increasing Mycenaean contact with or influence on the island in 1450-1400 and then 1400-1200 (PORTUGALI and KNAPP 73-78; PACCI 1986).

We can see Aegean influence, too, by looking at how Cypro-Minoan writing fits into historical developments in the greater Eastern Mediterranean world. The current picture is represented schematically in figure 4, adopting for convenient reference the standard division of Cypro-Minoan, first suggested by O. Masson and later refined primarily by E. Masson, into three distinct branches (CM 1, 2 and 3) and an archaic predecessor of CM 1 (HILLER 1985, 66-79; O. MASSON 1956, 199-201; E. MASSON 1974, 11-17; 1973, 99). Later in this paper I shall offer serious epigraphical and palaeographical reasons for calling these arbitrary divisions into question.

We have the sequence of linear writing systems evolving on the island of Crete in the Middle Bronze Age and even spreading into the Cyclades by MM III-LM I or the 17th and 16th centuries B.C. (OLIVIER 1986; PALAIMA 1982). There is no trace of Linear B until much later; but I have recently argued, on palaeographical, historical, and, for want of a better term, systemic grounds, that its creation be placed in LH II-III A:1, when we have the first clear indications of

---

Cypriote copper, an infiltration which stimulated native cultural developments on the island. BAURAIN 1984, 101-103.

the development of mainland palatial society and the beginnings of a marked outburst in Mycenaean trade and contact with the Near East and Anatolia (PALAIMA 1988b, 331-341 and n. 106). On Cyprus, however, the first traces of formal writing date conservatively to the end of the 16th century (BAURAIN 1980, 565-569, 580), i.e., to a period before the Mycenaean expansion[24] (CATLING 1973; PACCI 1986; PORTUGALI and KNAPP 1985, 60-64) and perhaps even before the Mycenaean acquisition of writing.

Nonetheless the affinities of the first full manifestation of formal writing on Cyprus are definitely with the Aegean scripts. This is the so-called archaic Cypro-Minoan tablet from Enkomi (figure 5 = Enkomi 1885) found in filling between floor levels, about mid-way through LC I B, so 1525-1475 B.C. (DIKAIOS 1963, 45-48; 1971, 882). The general similarities to Minoan linear writing are obvious, especially the flat-edged and flat-faced shape of the tablet, its conjectural restored size (ca. 11 cm. H x 7.5 cm. L x 3 cm. TH) and the linear forms of characters, most of which have suitable parallels in the now clearly established repertory of Linear A signs (figure 6). Reading right to left on the first line: AB nos. 57, 02, 54, —, — , 01, 41, 60 or, using Linear B values purely for the sake of reference, *ja*, *ro*, *wa*, —, —, *da*, *si*, *ra*; and left to right on the second line: AB nos. 77, 37 or 70, 37 or 70, 55, 04, 09, 37, again with Linear B values for reference only, *ka*, *ti* or *ko*, *ti* or *ko*, *nu*, *te*, *se*, *ti*; in the third line matchups are harder, but at least the fourth and sixth signs reading right to left have clear matches in AB nos. 01 or 10[25] (Linear B *da* or *u*) and 30 (Linear B *ni*) respectively. We might liken the second-last sign, again reading right to left, to Linear A AB 79 in the form in which it is attested in LM I B at Zakro on tablet ZA 4a.5, without being accused of drawing strained parallels. Differences from attested Minoan writing, specifically Linear A, have been stressed (GODART and SACCONI 1979) and even accepted in general historical syntheses (BAURAIN 1980, 568; 1984, 153-156; HOOKER 1985), but I do not find any of them compelling enough to dissociate the archaic Enkomi text from the Aegean tradition of writing or from Linear A in particular. These supposed differences are:

(1) the boldness of the ductus, i.e., of the way the characters are inscribed, in contrast to the usually exceedingly fine track of Minoan-Mycenaean styluses. RESPONSE: All this means is that the assumed Cypriote inscriber had a different

[24] NICOLAOU 1973, esp. 51-52 and 59, argues that Mycenaean presence in Cyprus begins in LH II-III A:1, i.e., early enough to have inspired the new Cypro-Minoan script and the new language which it represented. Yet Baurain's careful discussion of the dates of the Enkomi clay weight (?) and archaic tablet proves that they must precede the date of Mycenaean influence. The dates given for the clay weight (?) in GODART and SACCONI 1979, 128, is wildly incorrect. That Cypro-Minoan was used for a language newly introduced to Cyprus is, of course, an unnecessary assumption. An overview of Mycenaean presence in Cyprus, broken down by period, is provided by PACCI 1986. A reasonable number of habitation sites and cemeteries (c) have LH II B material: Enkomi, Hala Sultan Tekké, Pyla (c), Limassol (c), Skales (c). Ayia Irini and Enkomi have some LH II A.

[25] Particularly in the form attested on KN Zb 40.2 or HT 122a.1.

form of stylus,[26] and the relative size of the signs [.8-1.2 cm.] corresponds to those found in most Minoan-Mycenaean documents[27] as opposed to the smaller size of signs on later formal Cypro-Minoan texts from Enkomi.

(2) the supposedly intentional firing of this piece, again in contrast with the accidentally baked Linear A and Linear B texts. RESPONSE: I do not know how anyone who has studied clay tablet documents from the Aegean and the Near East can demonstrate conclusively whether a well-baked tablet has reached that state intentionally or not. Some of the tablets from the throne room at Mycenaean Pylos were baked unintentionally in the destruction of the Palace of Nestor with an intensity that has preserved them in the manner of kiln-fired sherds (PALAIMA 1988a, 137-139). Certainly, in the case of Enkomi 1885, its discovery in filling makes it impossible to determine whether it was preserved elsewhere by intentional or accidental firing. One may cite the case of the largest Enkomi CM 2 tablet, the two fragments of which appear to have been fired at different temperatures (MICHAELIDOU-NICOLAOU 1980, 11) and therefore no doubt accidentally, as a cautionary reminder against such assumptions.[28] In any event, the intentional preservation of a text has to do with the eventual application of an established script to a document that was important enough to preserve for a longer period of time. It has nothing to do with the original creation or adaptation of the script itself.

(3) the low percentage of sign matchups. RESPONSE: I find the number of probable parallels demonstrated above convincingly high for so brief a text; and we should rather stress the complete absence of *contemporary* Near Eastern archetypes for the forms of these signs.[29] There are 23 signs on the text, 21 on its recto, 2 on its *lat. dex.* Few of the signs can be considered probable duplicates: at most six (definitely the two on the *lat. dex.* and the first two signs

---

26 Bone styluses are known from Late Bronze Age levels at Enkomi, Palaepaphos, Kition and Maroni. For references, see KNAPP 1985, 248 and n. 157. For reasons to doubt whether the Enkomi styluses were used, or used exclusively, for inscribing tablets, see PALAIMA 1987, 510 and n. 28. KARAGEORGHIS 1976, 239, fig. 8, indicates how the styluses may have been able to produce the inscriptions on clay balls.

27 This point is well made in E. MASSON 1970, 66, and can now be confirmed by examination of the full corpus of Linear A clay documents (*GORILA* 1-3, 5) and Linear B palaeographical studies (OLIVIER 1967; PALAIMA 1988a).

28 Note that SCHAEFFER-FORRER 1978a, 93-94, insists that the Enkomi tablets were handed over by the scribes to be baked "en vue de les rendre solides et durables." This circularity of reasoning is disproved for two of these very pieces by Michaelidou-Nicolaou's observations on the firing temperatures of the two joining pieces of a single tablet. Even the better fired of the two joining fragments seems not to have been baked intentionally (MICHAELIDOU-NICOLAOU 1980, 11): "Le meilleur degré de cuisson de ce fragment [no. 1193] n'est pas intentionnel, mais accidentel, car il porte des traces de rubéfaction irrégulière caractéristique des vestiges de terres argileuses découvertes dans les niveaux archéologiques d'incendie."

29 The number of convincing parallels to Linear A certainly exceeds 3 out of 20 signs, *pace* HOOKER 1985, 178, where, however, he astutely reinforces Masson's observation about the singularity of the archaic Cypro-Minoan repertory of signs among Levantine and Anatolian scripts. BAURAIN 1980, 569-570, who would like to see a Syro-Levantine intermediary in the transmission of script to Cyprus, still must admit that there are no tablets in Ugaritic script attested at Ugarit prior to ca. 1365 B.C.

at the right of line .1; perhaps the second and third signs from the left on line .2). For 17 of the 20 potentially distinctive signs, one can propose parallel signs in Linear A, using little imagination and with a degree of probability which would convince all but the most perversely skeptical or biased scholars. I have already suggested another parallel to a specific variant of a Minoan sign form (AB 79). This would raise the number to 18. This is truly a high percentage (90%).

It is worth stressing, too, that one can, in most cases, find rather exact matches in the detailed palaeographical charts of Linear A sign variations now provided in *GORILA 5*, XXVIII-LII and in its three accompanying microfiches. It is absolutely wrong procedure to compare the Cypro-Minoan signs written by a specific hand on Enkomi 1885 to standardized Minoan characters. The significant range of variation among the forms of separate characters in the standard Minoan signary from site to site, period to period, material to material, and even scribal hand to scribal hand, makes clear that we have to keep in mind the possibility that Cypro-Minoan was patterned after a regional style of Linear A sometime in the LM I A or MM III period, a comparatively poorly documented phase in the development of the Minoan script. I advise any skeptical reader to look at the variations of Linear A signs AB 28, 37, 38, 39, 45, 54 and 65 in *GORILA 5*, XXXIII-XXXVIII. Some of the variants are so different from the standardized or archetypal forms that, if they did not occur on texts known to be Linear A, cautious scholars would undoubtedly doubt that even they were Linear A characters.

We also know nothing about the historical circumstances in which this isolated tablet Enkomi 1885 was produced. Was its inscriber expert, i.e., was he a professional scribe? If so, was he as inexperienced and relatively unaccomplished at writing as some of the minor hands in the Linear B administrations at Knossos and Pylos, or was he a master of a script which had been employed in Cyprus for some time? For what reason was the text produced? One that required special attention or one which might lead the writer to be less careful about sign shapes and overall tablet appearance? We find a wide range of variation in such characteristics in the Linear A and Linear B tablets. Only 5 of 23 signs (2 of 20 distinctive signs) on Enkomi 1885 are without reasonably demonstrable sign parallels in Linear A. Might these be supplemental signs such as those which were added, either immediately or over time, in the transition from Linear A to Linear B and even in the development of the Greek alphabet from Semitic predecessors?[30] Or might they be simply distorted or embellished versions of Linear A characters which are still less well attested, or were then not fully understood by the Cypriote borrowers of Linear A or by those who subsequently used and further transformed the new script? We know of Cypro-Minoan on the LC I A clay weight (?) from

---

[30] The Mycenaean supplementals and their relationship to Cypro-Minoan and later Cypriote Syllabic are treated in PALAIMA forthcoming. For a recent theory and discussion of older views about Greek alphabetic supplementals, see POWELL 1987.

Enkomi, not to mention the evidence of signs marked on LC I pottery; so we can posit at least a half-century of development within the Cypro-Minoan script by the time of Enkomi 1885. Such a span of time would be enough to produce peculiar palaeographical variants. Given all the unknown variables surrounding this text, the high percentage (90%) of sign matchups with Linear A actually speaks most forcefully in favor of seeing a clear link between the Minoan linear script and the origin of writing on Cyprus. It may even permit us to speak in terms of a more direct transmission of writing to Cyprus from Crete than one has heretofore assumed.

Still one has never spoken for Cyprus of a wholesale borrowing of script, with but minor alterations, in the manner of Mycenaean Linear B from Minoan Linear A. In the latter case, the homogeneity of mainland palatial culture, the strong impact of Minoan culture upon it, and the narrow range of desired applications of the new script are factors and motives radically different from those which we think are at work in Cyprus. A closer analogy perhaps would be the development of the Greek alphabet, wherein writing was adapted by a large number of independent, although culturally related, communities, apparently for very practical motives. The adaptation of the alphabet was achieved in a period of Phoenician-Greek interaction marked by an outburst of Greek trade activity and even colonization. It was effected, so far as we know, on the individual level rather than through any direct or coordinated initiative of ruling elites or developing political or economic administrations. In the case of the alphabet, one sees clear traces of experimentation and regional variation. Perhaps the same forces and factors were at work in early Late Bronze Age Cyprus. In this case, 50-75 years would doubtless produce significant innovations or variations in sign shapes in comparison with the signary of the mother-script, which itself was still developing.

(4) the intentional ruling into lines, although apparently after the text itself was inscribed.[31] RESPONSE: Most Minoan texts lack ruling; but some are ruled into sections, and some few even continuously. However, none has the long continuous sequence of presumably phonetic signs inscribed on Enkomi tablet 1885; and it takes no extraordinarily bold leap of imagination to assert that Minoan texts with complicated phonetic and syntactical units would have shown similar ruling.[32] Moreover, ruling is primarily an independent formatting development even in the Linear B texts. The fact that Linear B texts are consistently ruled, while Linear A texts are usually not, is no argument against the clearly established derivation of Linear B from Linear A. Nor should such an argument be seriously considered for archaic Cypro-Minoan.[33]

---

[31]See R. Janko, 1987, 315 and n. 22, for a discussion of this feature and its relationship to a CM 3 text from Ras Shamra.

[32] PALAIMA 1988b, 313-317, thoroughly reviews the evidence for ruling in Linear A.

[33] SCHAEFFER-FORRER 1978a, 94-96, uses arguments about the shape and formatting of Enkomi 53.5 and 20.01 to argue for a Near Eastern-Ugaritic origin of the CM II tablets. He mistakenly asserts that, in contrast to the Enkomi tablets, all Mycenaean tablets are uniformly turned left-to-right along the long axis in order to inscribe the verso. E. MASSON 1978, 51,

(5) the sinistroverse writing of line 1, suggested by the reverse orientation of several of the signs (E. MASSON 1970, 67), and I think proved by what Janko cleverly observes to be an *incipit* reference of two signs on the *lat. dex.* opposite the extreme righthand edge of line 1, where the two signs are repeated at the start of the text (JANKO 1987, 316-317). RESPONSE: Minoan-Mycenaean clay texts are uniformly left-to-right, but again the borrower of a script need not be a slavish adherent to such a principle–Enkomi 1885 in fact seems to be boustrophedon–and many of the later Cypro-Minoan texts appear to run consistently left-to-right, as does the earliest Cypriote Syllabic inscription, the late 11th century inscribed spit from tomb 49 at Paphos Skales, in defiance of later common Cypriote Syllabic practice (V. KARAGEORGHIS 1980, 131-136, figs. 12, 12c; E. MASSON 1987b, 376-377, with references). One would not, therefore, argue that Cypriote Syllabic is not related to Cypro-Minoan!

and (6) the absence of indications that this is an accounting document. RESPONSE: This again has to do with the applications of the new script and should not be used as an argument against the affiliation of Cypro-Minoan with Minoan Linear A. Moreover, the preservation of only three lines of text makes this irrelevant argument dangerous in its own terms, since one *could* have to do with a document of account with a full explanatory, narrative heading, for which practice there are sound Mycenaean and even Minoan parallels.[34]

We can then safely conclude that the genesis of formal script on Cyprus is somehow connected with the Aegean linear systems of writing. Yet what does this mean in terms of prospects for decipherment? How is the archaic system of formal script, of which Enkomi 1885 is our single, isolated example, connected with the Aegean tradition? Directly or through intermediaries? If intermediaries, are these Aegean, Anatolian or Near Eastern? How does this affect the complicated history of Cypro-Minoan writing in later periods both on Cyprus itself and the chief area where an offshoot is documented: Ras Shamra-

---

also views the turning of the Enkomi tablets along the horizontal axis as a Near Eastern feature. To the contrary, Linear B tablets can be turned along the short, horizontal axis, like the Enkomi tablets, and even along transverse axes from lower left to upper right and vice versa. See *Nestor* 1 (July 1962) 201, and PALAIMA 1988a, 104-107 (for variation within two closely related hands). Here one must stress also that it is no proper argument to say that the rectangular shape of the CM 2 documents is more Near Eastern because the majority of Linear A-Linear B documents do not have this shape. In fact, the Minoan-Mycenaean data are imbalanced by the typological variety of tablet shapes: labels, sealings and leaf-shaped texts serving specific functions. The longer lists, of which there are many whole series, are done on rectangular texts of this very type. Ugaritic influence on formatting at this stage is not at all unlikely: especially the un-Mycenaean system of placing entries in rectangularly ruled casements. This, however, does not prove that CM 2 is a special Ugaritic or Near Eastern offshoot of the CM script, which was already implanted in Cyprus for at least two centuries. The fact that I am using computer typesetting and formatting for this paper, a technique unknown to the Greeks and Romans, does not mean that I am no longer using the Greco-Roman alphabet!

34 See the long and purely lexical introductions on full accounting tablets from Pylos in *PTT* I: Jn 829.1-.3; Tn 316 v.1-.2; Un 267.1-.4; Un 718.1-.2; and An 519, 607, 654, 656, 657, 661. In Linear A, the long lexical entry on ZA Zb 3 (*GORILA* 4, 112-113) would certainly be misleading if the single ideogram and numerical entry were broken away.

Ugarit in northern Syria? Here we must turn to one problem of context: the context in which Cypro-Minoan has been studied.

Readers interested in a detailed summary of the history of early Cypro-Minoan scholarship may consult O. MASSON 1983, 30-38. Our purpose here is to analyze, within this history, the complications that have arisen for a clear understanding of the epigraphical data as a prerequisite for decipherment. During the last quarter of the 19th century, scholars in general linked the later Cypriote syllabic script, which was then the only form of Cypriote script well attested on the island, with Near Eastern writing systems. For example, because of its syllabic structure, it was connected with Old Persian syllabic cuneiform. However, by the first years of the 20th century, epigraphical and archaeological finds from the Bronze Age were to shift the focus of scholars interested in tracing the development of writing on Cyprus westward to the Aegean.

Already in 1900 on the basis of materials excavated on behalf of the British Museum, Sir Arthur Evans was to advance the idea that "the Mycenaean factor in the unwritten history of Cyprus assumes a new importance. The impress of this Aegean element is so strong that we find ourselves in [the] presence not of sporadic influences or isolated importations of objects, but of a distinct period in the insular civilisation to which the name Cypro-Mycenaean must henceforward be given." (EVANS 1900, 199) Evans was basing his opinion primarily on extensive finds of Mycenaean and Mycenaean-influenced objects and material remains from these excavations. But as the first great student of Aegean scripts, he also was struck, and convinced, by the resemblances he deduced among: (a) 15 distinct characters incised into three inscribed clay balls from Enkomi[35] (figure 7) and a gold ring from Hala Sultan Tekké (figure 8);[36] (b) those found on what he considered roughly contemporaneous tablets in the Cretan linear script which he had just discovered at Knossos; and (c) those of the later Classical Cypriote syllabary, already deciphered as Greek (EVANS 1900, 215-217). In his full treatment of Cretan hieroglyphic and Linear A published nine years later, he was to call the Bronze Age script of Cyprus Cypro-Minoan, in accordance with his own belief, developed during this interval, in the dominant influence of Cretan culture in the Aegean; and he was to compare this still limited corpus of inscribed Cypro-Minoan finds to the now more fully understood Cretan scripts, including linear script Class B. The results were hardly unequivocal, but Evans's chart of parallel sign forms led him to some extremely optimistic conclusions (EVANS 1909, 68-77, figs. 37-39): (1) 10 of the 15 known Cypro-Minoan characters were definitely paralleled ("an absolute conformity") in either Linear A or Linear B, while the remaining 5 could be matched with Cretan hieroglyphic prototypes; (2)

---

35 Four had been discovered in 1896, but only three were published and even those with incomplete and less than fully accurate drawings: an early, but typical example of the difficulty of gaining access, through normal scholarly publications, to Cypro-Minoan texts (E. MASSON 1971a, 11-13).

36 At first wrongly attributed by Evans to Enkomi, later to Maroni, attributions which misled Persson and others, including me in surveying this material historically, until corrected by O. MASSON 1957a, 20 n. 2.

two-thirds of the signs of the later Classical Cypriote syllabary were also derived from Linear A and Linear B, although a detailed comparison was postponed until the projected publication of the Linear B corpus; (3) the matches solely with Linear B and the archaeological indications of the influence of mainland culture in late Bronze Age Cyprus suggested that the mainland representatives of Minoan culture might have brought with them to Cyprus the model of a linear script which was already adapted to the Greek language; (4) yet tradition seemed to indicate that the Hellenization of the island was not this early, i.e., that the Cypriote syllabary and, by implication, the Cypro-Minoan script were "originally devised for a non-Hellenic language." As a consequence of this last point, Evans listed six perceived parallels between the Classical Cypriote script and non-Greek forms in the Lycian and Carian alphabets.

So already at this early stage in the study of the Cypro-Minoan scripts certain procedures were established: (1) the comparison, often extremely subjective, of sign forms first to determine the degree of relationship between scripts[37] and then, by introducing the Classical Cypriote syllabary, i.e., the final result of the development of writing on Cyprus, to suggest values for the signs of the Cypro-Minoan script; (2) the selective, if not arbitrary, pooling of different classes of epigraphical data, in this case the Hala Sultan Tekké gold ring (still something of an oddity, although O. MASSON 1957a, 20-22, has marshalled convincing evidence that the object itself is a genuine late Bronze Age artefact) and clay balls, in order to establish a sign repertory; and (3) the consideration of varying historical factors in explaining the advent, development, and applications of writing on Cyprus. It is interesting to observe that, in his earlier study, Evans took note of a copper ingot from Enkomi with an incised sign, which he identified as equivalent to later Cypriote syllabic *si* (EVANS 1900, 215, fig. 12). Yet this sign is nowhere discussed in his fuller treatment, perhaps because the form of the sign could not be easily paralleled in either of the Cretan linear scripts, or perhaps because Evans did not consider such an isolated mark writing *per se*, especially in comparison to the fuller sequences to which he had grown accustomed through his continuing research with Cretan writing, extending from hieroglyphic seals (similar to the Hala Sultan Tekké gold ring in sign layout) to full clay tablets (similar to the clay balls in execution). Evans himself makes no comment. We only note the omission here because the second possible explanation bears upon a question that became particularly crucial with the next major advance in Cypro-Minoan scholarship: how does one determine whether marks on an object

[37] EVANS 1909, 77-100, applied the same technique to Minoan and respectively Phoenician writing and signs on Iberic sherds. We now know, for example, that sign no. 15 from the Hala Sultan Tekké gold ring was matched with a Linear A fractional sign (a near impossibility), and that sign no. 1 is rather an Egyptian *ankh*, as Evans himself half-thought (EVANS 1909, 70 n. 3; 71 fig. 39). It is interesting to note that CASSON 1937, 86, excluded sign no. 15 and included sign no. 1 in his list, exactly opposite to O. MASSON 1957a, 22. EVANS 1935, 782-784, interpreted what we now know to be Cypro-Minoan signs on the silver bowl from Ugarit RS 389 (E. MASSON 1974, 19-20, fig. 5) as Linear B. BRICE 1961, 24, no. V 16 and plate XXXI, included the text in a catalogue of Linear A. We can thus see how precarious this procedure is, especially if one is influenced by preconceived opinion.

constitute a true inscription? Moreover the classification of the *ankh* symbol on the Hala Sultan Tekké gold ring as Cypro-Minoan was no doubt motivated by Evans's desire to expand the meager Cypro-Minoan sign repertory[38] and supported by his familiarity with Cretan hieroglyphs.

The 1930's were a decade of renewed interest in Cypro-Minoan, with some advances and some continuation of old problems. Among the advances one must consider the publication of Cypriote style signs painted on the bases of Mycenaean pots from Cyprus and Ras Shamra (SCHAEFFER 1936) and the compilation of a fuller Cypro-Minoan signary derived from a careful analysis of different categories of inscribed objects: incised or painted signs on vases of well-differentiated types; signs incised on clay balls and one on a vase before firing; signs on copper ingots and a bronze plaque in a private collection; signs on cylinder seals and the Hala Sultan Tekké ring (CASSON 1937).[39] Here careful attention was paid to the kinds of wares, the precise methods of making the signs, the find places and circumstances, and the exact number of attestations of individual signs. CASSON 1937, 108-109, also discussed and listed signs painted on Mycenaean wares imported, as he thought, from Cyprus into Palestine.

A first indication of real problems with Cypro-Minoan studies is furnished by Persson's studies of the clay ball inscriptions from Enkomi (PERSSON 1930 and 1932). Although, in his second publication, Persson produces as a positive result more accurate transcriptions of all four Enkomi clay balls plus a fifth from Hala Sultan Tekké, he also produces negative results by rushing into partial readings of the texts under study. He employs familiar tactics:

(1) the historical procedure: his views of the Mycenaeanization of Cyprus which allowed (2) Greek Cypriote syllabic values to be extended back to Cypro-Minoan and then even to Minoan-Mycenaean scripts;

(3) the arbitrary selection of epigraphical data: he interprets a pseudo-inscription on a sherd from Asine–the absence of tablets from the mainland was explained away by declaring that the Mycenaeans used ephemeral materials (wood, leather, palm leaves, papyrus)–by means of Classical Cypriote sign parallels (PERSSON 1930, 10-13, 17); and his other inscriptions chosen for "reading" are a potpourri, from the Knossian clay cups with painted Linear A inscriptions to some of the lexical units which Sundwall identified as occurring repeatedly on Linear A tablets (PERSSON 1930, 18-25);

---

[38] DANIEL 1941, 249-250, gives a succinct account of the limited Cypro-Minoan material and sign repertories of the early researchers.

[39] Casson relied on what Daniel calls the "almost unobtainable" publication MARKIDES 1916, which presented and analyzed Cypro-Minoan inscribed pottery from Arpera, Enkomi, and Markides's own excavations at Katydhata. MARKIDES 1916, 19-20, proposed adding 17 new signs from this material to Evans's list of 15 Cypro-Minoan characters. EVANS 1935, 758-763 and fig. 744, also provided a slightly updated list of signs from Cypro-Minoan inscriptions, including two more clay balls and a sherd.

(4) adducing text parallels: his "reading" of Mycenaean inscribed stirrup jars from Thebes by the same method, but with the support of supposed parallels for the type of text obtained, in this case on jars found in Syria-Palestine (PERSSON 1932, 272);[40]

(5) attributing a specific purpose to the inscribed objects which is in keeping with the texts obtained: his assertion that the clay balls functioned as weights (PERSSON 1932, 270-273);

and (6) even the acrophonic principle, whereby a sign is given the value of the first phoneme or syllable of the word for the object which the sign resembles in the fancy of the scholar and in the language that the scholar wants the script under study to represent (PERSSON 1930, 31-32).

We should note that PERSSON 1930, 32, includes the standard disclaimer that he has not achieved a full decipherment through his hodgepodge of readings. All of these problematic approaches to understanding Cypro-Minoan texts will recur, in one form or another, in the later attempts to read Cypro-Minoan to which I made oblique reference at the outset of this paper.

The real foundation for Cypro-Minoan scholarship of the last half-century was laid by J.F. Daniel (DANIEL 1941) who produced a truly analytical "corpus" which incorporated the abundant evidence of marked pottery, exploiting the full material from excavations at Kourion-Bamboula, and which classified signs according to the type of ware (Cypriote, Mycenaean, imported wheel-made red burnished) or object (cylinder seals, clay balls, copper ingot) and manner of marking (inscribed before or after firing, painted before or after firing). Daniel's study greatly expanded the repertory of Cypro-Minoan signs, and it forms the basis for what, until the present day, is considered the principal system of Cypro-Minoan writing: CM 1. Yet we should note that Daniel himself did not create a single unified sign repertory out of this heterogeneous material, preferring to let the categories stand separately. He did, however, grapple with the problem of how to define the formal Cypro-Minoan script. The first requirement was that a sign occur on an object "of indubitably Cypriote manufacture" (DANIEL 1941, 252). Signs of this type were grouped as Class I. Signs on other non-Cypriote objects would be included as Cypro-Minoan only if they corresponded to signs in Class I. He also enunciated (DANIEL 1941, 253) the following conditions for including a given sign within a single formal signary: (a) if it occurred in multi-sign inscriptions; (b) if it was identical to signs in multi-sign inscriptions (then still very few and brief: the clay balls, cylinder seals and

[40] It points out the hazards of proposing "readings" of an undeciphered script on the basis of such procedures to recall that PERSSON 1932, 272, "read" 'Kadmos ruler Thebes' on some of the Theban inscribed stirrup vases. He adduced parallels for this kind of text from the stamped handles of Palestinian vessels. We now know that the fullest stirrup jar inscriptions give normally two personal names and a Cretan toponym: Thebes and Kadmos nowhere appear in this class of inscriptions. It is typical of the lax methods behind such "readings" that PERSSON 1930, 28, neither informs us on which of the inscribed stirrup jars he reads these words nor provides us with a drawing of the inscriptions.

the gold ring); (c) if it was identical to signs used in Linear A, Linear B, or the Classical Cypriote script–this, according to Daniel, raised the likelihood of its having a phonetic value in Cypro-Minoan; (d) if the sign appeared with considerable frequency, thus increasing "the probability that it was in general currency." He used much greater restraint in deducing sign parallels among these various scripts, himself commenting negatively on the degree to which previous scholars had allowed for inversions and perversions of forms in tracing parallels (DANIEL 1941, 254-264).

The chronological span for the script was also of crucial importance for the different theories about its origin and impact. The stratified Kourion material made a rough estimate possible. The earliest pieces were datable to the late 16th and 15th centuries B.C. (LC I A:2-LC I B), but these marks were singletons (e.g., DANIEL 1941, 274, nos. 12, 21) and so simple in shape that they could not bear the burden of proof for the origin of formal script, especially since some of the marks catalogued by Daniel, even applying his four criteria listed above, were manifestly pure pot marks (DANIEL 1941, 253).

Daniel also paid careful attention to the kinds of epigraphical and palaeographical details which are of highest importance for understanding the evolution of any script. He attributed the differences between the signs of the Aegean linear scripts and the Cypro-Minoan inscriptions to differences in materials and techniques (DANIEL 1941, 253), factors taken into account too rarely nowadays: "The Minoan tablets were incised with a sharp tool in wet clay, a facile medium which led to a fluent and often florid style. The Cypro-Minoan inscriptions fall into two main technical groups. The Enkomi balls resemble the Minoan tablets in that they were inscribed in damp clay, but differ from them in being impressed with a dull tool rather than incised with a sharp one. This technique led to a graphic style which favored short strokes and the elimination of curved lines. Most of the other Cypro-Minoan inscriptions were deeply incised with a knife, or similar tool, in relatively hard materials, chiefly pottery. These, even more than the clay balls, call for a bold style and the avoidance of curves."[41] Thus Daniel explained the greater "linearization" of incised Cypro-Minoan sign-forms, in contrast to their Aegean counterparts, as a product of tools and materials rather than as the result of the influence of the techniques of Near Eastern writing.

Daniel's collection of signs, produced before the discovery of any lengthy, formal Cypro-Minoan inscriptions, nonetheless is the basis for the Cypro-Minoan signary, specifically that which is now known as CM 1. Some criticism was made of his system for excluding signs on non-Cypriote objects, since the number of attestations for signs of this kind was generally quite low (BUCHHOLZ 1954,

---

[41] I. Nicolaou in ÅSTRÖM and NICOLAOU 1980, 32, makes a keen observation about the difference in sign forms when incised by means of a needle-like pointed instrument on the lead sling bullets and when drawn in moist clay by the normal Cypro-Minoan stylus. E. MASSON 1985b, 149, observes that the mode of incision may have affected the sign forms on the gold rings from Kalavassos.

144). Nonetheless, in treating newer material, his procedures for incorporating signs into the Cypro-Minoan signary have been loosely followed, while his principle of constructing and maintaining separate categories on the basis of types of inscriptions has been largely abandonned. That is, one tends to call "Cypro-Minoan" any sign with a Daniel pedigree, whether of his Class I or not. Of course, the discovery of formal texts has deemphasized the importance of the very kinds of inscriptions which had been used to establish the sign repertory in the first place. Since the time of Daniel, the pot marks especially have tended to become a separate issue (e.g., BENSON and MASSON 1960; O. MASSON 1957b and 1966; ÅSTRÖM 1966 and 1969; MITFORD 1971; VERMEULE and WOLSKY 1976; DÖHL 1978 and 1979; PALAIMA-BETANCOURT-MEYER 1984; E. MASSON 1984 and 1988; GALLIS 1988; CATLING 1988; BENNET forthcoming). Also Daniel's epigraphical observations have been ignored to some extent, particularly in devising at least one of the other branches of Cypro-Minoan script, CM 2.

All this raises several problems. It is now impossible to distinguish the types of inscriptional attestations for signs in the published Cypro-Minoan signaries. One simply assumes that for CM 1 most of the signs come from the more formal types of texts of this class, e.g., on cylinder seals, clay balls, clay cylinders, metal vases, and in sequences of multiple signs on pots (see below), but there has been no separation of signs into classes nor has there been an obvious weeding out of CM 1 signs which are attested exclusively as pot marks or were included originally on the basis of one of Daniel's lesser criteria: mere frequency of occurrence or resemblance to signs in Linear A, Linear B, or Cypriote Syllabic.[42] Thus the corpus of Cypro-Minoan pot marks has expanded greatly since 1941 (see articles cited at the end of the preceding paragraph), in both the number of marked sherds or vases and their geographical spread, with little understanding of how this marking system relates to what one would consider writing *per se*. Moreover, there has not yet been any clear study of the development of CM 1 through time. In addition CM 1, CM 2 and CM 3 have been distinguished largely and admittedly through rather superficial judgments about the appearance of texts in the various categories and through historical-linguistic speculation (E. MASSON 1976, 139-140), ignoring for the most part the practical factors involved in determining sign forms which Daniel stressed. This has caused some clear instances of confusion in the wider literature among scholars attempting to make use or sense of Cypro-Minoan.

[42] The standard CM 1 signary is based on formal inscriptions, but also incorporates characters from pottery and other kinds of objects, without designating them as special (E. MASSON 1974, 12). A particular complication is that many signs of the standard signary are derived from inscriptions on clay balls which have been published in separate groups and according to different schemes of sign numeration (E. MASSON 1971a and 1971c). Thus it is impossible to check the source for characters in the standard general CM 1 signary (still that of E. MASSON 1974) without undertaking a painstaking process of elimination, inscription by inscription.

In fact, Daniel's "Prolegomena" has never been followed by a full analytical corpus, despite, or perhaps because of, the number of later separate and detailed publications of a much larger amount of significant Cypro-Minoan material, chiefly by the two foremost students of the script and its inscriptions, first Olivier Masson and, during the last 20 years, Emilia Masson. Their publications can be likened to individual, somewhat disconnected chapters in the story of Cypro-Minoan. The coherent book to follow Daniel's forward has yet to be written.

Our critical narrative history of Cypro-Minoan scholarship ends at this point, having touched upon some fundamental obstacles in approaching a decipherment, the last and most crucial being the absence of a corpus which would make all the essential data available to students of this script: not only the inscriptions themselves, but their types, dates, find-contexts, sign repertories, and palaeographical development, all in the manner of *GORILA*. Absence of a corpus has contributed I believe to the number of partial readings of Cypro-Minoan text material.[43] It is satisfying to some minds to work on narrow, esoteric problems and to suggest solutions which, while they cannot be corroborated, certainly cannot be absolutely disproved. Persson's work on the actual language of the select few Cypro-Minoan texts available to him offers one extreme example of what I would consider, quite frankly, meaningless speculation. Given the much larger body of Cypro-Minoan inscriptions now known, the scattered publications of inscriptions unfortunately offer an appealing opportunity to proceed in this way. The number of possible solutions increases, if one focuses solely on the CM 3 tablets from Ras Shamra or the clay cylinders from Enkomi and Kalavassos-Ayios Dhimitrios or the CM 2 tablets from Enkomi (see CHADWICK 1989) or selections from any of these groups. The Ras Shamra texts are ambrosia for certain would-be decipherers. The site is almost a literal Babel of scripts and languages: elements of the mixed population spoke or at least used Sumerian, Ugaritic, Canaanite, Babylonian, Hurrite, Egyptian, Hittite, and we may suppose Cypriote and conjecture Mycenaean Greek. The attested writing includes various forms of cuneiform, Hittite hieroglyphic, Egyptian hieroglyphic, Ugaritic alphabetic cuneiform, and Cypro-Minoan (SCHAEFFER 1956). Even the Cypro-Minoan might be of two sorts (see below). On the other hand, difficulties increase if one tries to confront all the Cypro-Minoan texts together, to limit the number of arbitrary value assignments by reducing sign parallels to those few which are most probable (cf. CHADWICK 1979, 139), to hold in check one's unprovable assumptions about the nature and purpose of the inscriptions at hand or about the language that may lie behind them.

For the sake of illustration, I shall now analyze one recent approach to the decipherment of Cypro-Minoan: FAUCOUNAU 1988. I have chosen it almost at random and without any malicious intent, since it was brought to my attention only recently when I received a group of offprints from the editor of the volume in which it appeared. Since then I have been in correspondence with its author,

43 Similar problems are created by the absence of a corpus for Cretan hieroglyphic. See OLIVIER, this volume.

who has sent to me a slightly corrected version of the text and several letters attempting the sort of historical justification of his decipherments which I have mentioned as the last in six stages of an ideal decipherment. Monsieur Faucounau's article is typical in concentrating on a few brief texts, to most of which we have already referred: the gold ring, two clay balls and a hematite cylinder seal from Hala Sultan Tekké; two of the clay cylinders from Kalavassos-Ayios Dhimitrios; and a reprise of the clay cylinder from Enkomi. Its flaws are also typical.

It behooves me here again to follow the model of the distinguished honoree of the symposium which inspired this volume. I apologize to Monsieur Faucounau for the following honest criticism of his work, and I assure him that I do not intend any of it as an *ad hominem* argument. I only undertake it because of his admirable willingness to discuss his ideas with me and because, in an assessment of the state of scholarship in a given field, one must be frank. Students of prehistoric scripts and languages are few. The conclusions and theories advanced by such students are often used by other specialists (archaeologists, prehistorians, art historians) who have varying levels of competence in and understanding of the data and methods by which conclusions and interpretations were reached.[44] One, therefore, has an obligation to be cautious and exacting in presenting information about prehistoric inscriptions. Otherwise, what I have referred to elsewhere as a microbic contamination of scholarship can occur. My own honest opinion is that in Cypro-Minoan studies we are faced with a potential epidemic, as this brief discussion will demonstrate.

Any reader, however uninformed, should be suspicious of Faucounau's opening reference to the decipherments of Cypro-Minoan writing systems as *faits accomplis*: CM 2 is declared to be a Hurrian syllabary, while the other branches are called Cypro-Semitic and are said to express an unknown language which is "une sorte de 'créole sémitique'." (FAUCOUNAU 1988, 239) Having one of the languages be a creole is a convenient tactic, because it broadens the range of possibilities for "readings" of these texts. We are then told, without being offered any further information, explanation, or references, that the three-sign inscription on the ring from Hala Sultan Tekké (figure 8) is in the Hurrian syllabary (CM 2) because the left-most sign on its surface (= right-most in the drawing of its impression in figure 8) is a "figure-eight." To understand this flat declaration of fact, one must search for oneself and eventually resort to E. Masson's accurate drawing of an inscription now classified as CM 2: Enkomi 53.5 (figure 10), where on lines 15 and 21 appears a sign (E. Masson no. 76), apparently unmatched in the other sub-systems of Cypro-Minoan, in the form of two square lozenges joined aslant one to the other at their respective lower right and upper left corners (see also E. MASSON 1987a, 193, fig. 3, 1B). Even

[44] I cite as an example the use made of a now generally discredited decipherment of Linear A as Semitic in BASS 1967, 77, 167; see especially p. 77 for Bass's confession of being totally unable to judge the decipherment in its own terms. It is interesting that Monsieur Faucounau has mentioned in a letter that the author of this discredited decipherment of Linear A is the only scholar to accept his Cypro-Minoan decipherment.

granting that these signs on the Enkomi tablet and the Hala Sultan Tekké ring are related–a not entirely improbable assumption, given the linear nature of CM 2 inscriptions–we would still have to ask whether, given the fact that the left-most sign on the ring impression (figure 8) is paralleled in CM 1 and the central sign in both CM 1 and 3 (see HILLER 1985, 62-65 for parallel sign lists), we are not dealing with an inscription of the CM 1 class, in which the right-most sign (in impression, figure 8)–rarely attested, if at all, in CM 2–is simply so far undocumented.

But even here we should not follow Faucounau in not exploring other alternatives. A reading of O. Masson's careful treatment of the gold ring (O. MASSON 1957a, 20-22, 27) provides us with specific parallels for all the signs on it. The left-most sign (in impression) is paralleled (oriented sinistroverse) on a cylinder seal from Ayia Paraskevi (O. MASSON 1957a, 17, no. 11) and (with the same sinistroverse orientation) as part of a dipinti inscription on a Mycenaean bowl from an LC II B context in Kourion Tomb 6 (= DANIEL 1941, 276-277, no. 76). The right-most sign (in impression), i.e., the "figure-eight" sign, is likened not only to the later curvilinear Cypriote Syllabic sign *le*, which suggests to Faucounau his value for this sign in Cypro-Minoan, but also to an angular sign in one case painted on Mycenaean ware and another time incised after firing on an LC II plain ware jug handle from tomb 5 at Kourion (= DANIEL 1941, 276, no. 50). Since the gold ring was discovered in a highly Mycenaeanized tomb context, the parallels to CM 1 dipinti marks on Mycenaean pottery should be given considerable attention. At least the unsubstantiated assumption that this ring inscription with its curvilinear "figure-eight" sign is CM 2 should be dismissed. The central sign is perfectly paralleled on a cylinder from Kourion (O. MASSON 1957a, 10-11, no. 4) and in all three Cypro-Minoan sub-systems.

The "reading" of the text is again flatly declared by Faucounau to be sinistroverse, without further explanation. One can only guess at the reasons. Perhaps the ring is considered to be a seal,[45] in which case the reversed impression (figure 8) read dextroverse (and therefore the ring inscription itself read sinistroverse) is the true reading? But if the direction of the right-most sign on the ring is normal (HILLER 1985, 62, E. Masson sign no.12), this would suggest that the text is to be read dextroverse on the ring itself. As mentioned above, the sign is found oriented sinistroverse on an actual cylinder seal where the inscription seems to have been part of the original, albeit crudely executed, design. This could be taken to imply that the reversed seal impression gives the proper orientation of the sign, i.e., dextroverse as on the surface of the Hala Sultan Tekké gold seal ring. The question of reading such inscriptions on seals at least deserves fuller study. Faucounau's Hittite-Luwian reading of the text of the ring and the very sequence in which he proposes the characters are to be read are both revealed to be pure assumptions–and not even easily defensible assumptions. My first moral is that even so restricted and isolated a three-character inscription does not permit a scholar to set up his own private universe of interpretation. It

---

[45] This is the opinion of O. MASSON 1957a, 22.

certainly does not give him the right to ignore the careful work of earlier scholars at presenting and editing the texts.

Faucounau's treatment of the clay ball and the hematite cylinder seal are equally flawed. The "readings" here depend on two optional identifications of signs to which he assigns the values *ke* and *ma* on the basis of presumed stemmata of formal evolution from Linear A and Linear B through Cypro-Minoan and into Cypriote Syllabic. Faucounau's chart is here reproduced as figure 11. It is sufficient to stress a point that is clear to anyone who has dealt firsthand with inscriptions, namely that palaeography depends on an intimate familiarity with the exact shapes of characters and their possible variations as they occur on the texts themselves. We made the point above, in discussing Enkomi tablet 1885, that the links with Linear A become startlingly clear when we compare the actual forms of signs found on Linear A documents with those found on the archaic Enkomi tablet. Those who argued for little resemblance had cavalierly compared the character forms on Enkomi 1885 to conventionalized Linear A characters. Using such a method, I would be hard-pressed to demonstrate that my own English handwriting made use of Roman alphabetic characters, so different is my developed hand from the standardized "pattern-book" written characters one learns in one's youth. Faucounau makes this same mistake. In the stemmata in figure 11, he begins with forms of the Linear A and Linear B characters that are so artificial and innacurate that the proposed succeeding development of the signs is immediately deprived of any value. In fact the hallmark of Linear B *ke* as opposed to *de* is that, in its upper portion, the outward slanting arms are dominant and the inverted triangle rests upon and between them, exactly opposite to Faucounau's drawing of *ke*.

Finally, I shall close this mini-review, by noting that, in examining Faucounau's study, we are entering a world without proper epigraphical transcriptions or drawings of texts (compare his fig. 3 and "transcription" of Kalavassos clay cylinder IV [FAUCOUNAU 1988, 247-248] with E. MASSON 1983, 132 IV, plate XVIII.7). The drawing of Kalavassos IV is inaccurate by even tolerant standards. Perhaps the reason for such fundamental epigraphical carelessness is betrayed by the way in which Faucounau dismisses the evidence for identification of the third character in the first line as something of little consequence. There is never a thought for any bit of evidence which does not conform or contribute to a preconceived system of decipherment. For some scholars obsessed with decipherment, it is unimportant to take pains to establish a true and accurate text. Thus, we find ourselves, in reading the work of such scholars, in one of those simultaneous universes where what E. Masson reads correctly as a fissure in the clay at the beginning of line 2 of cylinder IV, Faucounau can reinterpret as a determinative sign for a proper name. He does this by proposing a parallel on the Enkomi clay cylinder, but the "parallel" mark occurs neither in a comparable form nor in the same position relative to the lexical unit interpreted as a proper name. That is, Faucounau's new reading is based on a parallel which is no parallel at all!

Cylinder IV is interpreted by Faucounau as a foundation inscription, and the unmistakable numeral seven in its last line is rendered: "in the seventh year of the reign of Kukka-Zita." On what basis is one to opt for either this "kukk"y interpretation or that of E. Masson: "Il est fort probable que ce chiffre ne figure pas ici avec sa fonction réelle, à savoir numérique, mais plutôt comme un symbole, ayant la valeur rituelle bien connue de ce nombre" (E. MASSON 1983, 138)? Both alternatives are pure conjectures and do little to advance our real understanding of Cypro-Minoan. They can, however, do much to harm our reconstruction of Cypriote prehistory, by leading scholarship away from certainty and towards bald speculation masquerading as well-reasoned theory. All is possible in such a realm, even a consequent reinterpretation by FAUCOUNAU 1988, 250, of the Enkomi clay cylinder as a foundation inscription, not, as he originally thought, a proclamation. Moreover, a corrective insert in the personal offprint I received from the author now announces that the three-sign sequence on the second Hala Sultan Tekké inscribed clay ball (ÖBRINK 1979, 46 N 6035), for which no reference is provided, is no longer interpreted by him as a Cappadocian proper name written in the Hurrite CM 2 syllabary, but as a "lukki" proper name written in the Cypro-Semitic CM 1 syllabary. The principles of interpretation being used are so flexible and pay so little attention to the fundamental procedures of archaeological, palaeographical, epigraphical and linguistic research that one can change the meaning, language and script of whole texts as easily as one ignores archaeological contexts, parallels for sign identification, and the details of the physical texts being studied. The assumption that the Cypro-Minoan documents can be broken down into different sub-groups and different languages offers a wide field for epigraphical and linguistic speculation. The complicated cultural history of the island of Cyprus in the Late Bronze Age does little to limit the scope of speculation. What is true of Monsieur Faucounau is equally true of other theorists interested in Cypro-Minoan. Each can devise a not altogether implausible general historical framework which suits his speculations about the evolution of Bronze Age writing on Cyprus and the language(s) represented in the surviving inscriptions.

Existence of a corpus would certainly do much to clarify the conjectural division of the Cypro-Minoan script into subsystems and enable one to view the historical evolution of the script in thorough detail. One should mention here that O. MASSON 1957a, brought together all of the cylinder and signet seals bearing possible Cypro-Minoan signs;[46] and O. MASSON 1957b, assembled a bibliographically thorough index of all the Cypro-Minoan inscriptions then available, together with 29 photographic text figures of some of the more significant pieces, including the unprovenienced bronze plaque used by Casson in establishing his sign repertory (O. MASSON 1957b, fig. 30). These are still extremely important supplements to Daniel's work, even if admittedly no corpus

[46] VERMEULE and WOLSKY 1976, 72-75, fig. 3, no. 13, add a Cypriote manufactured lapis lazuli cylinder from Toumba tou Skourou discovered in a securely dated LH III A 2 context. It is clearly incised with a common Cypro-Minoan sign.

(O. MASSON 1957b, 9), as are the long series of individual publications of Cypro-Minoan material by E. Masson listed in the bibliography.

With this background let us now consider some of the problems with current approaches to the decipherment of Cypro-Minoan to which we have already alluded. From the period of the Enkomi clay weight (?) (LC I A = 1575-1525 B.C.) and archaic Cypro-Minoan tablet (LC I B = 1525-1475 B.C.) onward, Cypro-Minoan writing is widespread on the island of Cyprus and eventually is securely attested on tablets at the N. Syrian commercial center of Ugarit. Cypro-Minoan pot-marks have an even wider circulation from Syro-Palestine (COURTOIS 1978, 278-281) to Crete (BENNET forthcoming), now even turning up, it appears, in Late Bronze Age Thessaly, as well as at well-studied Mycenaean sites like Tiryns (GALLIS 1988; OLIVIER 1988, nos. 12-14, figs. 1-2, with references; PALAIMA 1988b, 334 and n. 97). One vision of the traditional scheme of writing on Cyprus and its relation to historical developments on the island is given in figure 9, taken from KNAPP and MARCHANT 1982, 22, chart 1. It should not be accepted as an accurate outline of writing in Cyprus, although the errors which it contains should be attributed to the problems we have so far encountered in Cypro-Minoan scholarship, rather than to any carelessness on the part of its authors.

The traditional scheme posits a single, general, long-lived and widespread system called Cypro-Minoan 1, the characters of which, found on a great variety of materials, maintain fairly linear forms throughout four centuries of use or more. As we have already seen, this style of script is found inscribed on vases, both before and after firing, both domestic and imported, mainly of the 13th-12th centuries. There are some few possibly earlier (14th century) examples of veritable multi-character pottery inscriptions and still earlier isolated pot-marks which do not necessarily constitute formal script or even a reflection of formal script: DIKAIOS 1971, 889 and plate 315, catalogues a single possible LC I A (1575-1525 B.C.) Cypro-Minoan pot mark and seven possible LC I B (1525-1425 B.C.) examples (cf. E. MASSON 1973, 92; ÅSTRÖM 1966, 190-191). This style of script also occurs (figure 1) on clay balls (from Enkomi, Kition and Hala Sultan Tekké, all on the eastern coast of the island), on clay cylinders (from Enkomi, north on the eastern coast; and Kalavassos-Ayios Dhimitrios, in the center of the southeastern coast), cylinder seals (from Kourion in the southwest; Enkomi; Verghi, a bit inland and almost equidistant between Enkomi and Hala Sultan Tekké in the east; Hala Sultan Tekké in the southeast; Sinda, directly west and inland from Enkomi; Ayia Paraskevi, in the north center of the island directly west of Sinda, almost equidistant between the northeastern and northwestern shores; Toumba tou Skourou, in the northwest, and perhaps even Ayia Irini, on the extreme northwestern coast[47]), copper ingots, ivory objects (E. MASSON

---

47 PECORELLA 1977, 22, no. 3:17, fig. 32: a cylinder seal with 4 linear signs incised in the field, from tomb 3 at Ayia Irini. VERMEULE and WOLSKY 1976, 72-75, fig. 3, no. 13: an inscribed Cypriote cylinder from an LH III A 2 context. PORADA 1976, 98-99, and E. MASSON 1976b, 130-131, discuss the hematite cylinder seal with five clear Cypro-Minoan signs from Tomb 2 at Hala Sultan Tekké (1400-1200 B.C.).

1985b), hemispheric bronze and silver bowls (one definitely from Enkomi, others likely to be from this site or from Kouklia[48] far in the southwest, one from Ras Shamra-Ugarit), even a jeweler's anvil.

The chronology of non-pottery finds is very difficult to establish, given the early date of acquisition or excavation of many of the inscribed objects, and the relative disinterest of recent researchers on Cypro-Minoan to investigate and report such information, when it is available. Yet contrary to the impression given by the placement of individual pieces on the chart in figure 9, most of the well-dated material comes from 13th to 12th century contexts. The earliest secure piece (figure 12), as we have already stated several times, now seems to be the inscribed clay weight (?) from Enkomi (BAURAIN 1980, 569).[49] The Kalopsidha vase has upon it four separate incised elements (figure 13); but, as is clear from a close reading of O. Massons's analysis (in ÅSTRÖM 1966, 136-137), only one of the elements is a sign in the Cypro-Minoan pot-mark signary, paralleled on tablet RS 17.06 from Ugarit. The other elements are two simple vertical bars, which were used to isolate the actual sign, and part of what appears to have been a simple "x" mark. The Kalopsidha vase, therefore, should not be used as an attestation of Cypro-Minoan script. Moreover, this piece, like so many others, does not have an entirely firm context: "The area where the handle was found was occupied from Middle Cypriote III to some time into Late Cypriote II, but there are some stray sherds from Late Cypriote III and the Iron Age...." Masson assigns it a tentative and general LC II date, i.e., anywhere in the 14th or 13th centuries B.C.

Otherwise several vases from tomb 11 at Katydhata (NW Cyprus) with multi-character inscriptions are also put forward as early (15th century) examples of formal script (HEUBECK 1979, 56; O. MASSON 1957b, 13, nos. 45 and 46, figs. 2 and 3). Here the true multi-character nature of the inscriptions is not in question, but the precise date of these vases is. Published early by Markides, they are plain white ware jugs "from tombs of the Late Bronze Period." (PERSSON 1937, 605). One should not place too much reliance on their general 15th century date, nor on the date of the clear six-character pithos inscription from Arpera (O. MASSON 1957b, 17, no. 174, fig. 7). The texts of these pottery inscriptions, taken from PERSSON's copy of the original Markides drawings, are given in figure 14. A final complicating factor is that E. MASSON 1974, 11-12 and fig. 1, uses the signs on the Enkomi clay weight (?), an Enkomi cylinder seal dated LC I (O. MASSON 1957a, 7-8, no. 1, fig. 1), and one of the Katydhata vases to form, along with characters on Enkomi 1885, her so-called archaic repertory of 30 signs. This is a *contaminatio* in terms of the types and materials of texts and even in terms of their dates, since the individual texts are assigned either firmly or

[48] E. MASSON 1973, 92. Unfortunately several of the inscribed bowls come from early excavations and are unprovenienced. One should not overlook, in this discussion, the importance of the inscribed Cypro-Minoan silver bowl from Ras Shamra: SCHAEFFER 1932, 22, plate XVI (1), and 23, fig. 15; SCHAEFFER 1956, 228 and n. 2.

[49] Clear photograph in SCHAEFFER et al., 1968, 266, fig. 3.

debatably to the 16th-15th centuries and the vase inscription could even be later. This contaminated signary should be treated with extreme caution.

The Enkomi clay cylinder (figure 15), measuring 54 mm. across and 40 mm. in diameter and containing 179 signs on 27 lines of text, was dated in the preliminary excavation report as "en gros du XIVe avant notre ère," without any details being given about context pottery or firm stratigraphy except that the immediate substratum contained MC III and LC I pottery (SCHAEFFER et al., 1968, 267-268 and fig. 5). No subsequent publication has improved on this rough date. One wonders then whether it should not be brought down closer to the more recently discovered cache of five such clay cylinders from Kalavassos-Ayios Dhimitrios, seemingly to be dated firmly to LC II C or ca. 1275-1225 B.C. (SOUTH 1983, 98-100; 1984, 21, 23-25). It is important to note here an important palaeographical feature of these cylinders: the miniscule nature of writing on them, signs being about 3-4 mm. high, despite which they retain the style of producing characters with linear forms by drawing the stylus through the clay surfaces.

The signs incised on vases and metal objects also retain a consistent linear style throughout the history of Cypro-Minoan. See, for example, the six- and five-sign inscriptions on pithoi respectively from Arpera and Enkomi (O. MASSON 1957b, figs. 7 and 14) and the fragmentary four-character inscription (figure 16) incised near the base of a deep bowl of buff ware, probably while the clay was hardening and the vase was upside down awaiting attachment of the base (DIKAIOS 1967, 80-84). This last inscribed vase has the advantage of a secure archaeological context which fixes it at a period when Mycenaean III C 1:b pottery was in circulation at the site, i.e., ca. 1230-1190 B.C. Signs on the ca. 68 securely dated clay balls from the Cypriote, French and Swedish excavations at Enkomi, Kition, and Hala Sultan Tekké also have a linear style despite the fact that they come from the latest phases of use of Cypro-Minoan and apparently span a considerable period of time from ca. 1250-1075 B.C. (E. MASSON 1971a, 28, 38 nn. 119-121; DIKAIOS 1971, 881-891, plates 318-319; KARAGEORGHIS 1976a, 238-239, fig. 8; ÖBRINK 1979, 3, 43, 46, 89, fig. 286). The two recently discovered gold rings from Kalavassos–Ayios Dhimitrios bear identical four-sign Cypro-Minoan inscriptions in a linear style. These appear in an upper register above a lower register with presumably decorative, or symbolic, designs. This pair dates from the 14th century (E. MASSON 1987b, 188, 194, fig. 4.1-2; E. MASSON forthcoming). We should note, too, that the twelve-sign Cypro-Minoan inscription on the carved ivory plaque in the figure of the god Bes from Kition, dated 1190-1150 B.C., also has characters in a perfectly linear style The same applies to the ivory pipe and bar from the same area of the site: Temple 4 Room 38C between floors III and III A (KARAGEORGHIS 1976a, 232-233, fig. 3; 1985, 116-117, nos. 4252, 4267, 4250; E. MASSON 1985a, pls. A and B).

In the traditional scheme, the second system, Cypro-Minoan 2, is reserved for four tablet fragments discovered at Enkomi. Their find-spots are known, but of little help for precise dating. Enkomi fragments 53.5 and 20.01 are said to be dated securely to no later than the general period defined by Schaeffer as LC III =

Dikaios's LC II B/II C, i.e., the long period ca. 1350-1200 (SCHAEFFER-FORRER 1978, 88-93). Enkomi fragments 1687 and 1193 are placed stratigraphically by Dikaios in his levels IIIA and end of IIIB respectively. Enkomi 1687 was found among vase fragments strewn as a bedding course for a hearth. That the tablet was deposited there intentionally as part of a foundation ritual is mere conjecture. In fact, Enkomi 1193, much worn on its surface and discovered in a destruction level, was undoubtedly "out of its original context and transferred from an earlier level," probably Level III A (DIKAIOS 1971, 885-887). Since Enkomi 1193 has now been joined to Enkomi 20.01, it is fairly safe to say that all these texts probably date to Dikaios's LC III A 2, i.e., ca. 1220-1190 B.C.

Now we come to our palaeographical crux. It is claimed that, with these four tablets and these tablets alone, the Cypro-Minoan signary on the island of Cyprus becomes cuneiformized. The writing on these four tablets then is thought to constitute a separate class and to represent a different language. Having surveyed the full corpus of Cypro-Minoan inscriptions and having examined the Enkomi texts first via the excellent photographs now in the PASP collection[50] and then by autopsy in the Cyprus Museum in Nicosia, I now find this classification very questionable. A close inspection of Enkomi 1687 (figure 17), the best preserved text, reveals that the characters are not formed much differently than those on CM 1 clay balls or even the CM 1 clay cylinders. What is different about the appearence of the signs has to do with palaeographical factors. On the Enkomi clay cylinder (figure 15), as well as on the smaller cylinders from Kalavassos-Ayios Dhimitrios, the small signs (ca. 4 mm.) have been incised on a drier clay surface. I think that this was necessary since the special curved (slightly convex) surface of these documents required the clay to be of a more permanent, almost fixed consistency before they could be properly formed, handled and inscribed. Thus the multiple elements of the signs tend to have a slightly more drawn aspect. However, the same shorter jab strokes are frequent for multiple horizontal and vertical elements within single signs. This is only natural when drawing miniscule strokes (some less than 3 mm.) with the fairly blunt Cypro-Minoan stylus.[51] The tablet surfaces, and the surface of Enkomi 1687 in particular, were much moister when the signs were inscribed. Thus the blunt and rather wide-pointed stylus (the *punkt*-mark at the end of line 20 of Enkomi 1687 is nearly 3 mm. in diameter) sinks more deeply into the clay when strokes are being made. Many, if not most, of the multiple horizontal and vertical strokes within single signs are no more than 2 mm. in length. One would be hard-pressed even with the much finer Linear B stylus to produce anything but the appearance of having quickly touched the stylus point into the clay surface and then having withdrawn it with a slight pull in one or the other direction. That is all that is required to produce such miniscule signs.

---

50 These were acquired through the kind assistance of the director, Olivier Picard, and the careful labors of photothecarian, M. Vitsilogiannis, of the École Française d'Athènes. Funding was provided by the Office of the Dean of the School of Liberal Arts at the University of Texas at Austin.

51 Illustrations of possible styluses in DIKAIOS 1969b, plate 158, 17 (807); plate 169, 1-3; KARAGEORGHIS 1976, 239, fig. 8.

Still there are several vertical strokes of some 4-5 mm. in length that are clearly *drawn* on the tablet surface.

I think that, with the characters on documents now classified CM 2, we are simply dealing with normal CM 1 of the smaller type seen on the clay cylinders.[52] On these four tablet fragments, the CM 1 signs are used in very small sizes in order to record very long texts efficiently and economically in terms of space and the number of documents required. The kind of casement formatting seen on Enkomi 53.5 (figure 18) does indicate that the Cypriote scribes were clever enough to borrow and develop formatting procedures suitable to their texts. Here the inspiration may indeed have come from cuneiform scribal practices.[53] There are good illustrations of such ruled columnar and casement formatting on Hittite-Luvian and Ugaritic cuneiform texts in WALKER 1987, 43, 45, figs. 23-24; and SCHAEFFER-FORRER 1978b, plate XLVI (RS 34.166). However, the characters of the script on these four Cypro-Minoan inscriptions are firmly within the Cypriote tradition, as they are when written even on media like cylinder seals where, if anywhere, the Near Eastern practice of inscribing very full cuneiform texts along with the scenes and designs on seals should have influenced the style of Cypro-Minoan characters. On the seals they remain immune to "cuneiformization," as do the signs on the CM 3 tablets discovered together with actual cuneiform documents at Ugarit. Because of the contexts of these CM 3 inscriptions, one would assume that the forms of signs on these tablets would come most directly under cuneiform influence. Yet they do not show any trace of Near Eastern influence (see below).

I believe that the signs on the texts now classed CM 2 likewise are not "cuneiformized." I therefore consider it a very dangerous procedure to study the four Enkomi tablets dated ca. 1200 B.C. as if they were a separate script and language. 39 of the 59 signs appearing on these 4 texts are clearly paralleled in documents now classed CM 1. Of the remaining 20 at least half could be considered, with little imagination, slightly altered variants of CM 1 signs. Given the differences in materials and methods of inscription and the greater chronological span for CM 1 as opposed to the intense chronological and geographical concentration of our four "CM 2" tablets, it is much safer procedure to consider their repertory of signs a local and temporal version of the standard CM 1 signary. I shall be bold enough to suggest that Daniel, with his habit of, and insistence on, paying careful attention to physical and epigraphical factors that

---

52 There is no compelling reason to see "cuneiformization" in the Kalavassos-Ayios Dhimitrios characters simply because they are made with small, fine and careful strokes (*pace* E. MASSON 1986, 181; 1987, 189).

53 For mistaken arguments about the supposedly non-Aegean shapes and rotation of the CM 2 tablets, see supra p. 139 n. 33. The physical description of the four CM 2 pieces and of the estimated sizes of the full tablets from which they come (E. MASSON 1976, 51) could actually be used to describe Mycenaean page-shaped tablets. In fact the flatness of the recto surface and the slight convexity of the verso is a hallmark of the Linear B page-shaped texts. Nonetheless KNAPP and MARCHANT 1982, 16, repeat that these fragments have a cuneiform "shape and ductus."

produce palaeographical variations, would have found favor with my sounding this note of caution.

Still one could point to the restricted number of characters (59) in the CM 2 repertory as an indication that it indeed constituted a distinct script system, in contrast to the 85-sign CM 1 system and the 44-sign CM 3 system. This, too, I think is dangerously misleading. We have seen (supra p. 124) that CM 1 is based on 713 signs of formal script (6 clay cylinders, 83 legible clay balls) supplemented by signs found on all the other kinds of objects surveyed at the outset. Thus CM 1's repertory has a much wider basis in terms of chronology, textual diversity, and sheer numbers of texts. We should recall the observation that only 46 signs were documented on the 26 clay balls in E. MASSON 1971a, while ca. 24 additional characters were supplied by the clay balls in E. MASSON 1971c. Thus does increasing merely the number of inscriptions increase the lexical and morphological diversity of their texts which in turn brings into play more of the characters of the writing system. Also the number of signs in the CM 1 repertory may be inflated by the inclusion of pot marks that should not be confused with characters of formal script. There may also be changes in the sign repertory because of development through time, since the formal CM 1 texts range at least from the mid-13th to the early 11th centuries B.C., and the Kalavassos-Ayios Dhimitrios rings seem to push formal CM 1 back into the 14th century. In Linear A, as we have mentioned (supra p. 138), the forms of individual signs show considerable variation corresponding to differences in the dates, media, scribes and find-spots of the texts. Only because of the larger number of documented occurrences, have we been able to identify quite different styles of actual characters as variants of the same sign in the official Linear A repertory.

Although on the CM 2 tablets we have some 1310 signs, there are, because of the joining of Enkomi 1193 and 20.01, only 3 separate and lengthy texts. These are obviously much different in nature and purpose than the clay balls and cylinders of CM 1. Enkomi 53.5 contains many repeated word units. E. MASSON 1976, 59, 67, 69, has demonstrated that each of the eleven legible casements on side a (figure 18) of this tablet ended with the same three lexical units in one of two sequences, and one can observe other repetitions on side b (figure 10). Such repetition, as well as the dating of these tablets to a restricted chronological period, certainly sets limits on the number of sign forms attested. One should note, as a cautionary parallel, that, despite the preservation of 28,500 signs on 1112 diverse tablets, five of the rarer characters of the standard Linear B signary (*18, *22, *47, *49, *87) are still not attested at Pylos.[54] These were undoubtedly peculiar to the Knossian-Cretan version of the syllabary and used mainly in Cretan anthroponyms and toponyms. Finally several of the signs in the CM 1 repertory appear to be slight variants of one another (HILLER 1985, 62-65: E. Masson nos. 12-14, 72-73, 81-84, 87-88). Yet another complication is E. Masson's recent hypothesis (E. MASSON 1985b, 151-154) that Cypro-Minoan employed small strokes ("épines") added to standard signs as diacritical marks. If

---

54 Statistics on numbers of signs in OLIVIER 1984, 13.

true, this would again greatly complicate the process of identifying the standard characters of the script. Thus the difference in the numbers of characters in these artificially devised repertories might be much less than it seems at first sight.

More remarkable and problematical still in this regard is the assignment of tablets from the site of Ras Shamra (Ugarit) on the Syrian coast to a third class of Cypro-Minoan script, CM 3. The main motive for this classification seems to have been geographical. Assigned to CM 3 are two of the four Cypro-Minoan tablets or tablet fragments from Ugarit, a cylinder seal from the site of Latakia 10 km. south of Ugarit, a pithos rim from Ugarit (COURTOIS 1978, 280-282, fig. 29.1 and .4; E. MASSON 1986, 180), and perhaps the silver bowl inscription from Ugarit, which we have already mentioned above (SCHAEFFER 1932, 23 fig. 15, pl. XVI). Yet the distinctions between this supposed system and CM 1 or 2 are not easy to discern. Consequently HILLER 1985, 72-74, and KNAPP and MARCHANT 1982, 22, mistakenly assign all four Ugaritic tablets to CM 3. Yet E. MASSON 1974, 23, and O. MASSON 1956, 247-250, especially 250, make clear that the inscriptions on the two smallest fragments (RS 19.01 and 19.02: figure 19) match up with the CM 1 signary.

The four signs of the inscription on the Latakia seal (figure 20), dated stylistically to ca. 1400 B.C., each can be matched with signs appearing on clay balls, or, in one case, a cylinder seal from Enkomi (BUCHANAN and MASSON 1968, 415). E. MASSON 1974, 24, stresses the slight singularity of the first character in assigning the seal inscription to CM 3. But a comparison of the particular sign (E. Masson no. 71) with similar signs in CM 1 (E. Masson nos. 69 and 70) makes this attribution suspect, especially given: (a) that Masson herself notes definite correspondences between the three other signs on the seal and those in CM 1 and 2; and (b) that all other inscribed cylinder seals are classified as CM 1 (or "archaic" if the assignment of the early Enkomi cylinder seal to this separate formative phase of script is justified on any other grounds than chronological). The unique aspect of the Latakia sign is the addition of vertical ticks to either side of the full central symbol. This may well be an embellishment or slight alteration of the standard CM 1 sign, rather than an entirely new character of a separate sign repertory. There are parallels for such embellishments in Linear A and B palaeography. In those systems, so far as we can tell, the embellished phonetic signs retain their identities and standard values.

The same case can be made for the silver bowl from Ugarit (figure 20a). The other metal bowl inscriptions from Enkomi are considered CM 1 (O. MASSON 1968). A numerical entry in the inscription on Enkomi bowl 16.63 (figure 21) in particular links up with RS 19.01 in CM 1 (PALAIMA forthcoming). On the bowl from Ugarit, the rightmost sign has a form very typical of CM 1 (E. Masson no. 102); the leftmost sign is a rigid linear variant of a CM 1 counterpart (E. Masson no. 91). One may therefore suggest that the central sign is a more elaborate, even calligraphic version of the simplified CM 1 sign E. Masson no. 2. In Minoan and Mycenaean palaeography, the shapes of signs inscribed on objects other than accounting documents, e.g., libation tables, painted inscribed stirrup jars, metal pins and other metallic artifacts, tend to deviate from forms found on clay administrative documents and to be closer to what we imagine were the original archetypes of the signs. This might have to do with the experience or inexperience of the artisan-inscriber. It certainly is affected by his desire to produce a text which contributes to the aesthetic impression of the object being inscribed. Signs on such artifacts give us our best clues as to what the careful "pattern book" shapes of the much simplified signs on tablets would be (PALAIMA 1988b, 307-310 and n. 44). In any event, it does not seem to me to be sound procedure to separate the cylinder seal and the silver bowl from other items in their classes solely or primarily on the basis that they were discovered not on Cyprus, but in northern Syria. Palaeography does not support such a radical step, nor does the distribution of the great majority of similar objects at sites on the island of Cyprus. These two pieces are, after all, very portable items. It is a more economical hypothesis to group them with their CM 1 counterparts.

This leaves the two tablets RS 17.06 (figure 22) and 20.25 (figure 23). As mentioned above, the shapes of the mere 219 characters on these two texts are not significantly different from those attested in CM 1. Of the forty-four signs in the signary devised for CM 3 by E. MASSON 1974, 24-46, figs. 14 and 18, ten are potentially unattested in CM 1. One of these (no. 51) is paralleled in CM 2. One (no. 20) is a reversed version of a CM 1 sign (no. 19). One (no. 105) occurs but a single time on each of the CM 3 tablets. It could be a palaeographical variant of the more frequent sign no. 104, which has a CM 1 equivalent. Nos. 71 and 3 occur on the Latakia cylinder seal and the Ugaritic silver bowl, and each can be interpreted as a variant of a standard CM 1 sign. No. 40 has been equated with CM 1 no. 32. No. 22 (occurring twice on RS 20.25) and no. 100 (occurring twelve times on the two CM 3 texts) closely resemble CM 1 nos. 21 and 99, which have so far been assigned no CM 3 counterparts. They are therefore likely to be equivalent. No. 94 (occurring twice on RS 17.06) has no obvious CM 1 parallel, while no. 58 (occurring three times on RS 20.25) contrasts directly with the CM 3 version of its closest possible CM 1 counterpart (no. 57) on the verso of RS 20.25. Thus we can say with tolerable certainty that only these last two signs from the forty-four sign CM 3 repertory are not so far paralleled in formal Cypro-Minoan texts from Cyprus. Given the limited documentation for these systems, this is a remarkably high percentage of matchable signs.

What can be said about the tablets themselves? RS 17.06 was found in a library composed of a large number of texts in Akkadian syllabic cuneiform and in the special Ugaritic alphabetic cuneiform (SCHAEFFER 1956, 228-229). The date of the collection of tablets is 13th century B.C., either second quarter or second half (SCHAEFFER 1956, 229; O. MASSON 1956b, 246). On the basis of differences between the twenty-five distinctive signs detected on RS 17.06 and the fifty-seven distinctive signs then distinguishable on Enkomi 1687 (DIKAIOS 1953, 236, fig. 3), O. MASSON 1956b, 239-240, 245, proposed that RS 17.06 represented a new unedited syllabary, albeit one squarely in the Cypro-Minoan tradition. He correctly emphasized the Near Eastern aspect of the tablet itself: in the convexity of both its recto and verso surfaces and in its small (40 mm. x 43 mm.), square shape, RS 17.06 resembles small Akkadian tablets from Ras Shamra.

E. MASSON 1974, 29-30, also places RS 20.25, discovered in another archives at Ugarit, physically in the Near Eastern tradition. Its shape and size (68 mm. x 58 mm. x 17 mm.) reminds her of oblong-formatted Ugaritic tablets. There are certain features of text formatting of RS 20.25 that are not attested in the formal CM 1 and CM 2 tablets: running the text over onto the edges, layout in simple linear "page" style, continuous ruling on RS 17.06, and the use of a special separator or terminator mark (a sinuous stroke surmounting a point) on RS 20.25. Again, however, we should recall the limited data with which we are working: a mere eight tablets or fragments of independent tablets total for all three systems. The fragment RS 19.02, which is associated with CM 1, has the same physical aspects and size as RS 20.25; its text also spills over onto the edges; its text has a linear "page" layout. Moreover, its excavator even thought the clay of the tablet exotic for Ugarit (E. MASSON 1974, 20). The archaic Enkomi tablet has rule lines, "page" layout, and two signs purposefully inscribed on its edge. The fact that the larger CM 2 tablets are divided into ruled left and right halves and even further into casements is undoubtedly a product of the peculiar texts they contain. Recall that each casement ended with the same three sign-groups in two different sequences. Even the special separator or terminator may be employed because of special textual requirements. E. MASSON 1974, 28, 38, has proposed that RS 17.06 is a letter, while RS 20.25 is a list of names in a set formula with patronymics. The CM 2 tablet Enkomi 53.5 on the other hand was considered most likely to be a hymn or medical text (E. MASSON 1978, 66-73). Such hypotheses, while still unprovable, are based on Masson's careful analyses of word and sign repetitions, on obvious differences in textual layout, and on analogies with Near Eastern texts. It is useful to remind ourselves again of formatting variations within the Linear A and B texts: some of smaller the Linear A tablets have a "page" layout, run-over of text onto their edges, and even ruling into lines or merely sections. It is very hazardous procedure to let the formatting of a mere eight tablets which were presumably inscribed with very different texts and for very different purposes be a main determining factor in distinguishing subsystems of an entire script.

My conclusions about the problems with the decipherment of Cypro-Minoan then are mainly cautionary. There is a good chance that the prevailing division of the script into four sub-systems (archaic, CM 1, CM 2 and CM 3) is invalid. Since we are dealing with so limited a corpus of formal and informal inscriptions, inscribed, as far as we can tell, for widely varying purposes over a span of some five centuries and distributed over a large number of sites on Cyprus and in N. Syria, we must be scrupulously cautious about the principles used to establish any sub-divisions. We have seen chronological clustering used to attribute a number of early texts to archaic Cypro-Minoan without considering the heterogeneity of the objects inscribed. We have seen general geographical location of find-spots used to group a cylinder seal, a metallic bowl and two tablets as CM 3. This meant divorcing the first two pieces from similar inscriptions in their respective classes which are clearly CM 1. Yet two other tablets from the same site are divorced from this geographical grouping, despite the clear similarities which one has in size, shape, formatting and manner of inscription. Style of inscription (ductus) and textual formatting have been used in treating texts of, and assigning texts to, every sub-system, in this case without considering the real validity of such features as means of achieving classification. In some cases erroneous assumptions were made about the existence or non-existence of these same features in Aegean, as opposed to Near Eastern, documents. Differences in the very contents of the formal inscriptions have been noted, but only in proposing possible interpretations of the inscriptions. Instead we should consider how the varying contents of our texts influenced the physical types and formats of our inscriptions or produced the restricted repertories of signs that have now been devised.

In order to make progress with Cypro-Minoan I suggest that we must carefully reassess the current classification schemes by focusing on (1) the signs themselves; (2) the epigraphical features, including differences in the materials and purposes of the inscribed objects, that affected their forms; and (3) the evolution and development of individual signs and the entire sign repertory through time and at different locations. This means that we must analyze the evidence from each class of inscriptions separately and systematically: pottery (incised and painted), cylinder seals, clay balls, clay cylinders, clay tablets, gold rings, etc. We must lay the palaeographical data out chronologically and geographically and discuss any information about the find contexts or original sources of the inscriptions that may have a bearing on palaeographical details. We should try to do this without any contaminating preconceptions about the life of the Cypro-Minoan script–I use the singular here intentionally and with conviction–from the time of its introduction into Cyprus under clear Minoan influence in the 16th century B.C.

The most remarkable feature about Cypro-Minoan, which is often lost in efforts to cuneiformize it or to rend it from its obvious Aegean roots, is how singular and distinctive it remains despite the many pressures and influences to which it must have been subjected until it finally transformed itself, as early as the 11th century B.C., into another equally distinctive and tenaciously independent script, the Cypriote Syllabary, which likewise resisted the influence of foreign scripts (cuneiform and the Greek and Semitic alphabets) from the 8th to the 3rd centuries B.C. In another context (PALAIMA forthcoming) I declared that it is a mystery why the inhabitants of Cyprus adopted an Aegean script, despite strong Near Eastern ties. It now seems clear to me that one reason for this choice is the intimidating linguistic and structural complexity of the cuneiform scripts at the period when Cypro-Minoan was developed. These systems required one to acquire a knowledge of (a) Sumerian and Akkadian; (b) some 300 signs with multiple syllabic values; and (c) specialized ideographic and determinative signs and conventions (DRIVER 1976, 65-68, 235-236; WALKER 1987, 33-34). The advanced and streamlined Ugaritic system of 31 signs (and a word-divider) is not attested until the 14th century (WALKER 1987, 44-46). Thus at the time when Cypro-Minoan was first formed, the Aegean script, Minoan Linear A, was the only script which provided a relatively easy and workable model. It has an open syllabary of some 90-110 signs. Each sign has a clearly established set of values. The orthographical conventions are relatively straightforward and seem to be determined by principles similar to fundamental properties specific to any given language (WOODARD 1989, has made a strong case for the "hierarchies of sonority and consonant strength"). Consequently the entire system can be applied efficiently to a new language (e.g., as was done with Mycenaean Greek) without requiring that one learn another language or languages in order to practice the art of writing. Such advantages would not have been forsaken lightly. Thus the Cypriote script preserved its independence: the Cypro-Minoan signs on 13th-12th century texts from Enkomi and Ugarit are not cuneiform or "cuneiformized" and they are not Mycenaean or "Mycenaeanized." They remain wholly Cypriote both in a decidedly Near Eastern environment and in a Cypriote community which experienced strong Mycenaeanization. The same is true for Cypro-Minoan pottery marks, whether they occur in Crete, mainland Greece, Cyprus or the Levant.

We need a unified and standardized corpus of Cypro-Minoan inscriptions that will allow us to see the whole script and its various classes of inscriptions–not sub-systems of the script itself–in a clear historical context. Until this is done, we shall continue to be plagued by piecemeal readings, guesses, and speculation. The groundwork has been laid by the careful work of dedicated scholars extending backward from E. Masson, O. Masson and V. Karageorghis to Dikaios and Ventris to Daniel and Casson to Schaeffer, to Markides and to Sir Arthur Evans. The 2500 signs now attested deserve to be drawn together and examined carefully as a whole. The fullness and variety of Cypro-Minoan inscriptions is encouraging. The lexical clues detected by E. Masson are encouraging. The continual new discoveries of inscribed materials in well-conducted excavations are encouraging. We must do for Cypro-Minoan what has been done for the other two Aegean linear scripts.

REFERENCES

ÅSTRÖM, P.

1966 A Corpus of Pot-Marks, *Excavations at Kalopsidha and Ayios Iakovos in Cyprus* (P. Åström ed.), SIMA 2, Lund, 149-192.

1969 Pot Marks of the Late Bronze Age from Cyprus, *Opuscula Atheniensia* 9, 151-159.

ÅSTRÖM, P. and NICOLAOU, I.

1980 Lead Sling Bullets from Hala Sultan Tekke, *Opuscula Atheniensia* 13, 29-33.

BASS, G. et al.

1967 *Cape Gelidonya: A Bronze Age Shipwreck*, Transactions of the American Philosophical Society N.S. 57, 8, Philadelphia.

BAURAIN, C.

1980 Chypre et le monde égéen, *BCH* 104, 565-580.

1984 *Chypre et la Méditerranée orientale au Bronze Récent*, Études Chypriotes VI, Paris, Diffusion de Boccard.

BENNET, J.

forthcoming Marks on Bronze Age Pottery from Kommos, *Kommos* I.

BENNETT, E.L., JR.

1963 Names for Linear B Writing and for Its Signs, *Kadmos* 2, 98-123.

1968 Review of Cyrus H. Gordon, *Evidence for the Minoan Language*, Ventnor N.J., 1966 in *Language* 44:1, 110-118.

BENSON, J.L. and MASSON, O.

1960 Cypro-Minoan Inscriptions from Bamboula, Kourion, *AJA* 64, 145-149.

BRICE, W.C.

1961 *Inscriptions in the Minoan Linear Script of Class A*, Oxford.

BUCHANAN, B. and MASSON, O.

1968 A Cypriote Cylinder at Yale (Newell Collection 358), *BCH* 92, 410-415.

BUCHHOLZ, H.-G.

1954 Zur Herkunft der kyprischen Silbenschrift, *Minos* 3, 133-151.

CASSON, L.

1937 *Ancient Cyprus*, London, 59-61, 72-109.

CATLING, H.W.

1973 The Achaean Settlement of Cyprus, *MEM*, 34-39.

1975 Cyprus in the Late Bronze Age, *The Cambridge Ancient History*[3], II, 2 (I.E.S. Edwards, C.J. Gadd, N.G.L. Hammond and E. Sollberger eds.), 188-216.
1988 Unpublished Finds from Cyprus: (I) Graffiti in the Late Cypriot Linear Script, *RDAC*, 325-327.

CAUBET, A. and COURTOIS, J.-C.
1986 Un modèle de foie d'Enkomi, *RDAC*, 72-77, pl. XIX.

CHADWICK, J.
1979 The Minoan Origin of the Classical Cypriote Script, *Cyprus-Crete*, 139-143.
1989 Review of J. Best and F. Woudhuizen eds., *Ancient Scripts from Crete and Cyprus*, Leiden, E.J. Brill, 1988 in *Antiquity* 63, 181.

COURTOIS, J.-C.
1978 Corpus céramique de Ras Shamra-Ugarit, SCHAEFFER 1978, 191-370.

Cyprus-Crete *Acts of the International Archaeological Symposium "The Relations Between Cyprus and Crete, ca. 2000-500 B.C.," Nicosia 16th April-22nd April 1978*, Nicosia, 1979.

DANIEL, J.F.
1941 Prolegomena to the Cypro-Minoan Script, *AJA* 45, 249-282.

DIKAIOS, P.
1953 A Second Inscribed Clay Tablet from Enkomi, *Antiquity* 27, 233-237.
1963 The Context of the Enkomi Tablets, *Kadmos* 2, 39-52.
1967 More Cypro-Minoan Inscriptions from Enkomi, *Europa: Studien zur Geschichte und Epigraphik der frühen Aegaeis* (W. Brice ed.), Berlin, Walter der Gruyter, 80-87.
1969a *Enkomi Excavations 1948-1958* I, Mainz, Verlag Philipp von Zabern.
1969b *Enkomi Excavations 1948-1958* III a, Mainz, Verlag Philipp von Zabern.
1971 *Enkomi Excavations 1948-1958* II, Mainz, Verlag Philipp von Zabern.

DÖHL, H.
1978 Bronzezeitliche Graffiti aus Tiryns I: vor dem Brand eingeritzte Zeichen, *Kadmos* 17, 115-149.
1979 Bronzezeitliche Graffiti und Dipinti aus Tiryns II: nach dem Brand eingeritzte und gemalte Zeichen, *Kadmos* 18, 47-70.

DRIVER, G.R.
1976 *Semitic Writing from Pictograph to Alphabet*[3] (S.A. Hopkins ed.), London.

DUHOUX, Y.
1978 Une analyse linguistique du linéaire A, *Études minoennes* I (Y. Duhoux ed.), BCILL 14, Louvain, 65-129.
1983 *Introduction aux dialectes grecs anciens*, Série pédagogique de l'Institut de Linguistique de Louvain 12, Louvain.

EVANS, A.J.
1900 Mycenaean Cyprus as Illustrated in the British Museum Excavations, *Journal of the Anthropological Institute of Great Britain and Ireland* 30 (N.S. 3), 199-220.
1909 *Scripta Minoa* I, Oxford, Clarendon Press.
1935 *The Palace of Minos*, IV, 2, London.

FAUCOUNAU, J.
1988 Deux études sur des inscriptions chyprominoennes, *Fucus: A Semitic/Afrasian Gathering in Remembrance of Albert Ehrman* (Y.L. Arbeitman ed.), Current Issues in Linguistic Theory 58, Amsterdam/Philadelphia, John Benjamins, 239-251.

GALLIS, K.
1988 Ενδείξεις για την εξάπλωση μέχρι της Θεσσαλίας ενός οργανωμένου συστήματος συμβόλων επί αγγείων κατά την εποχή του Χαλκού, *'Αρχαιολογία* 29, 58-63.

GEORGIOU, H.
1979 Relations Between Cyprus and the Near East in the Middle and Late Bronze Age, *Levant* 11, 84-100.

GJERSTAD, E.
1979 The Phoenician Colonization and Expansion in Cyprus, *RDAC*, 230-254.

GODART, L. and SACCONI, A.
1979 La plus ancienne tablette d'Enkomi et le linéaire A, *Cyprus-Crete*, 128-133.

GORILA 1-5 L. Godart and J.-P. Olivier eds., *Recueil des inscriptions en linéaire A* vols. 1-5, Études Crétoises XXI, 1-5, Paris, Librairie Orientaliste Paul Geuthner.

HEUBECK A.
1979 *Schrift*, Archaeologia Homerica X, III, Göttingen, Vandenhoeck & Ruprecht.
1983 Überlegungen zur Sprache von Linear A, *Res Mycenaeae. Akten des VII. Internationalen Mykenologischen Colloquiums in Nürnberg vom 6.-10.April 1981* (A. Heubeck and G. Neumann eds.), Göttingen, Vandenhoeck & Ruprecht, 155-170.

HILLER, S.
1985 Die Kyprominoische Schriftsysteme, *Archiv für Orientforschung* Beiheft 20, 61-102.

HOOKER, J.T.
1985 Minoan and Mycenaean Settlement in Cyprus: A Note, *Πρακτικά τοῦ Δευτέρου Διεθνοῦς Κυπρολογικοῦ Συνεδρίου* (Leukosia, 20-25 April 1982) volume I, Leukosia, 175-179.

JANKO, R.
1987 Linear A and the Direction of the Earliest Cypro-Minoan Writing, *Studies Chadwick*, 311-317.

KARAGEORGHIS, J.
1961 Histoire de l'écriture chypriote, *Κυπριακαί Σπουδαί* 25, 43-60.

KARAGEORGHIS, V.
1976a Le quartier sacré de Kition: campagnes de fouilles 1973-1975, *Comptes Rendus de l'Académie des Inscriptions et Belles-Lettres*, 229-245 (244-245 quote E. Masson's provisional assessment of the inscribed finds).
1976b *Kition. Mycenaean and Phoenician Discoveries in Cyprus*, London.
1980 Fouilles à l'Ancienne-Paphos de Chypre: les premiers colons grecs, *CRAI*, 122-136.
1981 *Ancient Cyprus. 7000 Years of Art and Archaeology.* Baton Rouge and London, LSU Press.
1982 Cyprus, *The Cambridge Ancient History*[2], III, 3 (J. Boardman and N.G.L. Hammond eds.), 57-70.
1985 *Excavations at Kition*, V, 2, Nicosia, Chr. Nicolaou & Sons Ltd.

KNAPP, A.B.
1983 An Alashiyan Merchant at Ugarit, *Tel Aviv* 10, 38-45.
1985 Alashiya, Caphtor/Keftiu, and Eastern Mediterranean Trade: Recent Studies in Cypriote Archaeology and History, *Journal of Field Archaeology* 12:2, 231-250.
1986 Production, Exchange, and Socio-Political Complexity on Bronze Age Cyprus, *Oxford Journal of Archaeology*, 5:1, 35-60.

KNAPP, A.B. and MARCHANT, A.
1982 Cyprus, Cypro-Minoan and Hurrians, *RDAC*, 15-30.

MARKIDES, M.
1916 A. Excavations, *Cyprus, Annual Report of the Curator of Antiquities*, 4-21, esp. 16-20.

MASSON, E.
1970 La plus ancienne tablette chypro-minoenne (Enkomi, 1955), *Minos* 10, 63-77.

1971a *Étude de vingt-six boules d'argile inscrites trouvées à Enkomi et Hala Sultan Tekké(Chypre)*, Studies in Mediterranean Archaeology 31:1, Göteborg, Paul Åströms Forlag.
1971b Rouleau inscrit chypro-minoen trouvé à Enkomi en 1967, *Alasia* I (C.F.A. Schaeffer ed.), Paris, 457-477.
1971c Boules d'argile inscrites trouvées à Enkomi de 1953 à 1969, *Alasia* I (C.F.A. Schaeffer ed.), Paris, 479-504.
1972 Les répertoires graphiques chypro-minoens, *Acta Mycenaea. Proceedings of the Fifth International Colloquium on Mycenaean Studies, held in Salamanca, 30 March - 3 April 1970* (M.S. Ruipérez ed.), *Minos* 11, Salamanca, 99-111.
1973 La diffusion de l'écriture à Chypre à la fin de l'âge du Bronze, *MEM*, 88-100.
1974 *Cypromìnoica. Répertoires. Documents de Ras Shamra. Essais d'Interprétation*, Studies in Mediterranean Archaeology 31:2, Göteborg, Paul Åströms Forlag.
1976a À la recherche des vestiges proche-orientaux à Chypre, *Archäologischer Anzeiger*, 139-165.
1976b Les témoignages épigraphiques, *Hala Sultan Tekke 1* (P. Åström, D.M. Bailey and V. Karageorghis eds.), SIMA 45:1, Göteborg, Paul Åströms Förlag, 130-135.
1979 Une inscription peinte d'Enkomi en caractères chypro-minoens, *RDAC*, 210-213, pl. 20.
1983 Premiers documents chypro-minoens du site Kalavassos–*Ayios Dhimitrios*, *RDAC*, 131-141.
1984 Les objets inscrits de Pyla-Kokkinokremos, *Pyla-Kokkinokremos: A Late 13th-Century B.C. Fortified Settlement in Cyprus* (V. Karageorghis and M. Demas eds.), Nicosia, 76-79.
1985a Inscriptions et marques chypro-minoennes à Kition, in KARAGEORGHIS 1985, 280-283, plates A-G.
1985b Les syllabaires chypro-minoens: mises au point, compléments et définitions à la lumière des documents nouveaux, *RDAC*, 146-154.
1986 Les écritures chypro-minoennes: Reflet fidèle du brassage des civilisations sur l'île pendant le Bronze Récent, *Acts of the International Archaeological Symposium "Cyprus Between the Orient and the Occident," Nicosia, 8-14 September 1985* (ed. V. Karageorghis), Nicosia, 180-200.
1987a Les écritures chypro-minoennes: État présent des connaissances et des ignorances, *Tractata Mycenaea. Proceedings of the Eighth International Colloquium on Mycenaean Studies held in Ohrid, 15-20 September 1985* (P.H. Ilievski and L. Crepajac eds.), Skopje, 189-202.
1987b La part du fond commun égéen dans les écritures chypro-minoennes et son apport possible pour leur déchiffrement, *Studies Chadwick*, 367-381.
1988 Marques chypro-minoennes à Maa-*Palaeokastro*, *Excavations at Maa-*Palaeokastro (V. Karageorghis ed.), Nicosia, Chr. Nicolaou & Sons Ltd., 399-400, pls. A-C.

forthcoming Vestiges écrits trouvés sur le site de Kalavasos-Ayios Dhimitrios, *Kalavasos-Ayios Dhimitrios* II, 38-40, pl. XIII, figs. 60-63.

MASSON, O.
1953 Les inscriptions étéochypriotes I.–Les pierres, *Syria* 30, 85-88, pls. XV-XVIII.
1956a Les écritures chypro-minoennes et les possibilités de déchiffrement, *Études mycéniennes. Actes du colloque international sur les textes mycéniens (Gif-sur-Yvette, 3-7 avril 1956)* (M. Lejeune ed.), Paris, Centre National de la Recherche Scientifique, 199-206.
1956b Documents chypro-minoens de Ras Shamra, *Ugaritica* III, Missions de Ras Shamra VIII (C.F.A. Schaeffer ed.), Paris, Libraire Orientaliste Paul Geuthner, 233-250.
1957a Cylindres et cachets chypriotes portants des caractères chypro-minoens, *BCH* 81, 6-37.
1957b Répertoire des inscriptions chypro-minoennes, *Minos* 5, 9-27.
1957c Les inscriptions étéochypriotes –II-IV II. Le texte des inscriptions d'Amathonte, *Syria* 36, 62-80.
1966 Fragments de Kalopsidha portant des signes chypro-minoens, *Excavations at Kalopsidha and Ayios Iakovos in Cyprus* (P. Åström ed.), SIMA 2, Lund, 136-137.
1968 Études d'épigraphie chypro-minoenne I. Trois bols de bronze du Musée de Nicosie, *Minos* 9, 66-72.
1971 Deux petits lingots de cuivre inscrits d'Enkomi (1953), *Alasia* I (C. F.-A. Schaeffer et al. eds.), Paris, 449-455.
1983 *Les inscriptions chypriotes syllabiques*, Études Chypriotes I, réimpression augmentée, Paris, Éditions E. de Boccard.
1988 Une inscription étéochypriote probablement originaire d'Amathonte, *Kadmos* 27, 126-130.

MASSON, O. and SZNYCER, M.
1972 *Recherches sur les Phéniciens à Chypre*, Publications du Centre de Recherches d'Histoire et de Philologie, Série II.3, Paris, Libraire Droz.

MEIGGS, R.
1972 *The Athenian Empire*, Oxford.

MEM *Acts of the International Archaeological Symposium "The Mycenaeans in the Eastern Mediterranean," Nicosia 27th March - 2nd April 1972*, Nicosia.

MICHAELIDOU-NICOLAOU, I.
1980 Regroupement de deux fragments de tablettes d'Enkomi avec écriture chypro-minoenne, *Studi Micenei ed Egeo-Anatolici* 21, 7-16.

MITFORD, T.B.
1971 The Cypro-Minoan Inscriptions of Old Paphos, *Kadmos* 10, 87-96.

1980 *The Nymphaeum at Kafizin. The Inscribed Pottery*, Berlin, Walter de Gruyter.

MITFORD, T.B. and MASSON, O.
1982 The Cypriot Syllabary, *The Cambridge Ancient History*2, III, 3 (J. Boardman and N.G.L. Hammond eds.), 71-82.

NICOLAOU, K.
1973 The First Mycenaeans in Cyprus, *MEM*, 50-61.

ÖBRINK, U.
1979 *Hala Sultan Tekke* 5, SIMA XLV:5, Göteborg.

OLIVIER, J.-P.
1967 *Les scribes de Cnossos*, Incunabula Graeca 17, Rome, Edizioni dell' Ateneo.
1975 Le disque de Phaistos, *BCH* 99, 5-34.
1984 Administrations at Knossos and Pylos: What Differences, *Pylos Comes Alive: Industry and Administration in a Mycenaean Palace* (C.W. Shelmerdine and T.G. Palaima eds.) New York, Archaeological Institute of America, 11-18.
1986 Cretan Writing in the Second Millenium B.C., *World Archaeology* 17:3 (1986) 377-389.
1988 Tirynthian Graffiti. Ausgrabungen in Tiryns 1982/83, *Archäologischer Anzeiger*, 253-268.

PACCI, M.
1986 Presenze Micenee a Cipro, *Traffici Micenei nel Mediterraneo* (M. Marazzi, S.Tusa and L. Vagnetti eds.), Magna Graecia 3, Taranto, 335-342.

PACKARD, D.W.
1974 *Minoan Linear A*, Berkeley, University of California Press.

PALAIMA, T.G.
1982 Linear A in the Cyclades: The Trade and Travel of a Script, *Temple University Aegean Symposium* 7, 15-22.
1987 Comments on Mycenaean Literacy, *Studies Chadwick*, 499-510.
1988a *The Scribes of Pylos*, Incunabula Graeca 87, Rome, Edizioni dell' Ateneo.
1988b The Development of the Mycenaean Writing System, *Studies Bennett*, 269-342.
forthcoming Ideograms and Supplementals and Regional Interaction among Aegean and Cypriote Scripts, *Minos*.

PALAIMA, T.G., BETANCOURT P.P. and MYER, G.H.
1984 An Inscribed Stirrup Jar of Cretan Origin from Bamboula, Cyprus, *Kadmos* 23, 65-73.

PECORELLA, P.E.

1977 *Le tombe dell'Età del Bronzo Tardo della necropoli a mare di Ayia Irini "Paleokastro"*, Rome.

PERSSON, A.W.

1930 *Schrift und Sprache in Alt-Kreta*, Uppsala Universitets Årsskrift, Program 3, 3-18.

1932 Some Inscribed Terracotta Balls from Enkomi, *Symbolae Philologicae O.A. Danielsson Octogenario Dicatae*, Uppsala, 269-273.

1937 More Cypro-Minoan Inscriptions, *The Swedish Cyprus Expedition Vol. III. Text* (E. Gjerstad et al. eds.), Stockholm, Victor Pettersons Bokindustriaktiebolag, 601-618.

PORADA, E.

1976 Three Cylinder Seals from Tombs 1 and 2 of Hala Sultan Tekke, *Hala Sultan Tekke 1* (P. Åström, D.M. Bailey and V. Karageorghis eds.), SIMA 45:1, Göteborg, Paul Åströms Förlag, 98-103.

1986 Late Cypriote Cylinder Seals Between East and West, *Acts of the International Archaeological Symposium "Cyprus Between the Orient and the Occident," Nicosia, 8-14 September 1985* (ed. V. Karageorghis), Nicosia, 289-299.

PORTUGALI, Y. and KNAPP, A.B.

1985 Cyprus and the Aegean: A Spatial Analysis of Interaction in the Seventeenth to Fourteenth Centuries B.C., *Prehistoric Production and Exchange* (A.B. Knapp and T. Stech eds.), UCLA Institute of Archaeology Monograph XXV, 44-78.

POUILLOUX, J.

1976 La rencontre de l'hellénisme et de l'Orient à Chypre entre 1200 et 300 av. J.C., *Assimilation et résistance à la culture gréco-romaine dans le monde ancien*, Travaux du VIe Congrès International d'Études Classiques (D.M. Pippidi ed.), Paris, Société d'Édition «Les Belles Lettres», 233-240.

POWELL, B.B.

1987 The Origin of the Puzzling Supplementals Φ X Ψ, *Transactions of the American Philological Association* 117, 1-20.

PTT I *The Pylos Tablets Transcribed. Part I: Texts and Notes* (E.L. Bennett, Jr. and J.-P. Olivier eds.), Incunabula Graeca 51, Rome, 1973.

RAISON, J. and POPE, M.

1978 Linear A: changing perspectives, *Études minoennes* I (Y. Duhoux ed.), BCILL 14, Louvain, 5-64.

SCHAEFFER, C.F.-A.
1932 Les fouilles de Minet-el-Beida et de Ras Shamra troisième campagne (printemps 1931), rapport sommaire, *Syria*, 13, 1-24.
1936 *Missions en Chypre*, Paris, 76-80; 119-121.
1956 Matériaux pour l'étude des relations entre Ugarit et Chypre, *Ugaritica* III, Mission de Ras Shamra VIII, Paris, Libraire Orientaliste Paul Geuthner, 227-232.
1978 *Ugaritica* VII, Mission de Ras Shamra XVIII, Paris, Libraire Orientaliste Paul Geuthner.

SCHAEFFER et al.
1968 Fouilles d'Enkomi-Alasia dans l'île de Chypre, campagne de 1967, *Syria* 45, 263-274.

SCHAEFFER-FORRER, C.F.A.
1978a Commentaires sur les problèmes d'épigraphie chypriote, *Journal des Savants*, 87-104.
1978b Épaves d'une bibliothèque d'Ugarit, SCHAEFFER 1978, 399-474.

SOUTH, A.K.
1983 Kalavasos–*Ayios Dhimitrios* 1982, *RDAC*, 92-116.
1984 Kalavasos–*Ayios Dhimitrios* 1983, *RDAC*, 14-41.

STUBBINGS, F.H.
1951 *Mycenaean Pottery from the Levant*, Cambridge, 45-52.

Studies Bennett J.-P. Olivier and T.G. Palaima eds., *Texts, Tablets and Scribes*: *Studies in Mycenaean Epigraphy and Economy Offered to Emmett L. Bennett, Jr.*, Suplementos a Minos 10, Salamanca, 1988.

Studies Chadwick J.T. Killen, J.L. Melena, J.-P. Olivier eds., *Studies in Mycenaean and Classical Greek Presented to John Chadwick*, *Minos* 20-22, Salamanca, 1987.

VERMEULE, E. and WOLSKY, F.
1976 Pot-Marks and Graffiti from Toumba tou Skourou, Cyprus, *Kadmos* 15, 61-76.

WALKER, C.B.F.
1987 *Cuneiform*, Reading the Past 3, Berkeley, University of California Press.

WATROUS, L. VANCE
1985 Late Bronze Age Kommos: Imported Pottery as Evidence for Foreign Contact, *A Great Minoan Triangle in Southcentral Crete*: *Kommos, Hagia Triadha, Phaistos* (J. and M. Shaw eds.), *Scripta Mediterranea* 6, Toronto, Canada.

WOODARD, ROGER D.
1989 Greek Orthography and Syllabic Structure: The Case of Mycenaean and Classical Cypriot, *Abstracts* of the One Hundred and Twentieth Annual Meeting of the American Philological Association, Baltimore, Maryland January 5-8, 1989, Scholars Press, Atlanta, 37.

Program in Aegean Scripts and Prehistory
University of Texas at Austin
Austin, Texas 78712-1181 USA

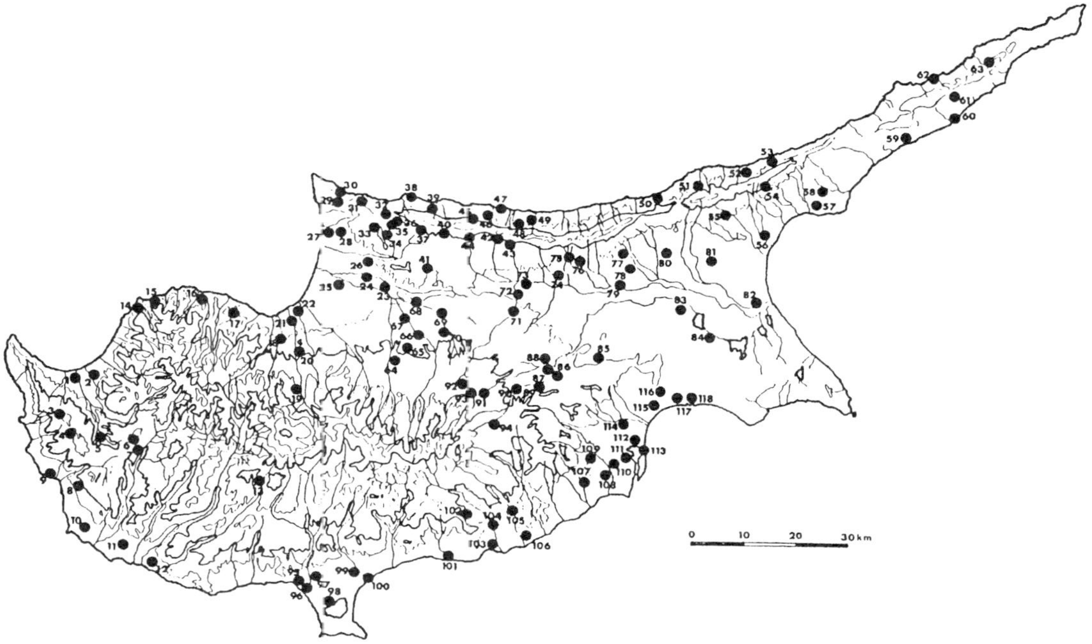

Figure 1 Map of Cyprus with Late Cypriote Centers (after BAURAIN. 1984, 72, map 7)

Site	No.
Arpera	108
Athienou	85
Ayia Irini	28
Ayia Paraskevi	near 72
Enkomi	82
Hala Sultan Tekké	111
Kalavassos	104
Kalopsidha	84
Katydhata	20
Kouklia-Palaepaphos	12
Kourion	96
Larnaka (Kition)	113
Limassol	100
Maroni	106
Morphou-Toumba tou Skourou	25
Nicosia	72
Pakhyammos	15
Sinda	83
Verghi	115

No.	Site
12	Kouklia-Palaepaphos
15	Pakhyammos
20	Katydhata
25	Morphou-Toumba tou Skourou
28	Ayia Irini
72	Nicosia
near 72	Ayia Paraskevi
82	Enkomi
83	Sinda
84	Kalopsidha
85	Athienou
96	Kourion
100	Limassol
104	Kalavassos
106	Maroni
108	Arpera
111	Hala Sultan Tekké
113	Larnaka (Kition)
115	Verghi

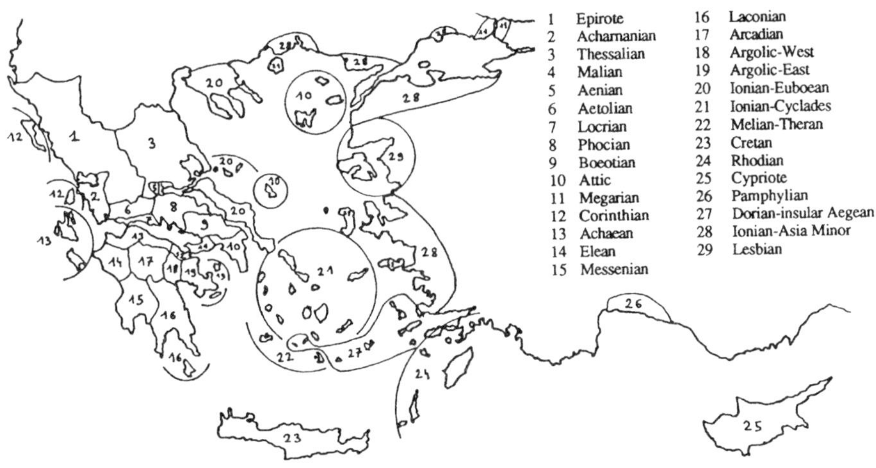

figure 2 Dialect Map of Greece in 5th Century B.C.
(after DUHOUX 1983, 8, fig. 1)

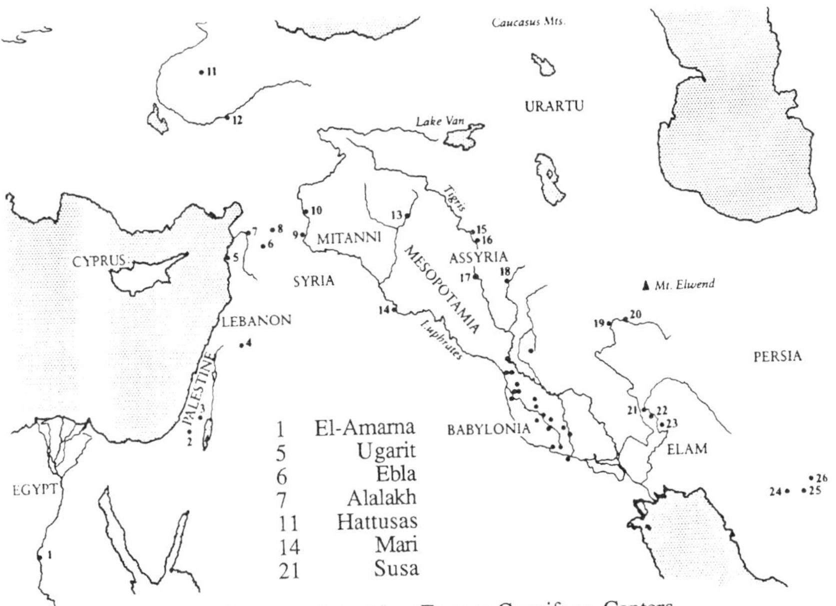

figure 3 Cyprus and the Near Eastern Cuneiform Centers
(after WALKER 1987, 8)

	Crete	Cyclades	mainland	Cyprus	Enkomi	Ugarit
19th c.	b. hieroglyphic/ proto-Linear A					
18th c.	b. Linear A					
17th c.		b. Linear A				
16th c.				—archaic CM/CM 1—		
15th c.	e. hier./ Linear A	e. Linear A	b. Linear B ?	——CM 1——		CM 1?
14th-13th c.	Linear B		Linear B	CM 1	CM 2	CM 3
11th?-3rd c.				Cypriote syllabary		

Figure 4. Schematic chart of chronology and relations among Aegean and Cypriote scripts. (b.=begin / e.=end)

figure 5 Enkomi no. 1885 archaic Cypro-Minoan (after JANKO 1987, 317, fig. 1)

TABLEAU DES SIGNES STANDARDISÉS DU LINÉAIRE A

AB 01	AB 21	AB 31	AB 54	AB 76	AB 123
AB 02	AB 21^{f}	AB 34	AB 55	AB 77	AB 131a
AB 03	AB 21^{m}	AB 37	AB 56	AB 78	AB 131b
AB 04	AB 22	AB 38	AB 57	AB 79	A 131c
AB 05	AB 22^{f}	AB 39	AB 58	AB 80	AB 164
AB 06	AB 22^{m}	AB 40	AB 59	AB 81	AB 171
AB 07	AB 23	AB 41	AB 60	AB 82	AB 180
AB 08	AB 23^{m}	AB 44	AB 61	AB 85	AB 188
AB 09	AB 24	AB 45	AB 65	AB 86	AB 191
AB 10	AB 26	AB 46	AB 66	AB 87	A 301
AB 11	AB 27	AB 47	AB 67	A 100/102	A 302
AB 13	AB 28	AB 49	AB 69	AB 118	A 303
AB 16	A 28b	AB 50	AB 70	AB 120	A 304
AB 17	AB 29	AB 51	AB 73	A 120b	A 305
AB 20	AB 30	AB 53	AB 74	AB 122	A 306

figure 6 Linear A phonograms
(after *GORILA 5*, xxii)

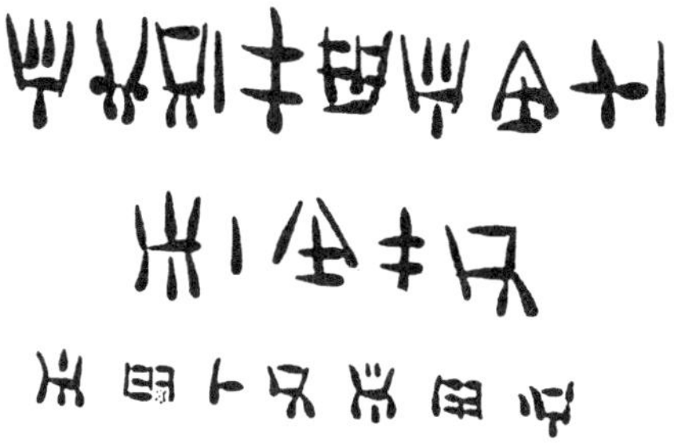

figure 7 Clay Balls nos. 1, 2 and 4 from Enkomi (after E. MASSON 1971a, 11-12, figs. 1, 2, 4)

figure 8 Gold Ring from Hala Sultan Tekké (after O. MASSON 1957a, 21, fig. 15)

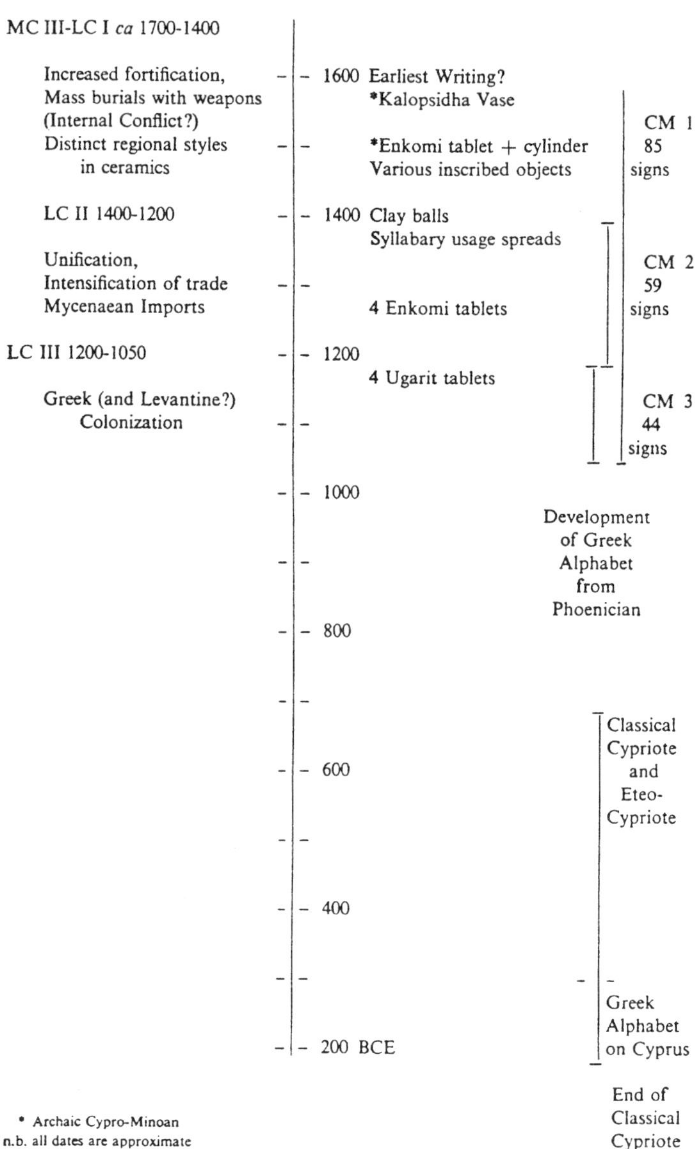

figure 9 Standard (Erroneous) Chronology of Cypro-Minoan Script (after KNAPP-MARCHANT 1982, 22, chart 1)

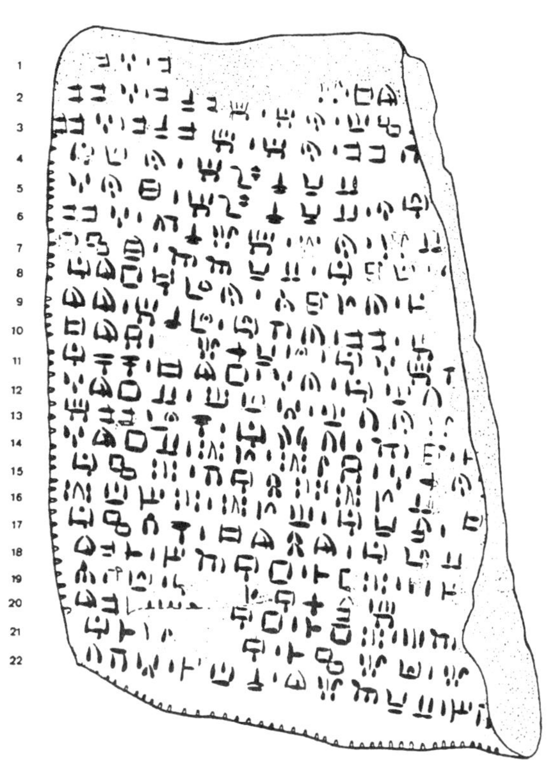

figure 10 Enkomi 53.5 side b: Cypro-Minoan 2 Tablet (after HILLER 1985, 69-70, fig. 7)

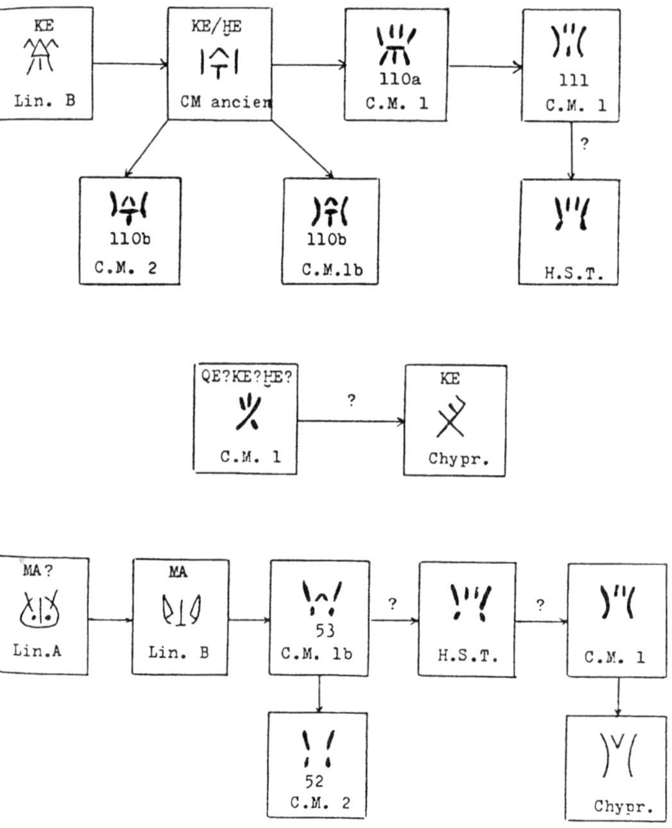

figure 11 Flawed Palaeographical Development Schemes (after FAUCOUNAU 1988, 243, fig. 2)

figure 12 Inscribed Clay Weight from Enkomi LC I A (1575-1525 B.C.)
(after BAURAIN 1984, 155, fig. 22)

figure 13 Kalopsidha Vase Inscription
(after ÅSTRÖM 1966, plate 44 fig. 133)

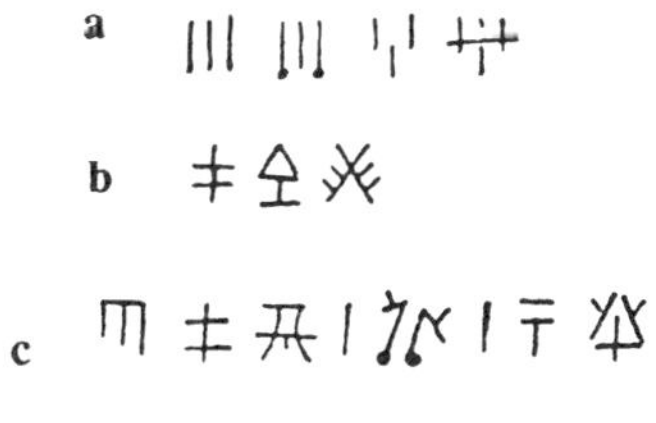

a

b

c

figure 14 Vase Inscriptions from Katydhata (a, b) and Arpera (c)
(after PERSSON 1937, 606, figs. 2b, 3, 9)

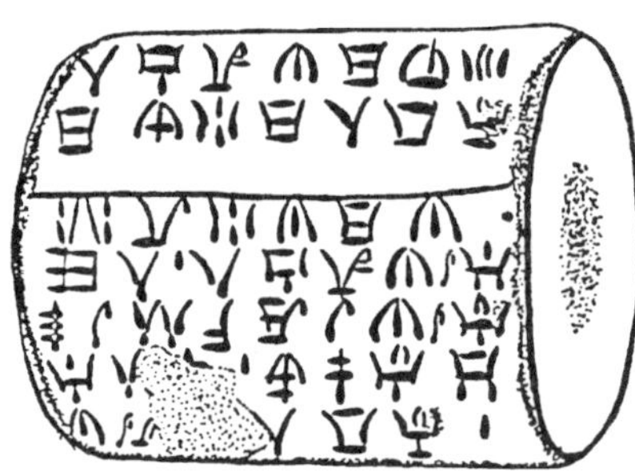

figure 15 Enkomi Inscribed Clay Cylinder
(after Hiller 1985, 67, fig. 4)

figure 16 Inscription on Deep Bowl from Enkomi ca. 1230-1190 B.C.
(after DIKAIOS 1967, plate VI a; 1971, plate 319, fig. 130)

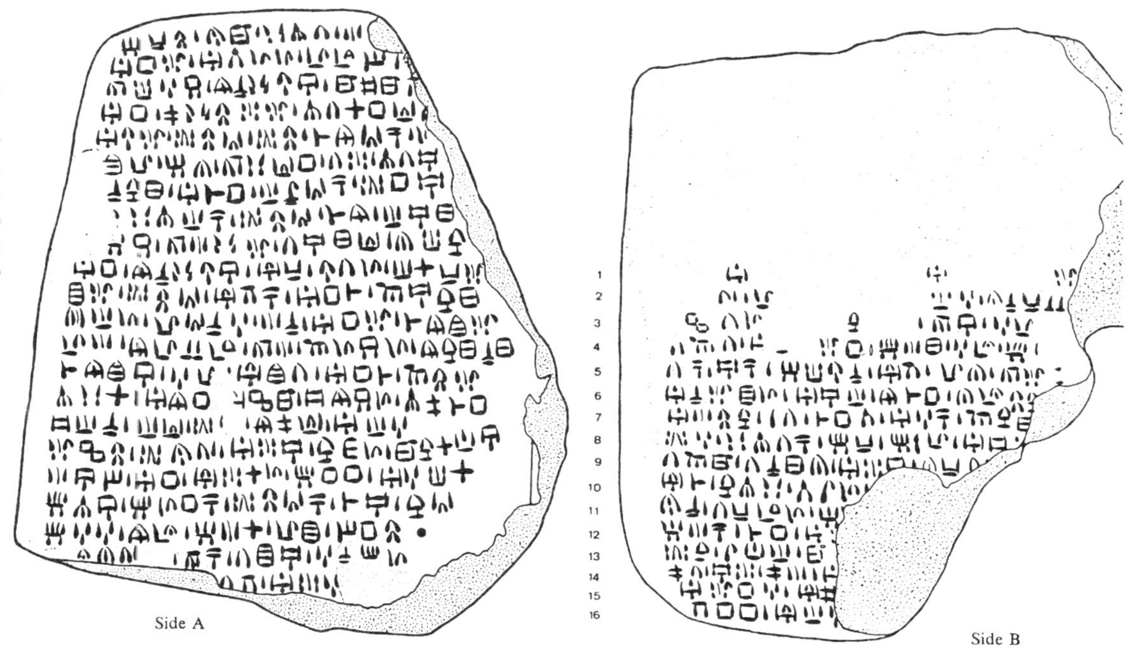

figure 17 Enkomi 1687: Cypro-Minoan 2 Tablet
(after DIKAIOS 1971, plate 318, figs. 3-4)

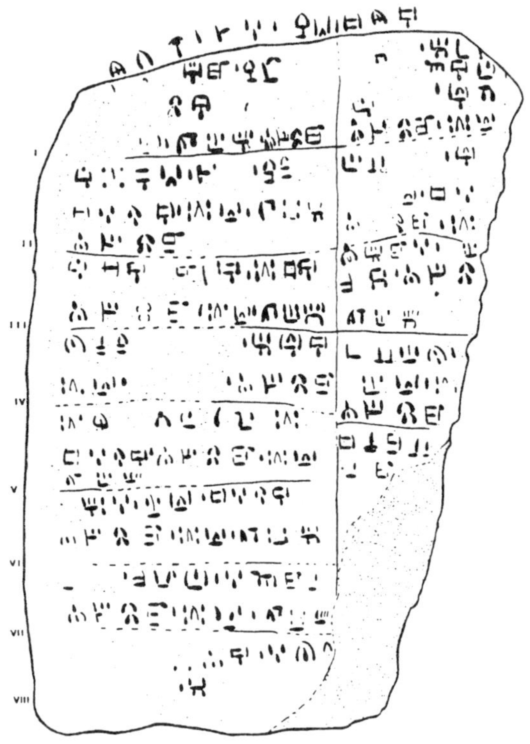

fig. 18 Enkomi 53.5 side a: Cypro-Minoan 2 Tablet
(after HILLER 1985, 69, fig. 7)

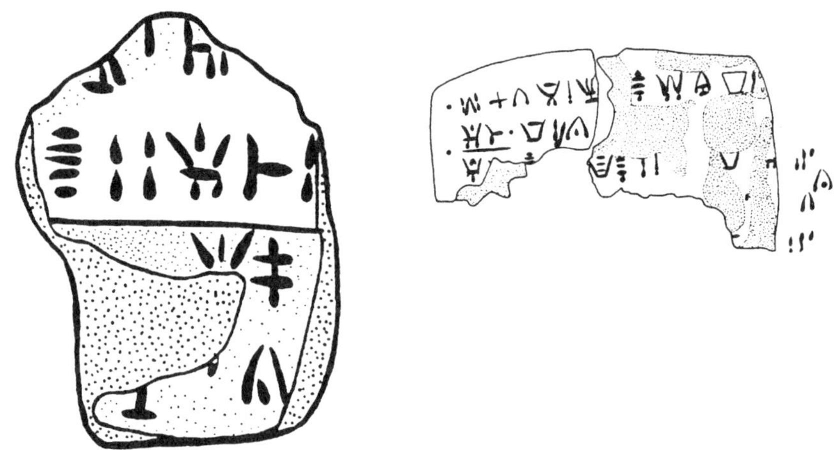

figure 19 RS 19.01 and 19.02: Cypro-Minoan 1 tablets from Ugarit
(after E. MASSON 1974, 21-23, figs. 7 and 9)

figure 20 Inscription on Cylinder Seal from Latakia (Newell Coll. 358) (after E. MASSON 1974, 24, fig. 10)

figure 20a Inscription on silver bowl from Ugarit (after *Syria* 13 [1932] 23 fig. 15)

figure 21 Inscription on silver bowl from Enkomi 16.63 (drawing by Nicolle Hirschfeld)

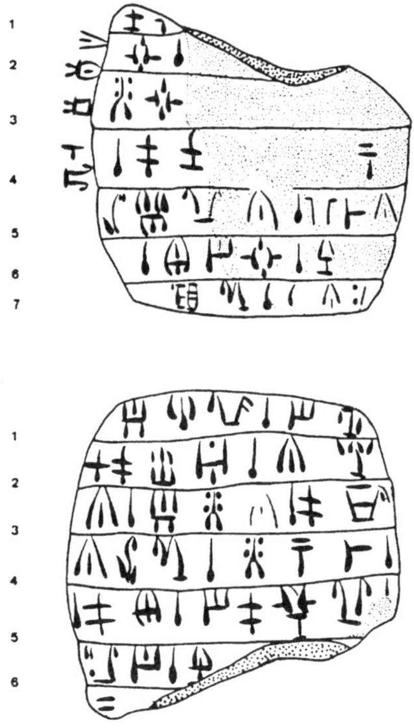

figure 22 RS 17.06: Cypro-Minoan 3 Tablet from Ugarit (after HILLER 1985, 73, fig. 11)

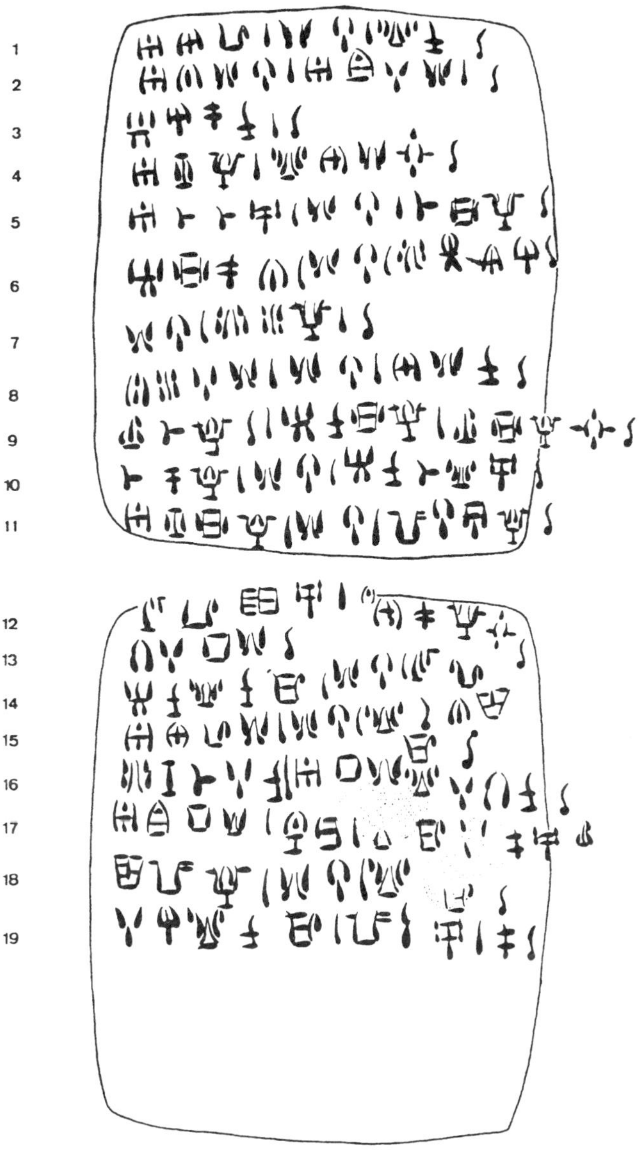

figure 23 RS 20.25: Cypro-Minoan 3 Tablet from Ugarit
(after Hiller 1985, 74, fig. 12)

BCILL 49 : *Problems in Decipherment,* 189-216.

'DECIPHERING' ETRUSCAN

Giuliano BONFANTE
Academia Nazionale dei Lincei

Larissa BONFANTE
Department of Classics
New York University

Emmett Bennett expressed the hope that the papers presented at the Burdick-Vary Symposium on "Problems in Decipherment" would address specific problems and the methods by which they can be overcome. The following brief account of the state of Etruscan language study today will accordingly focus on problems and attempted solutions.

First, the problems. 1. The language is different from any other in Europe or elsewhere. In direct contrast with Linear B, which turned out to be an unknown script used for a known language, Etruscan is an unknown language written in a known script: the alphabet. 2. No literature survives: we have no narrative texts, no history, poetry or drama. 3. The 13,000 Etruscan inscriptions that have come down to us are mostly short: dedications, or epitaphs, with names, human and divine, titles, and a few common nouns, numbers and verbs. The longer inscriptions are technical: religious texts, prayers, rites, and contracts.

Attempting to solve these difficulties, scholars have studied the Etruscan language in a variety of ways, using bilingual inscriptions and glosses as well as cultural-archaeological, linguistic or etymological methods (PALLOTTINO 1978, 197-208; G. BONFANTE and L. BONFANTE 1985, 75-86).

1. Bilingual texts include the three gold tablets from Pyrgi, the port of Caere, found in 1964, written in Phoenician and Etruscan, as well as some 30 Etruscan-Latin inscriptions. There are also numerous "picture bilinguals" in which labels or captions identify pictures on wall paintings or engraved mirrors (PFIFFIG 1969, 12). Particularly promising is the comparison of Etruscan religious inscriptions with those of their neighbours, "quasi-bilinguals" (PALLOTTINO

1984, 414), such as the Umbrian Iguvine Tablets (written partly in an Etruscan alphabet, partly in a Latin alphabet), evidently similar to those of Etruria in structure and content (PROSDOCIMI 1972, 1984; RIX 1985, 21-37; BOURGEAUD 1982). Francesco Roncalli has used this method for the text of the linen bandages originally wrapped around an Egyptian mummy in Zagreb, for which recent cleaning and restoration have also yielded better readings (RONCALLI 1985).

2. *Glosses* comprise the only non-monumental evidence (*TLE* 801-858). A number of Etruscan words in Greek and Latin texts explained by ancient authors refer, as Mario Torelli has shown (TORELLI 1976, 1001-1004), to the *disciplina etrusca,* the religious sphere of divination which the Romans imported from their technically proficient neighbours: they deal with birds, plants and rituals. Only in a few cases is the study of these glosses useful for our knowledge of the Etruscan vocabulary. Some are authentic, as in the case of *atrium, aisar,* "gods," *clan,* "son." Often ancient sources are confirmed. The most interesting case is that of *arimos,* "monkey" (*TLE* 811). We know from Vergil (*Aen.* 9, 715) that the ancient name of Ischia was *Inarime.* Obviously this was its ancient Etruscan name: "monkey island," equivalent to *Pithekoussai,* the name the Greeks used for their most ancient colony in the West. The "Island of Monkeys" may have been named from a population of monkeys once to be found on it, as in Gibraltar (RIDGWAY 1984, 49-50, but see G. BONFANTE and L. BONFANTE 1983, 59).

Some glosses are false. *Balteus* cannot be Etruscan since Etruscan had no voiced stops (*g, d, b*) but only voiceless stops (*k, t, p*). Greek glosses mistake Latin *deus,* "god," *kapra,* "goat," for Etruscan: *δέα· θεὰ ὑπὸ Τυρσηνῶν* and *κάπρα· αἴξ Τυρρηνοί* (*TLE* 828, 820). These words must have reached the Greeks when Rome was under Etruscan domination or influence; for the Greeks, Rome was then Etruscan (just as for some people now Corsica or Alsace are French). We must eliminate the words *balteus, agaletora, andas, burros, cassidam, damnos, drouna, phaboulониam, gapos, falado, gnis, subulo. Nepos* is obviously Latin. That the Etruscans used *t* instead of *d* is proved by some Latin words of Greek origin (*sporta*), by Varro (*L.L.* 6.4), and by Macrobius (*Saturae* 1, 15, 14-17), who asserts that the Etruscans said *Itus* while the Sabines said *Idus*. This is in fact one of the few words known from the glosses that may with some probability be attributed to Etruscan.

As for *Italos*: *Τυρρηνοὶ γὰρ ἰταλὸν τὸν ταῦρον ἐκάλεσαν* (*TLE* 839), this is obviously *vitulus*, of Latin or Oscan origin, mediated through Greek (by which the loss of the initial digamma is explained). From here comes the name of Italy, Latin *Italia* (with short *i*, short *i*: we read *Viteliu* but also *Italia* on the Oscan coins of the Italic League during the war against Rome, 90-89 B.C.) (G. BONFANTE and L. BONFANTE 1985, 60).

Recently the linguistic study of the language, especially the internal study of names and syntax, has made important contributions to our understanding of the language (RIX 1963; DE SIMONE 1985). DE SIMONE's book on the transformations of Greek words brought into Etruscan marked an important step in the study of Etruscan pronunciation (DE SIMONE 1968).

Least to be trusted is the so-called "etymological" method dear to the hearts of amateurs, whereby Etruscan is compared to all languages, from Albanian to Turkish, Hebrew, etc. Such a method, which tends to consider only the vocabulary, is today discredited by serious scholars. In fact, Giuliano Bonfante, an Indo-Europeanist, has recently turned his attention to the study of Etruscan because he can tell us what it is *not* (G. BONFANTE and L. BONFANTE 1983, 1985). The most fruitful method has been the cultural-archaeological, in which an inscription is considered in its historical context, and in close relation with the monument or object on which it appears. In recent times Pallottino has repeatedly urged such an approach (PALLOTTINO 1984, 414-420, with bibl.; BANTI 1969, 282); a good example of inscriptions studied in such a manner has been that of the Pyrgi tablets. In fact, the discovery of this long-sought, long-awaited bilingual, in 1964, can be seen to have marked a turning point. It coincided with, and in part was responsible for, a new focus in the study of the Etruscan language. This can be summarized under three headings.

(1) A view of the historical, geographical context of the inscriptions as made in Italy at a specific time contributed to the growing consciousness of the Etruscans as deeply involved in ancient Italy as well as in the ancient Mediterranean. Scholars are now studying the development of the Etruscans in history, like that of any other ranking civilization, and the variety to be discovered in the different Etruscan cities (BANTI 1969) and in different periods (TORELLI 1986, 47-65; GRANT 1980). Far from any hint of isolation, it is their lively commercial, cultural, and political relations that are being documented at a rapidly increasing rhythm. We can trace their contacts with Greeks, Phoenicians, Latins, and other inhabitants of Italy and Europe (RIDGWAY 1984; TURFA 1986) down to the end of the Etruscan language.

(2) A new study of monuments, known, often, for a hundred years or more, resulted in discoveries fully as important as those from newly excavated material. In fact, an archaeological and historical context can often be recovered for objects originally uprooted from their proper environment. This is true of non-inscriptional material in museum basements (e.g., SWADDLING 1985), as well as important inscriptions, for instance the Zagreb mummy wrappings, the Capua tile, the Perugia cippus (RONCALLI 1985), or the Piacenza liver (VAN DER MEER 1987). Monuments long hidden from the eyes of the public (the Zagreb mummy wrappings, the Capua tile) were exhibited in the underground rooms of the Rocca Paolina in Perugia in 1985, the first year of the *Progetto Etruschi*. The exhibit *Scrivere Etrusco*, which caused Massimo Pallottino to refer to the Etruscans as "the people of the book," reminded visitors of the variety of writing to be found in ancient Italy: Greek, Etruscan, Phoenician, Aramaic (McCARTER

1975, BUCHNER 1978, GARBINI 1979), Egyptian, Latin, etc. (RONCALLI 1985, CRISTOFANI 1988).[1]

(3) *Corpora* dating back to the 19th century have been started up again, and new ones have been inaugurated in an unprecedented era of international collaboration. This situation can in large part be attributed to the enthusiasm, energy and vision of one man, Massimo Pallottino, who, as President of the Istituto di Studi Etruschi ed Italici, has brought together scholars from many countries, identified areas which needed attention and directed numerous projects. Fascicles of the *CIE* are once again appearing after a long hiatus. The *Thesaurus* as well as Pallottino's own *TLE* are indispensable for any study of the language; the *REE* and the *CSE* all keep us abreast of available material. A full-fledged grammar of Etruscan (PFIFFIG 1969) has appeared: though criticized by specialists as overly optimistic, it has stimulated further study and can be counted among the *strumenti di lavoro* now available.

How have such new directions, contributions, discussions and discoveries affected Etruscan studies?

The Etruscans are now more securely located in Italy and in the wider world of the Mediterranean. From at least 1000 B.C. to 100 B.C. they held the most fertile land, the best harbors, and the rich mineral resources of central Italy, and developed a recognizable culture *in situ*. A comparison with the Basques, whose pre-Indo-European language was evidently preserved by their isolation in mountain ranges, is scarcely valid. There is much to be studied still about the growth of settlements into urban centers already in the Villanovan period, before the Greeks arrived, bringing, as a precious part of the "Orientalizing" ferment, the gift of the alphabet. The role of Sardinia and of the Phoenicians–who never had a "Dark Age" in this period–in bringing technical expertise to Italy and the fame of the Etruscans to Greek ears, as recently suggested (RIDGWAY 1984), paints a far more complex picture than that of the previous Etruscan "enigma." Scholars have been heeding, and even the public has been made aware, during the "Year of the Etruscans," of Pallottino's warning to substitute a view of the Etruscans' development for the sterile problem of their "origins." Problems remain, but the questions being asked are capable of answers, or at least lead back to a reality that can be documented by archaeological, historical and linguistic investigations, and a closer study of monuments actually available to us.

The alphabet, a prestigious sign of the new Orientalizing style as well as a status symbol, appears on objects placed in rich Orientalizing tombs of the seventh century (fig. 1). Such "model" alphabets, taken directly from the Greek alphabet as brought West by the Euboeans (CRISTOFANI 1987; PROSDOCIMI 1985; LEJEUNE 1985), bear witness to the speed with which this new development or

---

[1] The exhibit will travel to Yugoslavia and Berlin. A modified version, *Umbri Etruschi*, opened in the Vatican in the Fall of 1988, moving on to Copenhagen, Budapest, Cracow, Leningrad, and New York.

discovery (BERNAL 1987) was adopted; while actual Etruscan inscriptions (there are to date 75 of them from the seventh century, a quantity comparing very respectably with Greek inscriptions from this period: BUNDGÅRD 1965; CRISTOFANI 1987a, 127-131) show the steps in the adaptation of the letter alphabet to the Etruscan language. Etruscan had no voiced stops (*b*, *g*, *d*) and no "o": "u" was regularly substituted (Pliny, *apud* Priscian II, 26, 16; G. BONFANTE and L. BONFANTE 1983, 66-67; 1985, 92; PFIFFIG 1969, 29). They invented, adopted or inherited the letter *8* to express the sound of "*f* ," unknown in Greek but shared by the Lydian alphabet in northwest Anatolia (SOMMER 1930, 11-17; JENSEN 1969, 512-513; BERNAL 1987, 7; AGOSTINIANI 1986, 19). We owe the sound of "*f* " to the Etruscans who passed on the sound in Italy to the Latins, the Oscans, the Umbrians, the Veneti, and beyond, in northern Europe (G. BONFANTE 1983 [1985], 161-166).[2]

At Kaminia in Lemnos, excavations over a century ago, in 1885, uncovered an inscription in a language similar to Etruscan (fig. 2). In 1928 Italian archaeologists found fragmentary inscriptions on sherds: these were of vital importance, for the fact that they were locally made showed that the language was spoken *in situ* (DELLA SETA 1937, 119-146). The largest, a funerary stele dating from the sixth century B.C., shows surprising connections with Etruscan material. The type of funerary stele is not unlike north Etruscan examples such as that of Aule Feluske, Avile Tite, Larth Tharnie and Larth Ninie, ranging in date from ca. 600 B.C. through the sixth century B.C. (figs. 3-6). On each, a warrior is represented together with his armor and identified by an epitaph (G. BONFANTE and L. BONFANTE 1983, 110-113; 1985, 140-143). Iconographic similarities have been noted between such stelae and funerary sculpture from Southwest Anatolia (e.g., a relief stele from Xanthos in Istanbul) (PALLOTTINO 1963, 143-153).

Recently scholars have once again taken up the question of the language of the Lemnos stele and its relation to Etruscan, particularly in light of the advances made in Etruscan linguistics in the last twenty years (LEJEUNE 1980; HEURGON 1980, 1985; DE SIMONE 1986, 723-725; AGOSTINIANI 1986, 15-46). The inscription consists of two parts, inscribed in front (A), and on the side (B) of the stele. Various explanations[3] have been offered for the puzzling presence of two separate, apparently independent epitaphs (AGOSTINIANI 1986, 17-18).

A. holaieṡ:naphoth:
ṡiaṡi:
maraṡ: mav
sialchveiṡ:aviṡ

[2] The only three languages to use the sign *8* for *f* are Etruscan, Oscan, and Lydian. Thus the sign, which also came from Etruria, spread in a much more limited area than the sound.

[3] Examples of epitaphs written at different times, or lines added to pre-existent epitaphs, are known to us: in Roman times, for example, Publius Scipio (TATUM 1988, 253-258).

evistho:seronaith
śivai

aker:tavarśio
vanalasial:seronai:morinail

B. holaieśi: phokiasale: śeronaith:evistho:toverona [...]
rom: haralio: śivai: epteśio:arai:tiś:phoke
śivai:aviś:sialchviś:maraśm:aviś:aomai:

Alphabet and language are similar. As in Etruscan, signs for the voiced stops (*b*, *g*, *d*) are missing. Missing is also the letter *z*. In contrast to Etruscan, which loses *o* but substitutes *u*, the stele has *o* but no *u*. (The two are the same phoneme.) There are signs of punctuation between syllables, as occasionally in Etruscan (DE SIMONE 1986, 723, for Lemnian; G. BONFANTE and L. BONFANTE 1985, 63, 72-73). Vocabulary and syntax are strikingly close. Numerals, for example: on the Lemnian stele, the age of the deceased, indicated by *śivai aviś sialchviś* (also *sialchveiś*), can be paralleled by Etruscan *zivas avils sealchls*, translatable as "having lived 40 years."[4] Lemnian and Etruscan are both distinguished in this way as non-Indo-European. From "30" onward, the tens in Etruscan are formed by the suffix *-alch*; for example, *ci*, "3" > *ci-alch*, "30"; *śa* "4" > **śa-alch* (> *śealch*), "40"; etc. *Naphoths*, "grandson" or perhaps "descendant," is close to Etruscan *nefts* or *nefś* (cf. the ending of *prumaths*, "grandnephew") (LEJEUNE, in HEURGON 1980, 604). Both Lemnian and Etruscan have *-m* as copulative suffix, "and." Similar too are the formulae *Holaieśi Phokiasale*, "to Holaie of Phokis," and *Larthiale Hulchniesi* "to Hulchnie, son of Lars," in Etruscan in the Tomb of Orcus. (These have been interpreted as eponymous dates, comparable to *M. Messalla M. Pisone consulibus* in Latin, by Rix (RIX 1968; DE SIMONE 1986, 724.)

How can such striking similarities be explained? There is as yet no satisfactory solution as to the historical context in which they could be understood. Most recently AGOSTINIANI (1986, 16, 42) has thought Lemnian reflects an archaic form of Etruscan, preceding the sixth-century date of the stele. Michel Gras once suggested an Etruscan commercial settlement on the island in the sixth century B.C. as the event that might have given rise in antiquity to the tradition of the Tyrrhenian-Pelasgians of Lemnos (GRAS 1976, 367; but see now GRAS 1985, 615-632). HEURGON also (1980, 1985) tries to find a historical context–the Persian wars and the conquest of Lemnos by Darius in the last quarter of the sixth century B.C.–to fit the date of the stele. Agostiniani's findings, if accepted, would force scholars to find an earlier context for any "settlement" of Etruscans on Lemnos, for the language would be far more archaic than the date of the monument itself, and to think of a different scenario to account for such a remarkable connection, as well as such ancient traditions as Thucydides' reference

[4] But AGOSTINIANI 1986 and DE SIMONE 1986 translate *śealchls* as "60" rather than "40" (see above for references).

to Tyrrhenians in Lemnos (4.109.4: "A Pelasgian element, formed by those Tyrrhenians who once inhabited Lemnos and Athens. . ."; cf. Diodorus 9.10.6).

Relations with other peoples of the Mediterranean are more clearly documented. The most exciting find of the last quarter-century was, of course, the long-sought bilingual, which turned up in 1964 in the form of three gold tablets from Pyrgi (fig. 7). The Phoenician one has recently been on exhibit in Venice (MOSCATI, in *I Fenici*, 1988, 54-56). Dating from around 500 B.C., it brings us into the midst of Etruscan and Roman history. The longer inscription reads:

ita. tmia. icac. heramasva [.] vatieche unialastres.
themiasa. mech. thuta. thefariei. velianas. sal.
cluvenias. turuce. munistas. thuvas tameresca.
ilacve. tulerase. nac. ci. avil. churvar. tesiameitale.
ilacve. alsase nac. atranes. zilacal. seleitala. acnasvers.
itanim. heramve. avil. eniaca. pulumchva.

"This is the temple (or chapel, *cella*) and this is the place of the statue (?) which he has dedicated to Uni-Astarte, the Lord of the people (or king, or tyrant), Thefarie Velianas, *sal cluvenias*, he gave it, this one place (?); since on the one hand she raised him for three years in this way, *churvar tesiameitale*, and since on the other hand he has been protected, here is the statue; and may the years be as many as the stars."

The Phoenician text says:
"To the Lady Astarte. This is the sacred place made and given by Thefarie Velianas (TBRY' WLNŠ), king over Cisra (KYŠRY') in the month of Zebah (ŠMŠ) as a gift in the temple and in the enclosure(?); because Astarte has favoured her votary in his kingdom for three years in the month of KRR on the day of the burial of the deity. And the years of the statue of the divinity shall be as many years as these stars."

The tablets have been much discussed, and scholars have pointed out: (1) their historical importance (the confirmation of Polybius, 3.22.4-13, who quotes the text of a treaty of 509 B.C. between Rome and Carthage); the character of Thefarie Velianas (Tiberius), King, *mlk* (*zilath* in Etruscan) over Caere; (2) their religious importance–*Uni Ishtar*: Astarte, anyone would have thought, would be identified with Turan, Aphrodite/Venus; yet the importance of Uni, the mother goddess in Italy, is hereby confirmed epigraphically, as it is iconographically; (3)

confirmation of the numbers. We knew the first six numbers, written out on the six faces of the famous Tuscania dice: *thu, zal, ci, sa, mach, huth* (fig. 8). (These, by the way, are clearly different from any other Indo-European language, and help to prove the non-Indo-European character of Etruscan.) But until the Pyrgi tablets, we were not certain of the order. Now *ci* on the Etruscan text, "three years," *ci avil,* obviously corresponds to "three" in the Phoenician text, written out and marked by three bars, *///,* for greater clarity. Since we know that each of the two faces on the dice added up to seven *(Anth.Pal.* 14.8), the order of the numbers is set: *thu* is 1; *zal* is 2; *ci* is 3; *sa* is 4; *mach* is 5; *huth* is 6.

Greek-Etruscan relations are attested by far more consistent evidence. We know how the Etruscans spoke and what they looked like because they adopted from the Greeks the alphabet and the human figure in art. From 700 B.C. onward, imports of Greek art, and Greek artists and craftsmen, were massive. The largest percentage of Greek vases with known provenience–some 75 percent–come from Italy. They are often the most beautiful, purchased by wealthy Etruscans, who sometimes dedicated them to their own divinities in local sanctuaries. Such votive inscriptions, though short, provide us with examples of Etruscan, showing it was an inflected language.

From Tarquinia comes a vase by Oltos with a dedication in Etruscan to the Dioscouroi: *itun turuce venel atelinas tinias cliniiaras,* "This gave Venel Atelinas to Tinia's sons" (*TLE* 156). *Tinia* is Zeus. We see an example of Etruscan "grammar": *clan* = "son"; *clenar* (nom. pl.) = "the sons"; *cliniiaras* (dat. pl.) = "to the sons." There are also the *Bild-Bilinguen,* "picture bilinguals," on vases as well as on wall paintings from Tarquinia and engraved bronze mirrors. A red-figure Etruscan vase from the fourth century B.C. shows Admetus bidding farewell to Alcestis (fig. 9). The two are labelled, *Atmite, Alcsti,* and the scene is explained: *Eca ersce nac achrum flethrce,* "she went to Acheron [and] sacrificed [herself]" (*TLE* 334). *Atmite,* masculine singular, has the regular ending in *e,* contrasting with the feminine *Alcsti,* ending in *-i.* The active third person ending for past perfect verbs, as above *turuce,* "gave," *flethrce,* "sacrificed," contrasts with the passive, *-che* (*zichuche,* "was written").

Greek gods and heroes, as we have seen, were adopted by Etruscan artists and by the aristocrats who commissioned luxury items such as the characteristic bronze mirrors, highly polished on the reflecting surface and engraved on the back with mythological scenes (more rarely, with scenes of daily life). Some 3,000 of these have come down to us, and are being published in the *Corpus Speculorum Etruscorum, CSE.* Often the figures are merely labeled: one mirror shows *Aplu, Tinia, Turms*: Apollo, Zeus, and Hermes. But some scenes are quite original, for example, the handsome mirror from Volterra (fig. 10) with the purely Italic scene of an enthroned Hera (Uni/Iuno) nursing a fully-grown, bearded Heracles in the presence of a solemn assemblage of divine witnesses, one of whom–recognizable by his trident as Poseidon/Neptune–points to the official document of this adoption which reads, *Eca sren tva ichnac hercle unial clan thrasce,* roughly, "This picture shows how Heracles, Uni's son, drank milk"

(*TLE* 339). This remarkable picture is only one of many proving the importance of mother goddesses, *kourotrophoi*, and specifically *nutrices*, in Italy, in direct contrast to the situation in Greece, where nursing scenes are all but non-existent (L. BONFANTE 1988).

A number of monuments have received renewed attention. Three, one from the fourth century B.C. and the other two from the Hellenistic period, are worth looking at more closely. The François Tomb, with its "historical" cycle of paintings, has been the subject of an exhibit and catalogue featuring in particular the picture of the triumphing general, Vel Saties, shown with his assistant, Arnza ("Little Arnth"), in the act of reading the omens (fig. 11) (BURANELLI 1987). Such divination, reading the divine will by signs in the sky or in a kosmos reflected here on earth, was an Etruscan specialty. Roman tradition presents us with a Tanaquil who used such knowledge to help her husband found the Tarquin dynasty at Rome. Livy tells us (9.36) that in the fourth century B.C., Roman aristocrats sent their sons to Caere to learn "letters," as they later sent them to Athens; it is quite possible that it was this kind of technical knowledge, so necessary for a successful statesman and general, that they were sent to study.

Van der Meer (1987) has recently published an exhaustive study of the most remarkable document to have come down to us in connection with this Etruscan specialty, the bronze model of a sheep's liver from Piacenza (fig. 12) with divisions reflecting the sections of the sky and 28 names of divinities, some of which are known to us from other sources: *tin* = Iuppiter, *uni* = Iuno, *catha* = the sun god, *cel* = a mother goddess, *selvan* = Silvanus, *fufluns* = Bacchus (cf. *Fuflunia, Populonia*, "city of Bacchus"), *herc* = Heracles, *usil* = the sun, *tiur* = the moon. His conclusion, based on a review of a variety of evidence, is that many of the divinities are local Italic gods, and that the liver is late (about 150 B.C.).

New material continues to appear. A handsome bronze figurine of a nude male athlete in a private collection in America, ca. 300 B.C., was included in a recent exhibition (fig. 13). The votive inscription (CLEVELAND 1988, No. 17) incised on its side–an archaic Greek practice which continued to a late date in Etruscan art–is one of ten dedications to Silvanus: *ecn turce aule havrnas tuthina apana selvansl tularias*, "this gave Aule Havrnas, a paternal gift (?) to Silvanus of the boundaries" (DE SIMONE 1985, 1988; VAN DER MEER 1987, 65-66).

Etruscan can be interpreted only through Etruscan, not through any kind of "etymological" method which claims connections to Albanian, Basque, etc. The language shows traces of influence from neighbors. It evidently developed in central Italy, during the Iron Age, Villanovan period, which might be called "proto-Etruscan." In other words, Etruscan was a language which had been spoken, and inevitably changed, in Italy, by people who lived there for several centuries, before it appeared on the inscriptions which have come down to us.

Greek words had found their way into Etruscan before 600 B.C. These were mostly words for pots, containers, and wine drinking: *thina* from Greek δῖνος, *lechthum* from Greek λήκυθος, *culichne* from Greek κύλιξ; and the important word for "oil," ἔλαιον. Umbrian gives *klètra*, "litter" or "basket" (a word found on the Zagreb mummy wrappings).

Etruscan words in Latin date from an early period (DE SIMONE 1987), like the Etruscan fashions which became Roman ritual garments in the seventh and sixth centuries B.C., a time of Etruscan cultural dominance (L. BONFANTE 1975, 101-104). A partial list will illustrate the "civilized" character of this type of vocabulary: *lanterna, cisterna, taberna, histrio* ("histrionics"), *Phersu* > *persona*, "mask" or "character" (in a play), "Ides," Etr. *itus*, "month," *populus*, *forma* (< μορφή, with inversion of consonants). *Litterae* (from διφθέρα), "letters," *cera*, *stilus*, all testify to the importance of the Etruscans' introduction of writing to Rome. *Lucumo*, "king" or "magistrate," is the name of Tarquin in Livy; *atrium* and *cella* refer to architecture; *classis*, *turris*[5] to naval or siege warfare. *Triumphus*, the name of the highest honor to which a Roman could aspire, came from the Greek θρίαμβος by way of the Etruscan *triumpe* (with an expected change from *b* to *p*, then to *ph*). Ritual fashions, *laena* (from Greek χλαῖνα), *tutulus*, recall their Etruscan past (G. BONFANTE 1985b-c, 1987). *Rasenna*, the Etruscans' name for themselves, survives in several toponyms in Tuscany (*ThLE* 1978; PIERI 1969, s.v. "Rasna"). The total vocabulary is not large: only some 250 words, aside from proper names. From these, however, we can tell something about the nature of the language.

It is non-Indo-European. The common words, clearly connected in the various IE languages, are quite different in Etruscan. "Father," "mother," "son," "daughter," "brother," "king," and "god," are *apa, ati, clan, sech, ruva, lauchum, ais*; quite unrelated to Latin *pater, mater, filius, filia, frater, rex*, or *deus*, for example. The numbers too, we have seen, are different: not only the first six numbers, but the formation of the tens. The numbers from "seventeen" to "twenty" are formed by subtraction, as in Latin (*duo de viginti*): this may in fact be a borrowing in Latin from Etruscan.

It was an inflected language, with cases clearly marked for nouns (*clan, clenśi*, dat.; loc. *clenthi*, plural *clenar, clenaraśi*) and tenses for verbs (*tur*, "give"; *turuce*, "gave," vs. *zichuche*, "was written").

The pronunciation was harsh, without *b, d, g*, and with the sounds *kh* (*ch*), *th*, and *ph*. These are relatively rare sounds in languages in general. The Latin alphabet owes its letter *C* (in contrast to the Greek *Γ, gamma*) to the Etruscan intermediary. Some have suggested that the modern "gorgia toscana," so obvious in Florence and Siena today ("Coca Cola" = "hoha hola") derives from Etruscan (see AGOSTINIANI, GIANNELLI 1983). The loss of vowels after the first syllable, resulting in clusters of consonants, is due to the intensive stress accent which around 500 B.C. affected Etruscan as well as other languages of Italy

[5] *Turris*, which came by way of Etruscan (SKUTSCH 1907), gave the Etruscans their name, Τυρσηνοί.

(Latin, Umbrian, Oscan, Sabellian). Thus we have *Alexandros* > *Alcsentre*, *Ramutha* > *Ramtha*, *Clytaimestra* > *Cluthumustha*, *Clutmsta* (HEURGON 1961, 303, on the possible influence of the Etruscan theater).

Etruscan must clearly be studied in its historical context, not as a puzzle waiting to be solved by the fortunate find of another Rosetta Stone. Such a historical context lies behind Roncalli's view of an area rich in religious sanctuaries–around Lake Trasimene, including Chiusi, Cortona, Perugia, Gubbio–as the provenance of the longest religious texts: the Iguvine Tablets, the Perugia cippus, the Zagreb mummy wrappings, the Piacenza liver (RONCALLI 1987). Various votive inscriptions, similar to the dedication to Selvans (see above), come from this area, as various others must have for which we have today no provenance.

From this inland area came some of the latest inscriptions, on funerary urns from Volterra, Perugia and Chiusi. These allow us to study the gradual Romanization of the area. From Perugia and Chiusi come bilingual texts, in Etruscan and Latin, from the last years of the Etruscan *nomen*, as well as epitaphs of married couples, and brothers, one of whom has it inscribed in Latin, the other in Etruscan (KAIMIO 1972, 85-245). From the region of Perugia, too, comes the *Arringatore*, usually dated ca. 100 B.C., just about the time when all of Italy received Roman citizenship. (It could, however, be earlier: COLONNA 1988.) Marking this transition from Etruscan to Roman is the Etruscan inscription of the border of his toga, contrasting with the insignia of his Roman citizenship (he wears the ring, the laced high *calcei*, the tunic with stripes, the bordered toga *prœtexta* of a Roman magistrate).

The characterization of the Etruscans as "People of the Book", a welcome change from the cliché of their enigmatic smile and mysterious origin, has resulted from the recent focus on Etruscan writing and the central place it held in their culture. It is this realization of its historical and religious importance, as much as the linguistic studies, that have created the optimistic climate within which so much progress is being made.

REFERENCES Includes recent bibliography and items not listed in *EL*.

AGOSTINIANI, L.
1982 *Le iscrizioni parlanti dell'Italia antica*. Florence.
1984 La sequenza *eiminipicapi* e la negazione in etrusco, *AGI* 69, 84-117.
1986 Sull' etrusco della stele di Lemno e su alcuni aspetti del consonantismo etrusco, *AGI* 71, 15-46.

AGOSTINIANI, L. *and* GIANNELLI, L. editors.
1983 *Fonologia etrusca, fonetica toscana: Il problema del sostrato,* Florence. On the *gorgia toscana* and its ultimately Etruscan origin.

AIGNER FORESTI, L.
1974 *L'origine degli Etruschi,* Vienna.

ANRW H. TEMPORINI (ed.), *Aufstieg und Niedergang der Römischen Welt* I, Berlin-New York.

BANTI, L.
1969 La scrittura e la lingua. *Il mondo degli Etruschi*, Rome, 255-282.

BERNAL, M.
1987 On the Transmission of the Alphabet to the Aegean Before 1400 B.C. *BASOR* 267, 1-19. Controversial: includes summary of studies and bibliography on the subject.

BONFANTE, G.
1981 The Spread of the Alphabet in Europe: Arezzo, *Erz*, and Runes, in L. BONFANTE 1981, 124-130.
1983 [1985] Il suono *F* in Europa è di origine etrusca? *StEtr* 51, 161-166.
1985a Sull'origine delle rune. *RendLincei* 40, 145-146.
1985b Etruscan Words in Latin. *Word* 36, 203-210.
1985c L'étimo di *elementum. RendLincei* 40, 105.
1987 L'étimo del latino *forma. ParPass* 232, 37-38.
1988 Note sulla grafia etrusca. *AGI* 73, 54.

BONFANTE, G. *and* BONFANTE, L.
1983 *The Etruscan Language: An Introduction,* Manchester, New York, with previous bibliography (=*EL*) .
1985 *Lingua e cultura degli Etruschi*. Rome; revised translation.

BONFANTE, L.
1975 *Etruscan Dress*. Baltimore, *Vocabulary*, 101-104.
1981 (ed.), *Out of Etruria: Etruscan Influence North and South. BAR*, Oxford.
1982 Inscriptions, in DE GRUMMOND 1982.

1986 (ed.), *Etruscan Life and Afterlife. A Handbook of Etruscan Studies*, Detroit.
1987 Review of RIDGWAY 1984. *AJA* 91, 151-153.
1988 Iconografia della madre in Etruria. *La donna in Etruria* (A. RALLO ed.), Rome.

BOURGEAUD, W.A.
1982 *Fasti Umbrici. Études sur le vocabulaire et le rituel des tables eugubines.* Ottawa.

BUCHNER, G.
1978 Testimonianze epigrafiche semitiche dell' VIII sec. a.C. a Pithekoussai. *ParPass* 33, 130-142.

BUNDGÅRD, J.A.
1965 Why did the art of writing spread to the West? Reflexions on the alphabet of Marsiliana. *Analecta Romana Instituti Danici* 3, 11-72.

BURANELLI, F.
1987 *La tomba François,* exhibit catalogue. Vatican,180, no. 68.

CIE *Corpus Inscriptionum Etruscarum*. Leipzig, Florence, 1893-1987.

CLEVELAND
1988 *The Gods Delight: The Human Figure in Classical Bronze.* Exhibit Catalogue, Cleveland.

COLONNA, G.
1978 I cosiddetti dadi di Tuscania. *StEtr* 46, 115. The "Tuscania dice" do not come from Tuscania.
1982 Un'iscrizione di Talamone e l'opposizione presente/passato nel verbo etrusco. *ParPass* 202, 5-11.
1988 The *Arringatore*. Personal communication.

CRISTOFANI, M.
1972 Sull'origine e la diffusione dell'alfabeto etrusco. *ANRW* I_2, 469-489.
1973 *Introduzione allo studio dell'Etrusco*. Florence.
1978 L'alfabeto etrusco. *Popoli e civiltà dell'Italia antica,* vol. 6, 401-468.

1979 Recent Advances in Etruscan Epigraphy and Language, in *Italy Before the Romans* (D. and F.R.S. RIDGWAY eds.), London, New York, San Francisco.
1982 Contatti fra Lazio ed Etruria in età arcaica: documentazione archeologica e testimonianze epigrafiche. *Alle origini del latino. Atti del Convegno della Società Italiana di Glottologia,* Pisa 1980, 27-42.
1983 *Gli Etruschi del mare.* Milan, 56-60.

1985 Prospettive per l'etrusco. *L'etrusco e le lingue dell'Italia antica*, Atti Pisa 1984 [1985], 11-20.
1987a Saggi di storia etrusca arcaica. *Archaeologica* 70, Rome.
1987b Antroponimia e contesti sociali di pertinenza. *AION* 3, 1981, 47-79 = CRISTOFANI 1987a, 107-135.
1987c La formazione della scrittura, in *Atti del Convegno, La scrittura in Etruria*, Orvieto, October 1985 (forthcoming) = CRISTOFANI 1987a, 25-37.
1988 La scrittura nell'Italia antica. *Archeo, Dossier* marzo, 3-66. Contains color photographs; based on RONCALLI 1985.

CSE *Corpus Speculorum Etruscorum Denmark* I, 1981; *Italia* I, 1981; *The Netherlands*, 1983; *DDR* I, 1986; II, 1987; *Bundesrepublik Deutschland* I, 1987; *USA* I, 1987.

DE GRUMMOND, N.
1982 *A Guide to Etruscan Mirrors*, Tallahassee, Florida.

DELLA SETA, A.
1937 Iscrizioni tirreniche di Lemno, in *Scritti in onore di B. Nogara*, Rome, 119-146.

DENNIS
1883 *Cities and Cemeteries of Etruria*[3], London.

DE SIMONE, C.
1968 *Die griechischen Entlehnungen im Etruskischen* I, Wiesbaden.
1985 L'ermeneutica etrusca oggi. *Atti II Congresso Internazionale di Studi Etruschi*, Florence, May-June 1985 (forthcoming).
1986 La stele di Lemnos, in *Rasenna* (Milan 1986) 717-725. Wonderfully clear description and analysis.
1987 Gli imprestiti etruschi nel latino arcaico, in *Alle origini di Roma*. Atti Pisa Settembre 1987 (E. CAMPANILE ed.), 27-41.
1988 in Rivista di Epigrafia Etrusca, *StEtr* 54 (1988), forthcoming. On the inscription of the bronze statuette with dedication to Selvans (CLEVELAND 1988, No. 17).

DEVOTO, G.
1944 [1983] *Storia della lingua di Roma*, 1940, 1944, reprint 1983.

DURANTE, M.
1982 Il latino preletterario, in *Alle origini del latino. Atti del Convegno della Società Italiana di Glottologia*. Pisa 1980, 65-78, esp. 75. The word *classis* came into Latin from Etruscan.

EL See BONFANTE. G., and BONFANTE. L. 1983.

EMILIOZZI MORANDI, A.
1983 L'archeologo, in *La figura e l'opera di Francesco Orioli (1783-1856)*, Atti del III Convegno Interregionale di Storia del Risorgimento del Comitato di Viterbo, ottobre 1983, 3-17, with bibliography of ORIOLI: gem with *abacario*, Paris, Bibl. Nat.

ERNOUT, A.
1930 Les éléments étrusques du vocabulaire latin. *BSL* 30, 82-124.

ERNOUT, A. and MEILLET, A.
1959 *Dictionnaire étymologique de la langue latine*, fourth edition, reprinted 1967, *s.v. laena, persona, triumphus, littera, taberna, histrio.*

ES GERHARD, E., *Etruskische Spiegel,* Berlin 1840-97.

GARBINI, A.
1978 Un'iscrizione aramaica a Pithekoussai. *ParPass* 33, 143-150.

GRANT, M.
1980 *The Etruscans,* New York.

GRAS, M.
1976 La piraterie égéenne en mer Égée: mythe ou réalité? *Mélanges Heurgon.* Rome, 341-369.
1985 *Trafics tyrrhéniens archaïques,* Rome.

HÄGG, R.
1983 (ed.), *The Greek Renaissance of the Eighth Century: Tradition and Innovation,* Stockholm. Includes W. BURKERT, *Oriental Myth and Literature in the Iliad* (on Bellerophon's letter), 51-56; A. JOHNSTON, *The Extent and Use of Literacy; the Archaeological Evidence,* 63-68.

HAMMARSTRÖM, M.
1931 Review of SOMMER 1930, in *Gnomon* 7, 92-95.

HAYNES, S.
1987 *The Augur's Daughter,* London. Translation of *Die Tochter des Augurs,* Mainz 1981.

HEURGON, J.
1961 Les lettres étrusques, in *La vie quotidienne chez les Étrusques*, Ch. 8, 270-328.
1980 A propos de l'inscription *tyrrhénienne* de Lemnos. *CRAI*, 578-600.
1985 A propos de la stèle tyrrhénienne de Lemnos. *Atti II Congresso Internazionale Studi Etruschi,* Florence 1985 (forthcoming).

I FENICI

1988 *I Fenici*, Exhibit Catalogue, Venice. (*The Phoenicians*, English translation.)

JANNOT, J.-R.
1985 Un avatar étrusque du mythe grec: Actéon, Calu et le jeu de Phersu, *REL* 62 (1984), 45-56, esp. 51, n. 26, on *Phersu, persona* (with previous bibliography).

JENSEN, H.
1969 *Sign, Symbol and Script: An Account of Man's Efforts to Write*, New York.

KAIMIO, J.
1972 The Ousting of Etruscan by Latin in Etruria, in *Studies in the Romanization of Etruria*. Acta Instituti Romani Finlandiae, V, 85-245.

KEYSER, P.
1988 The Origin of the Latin Numerals 1-1000, *AJA* 92, 529-546.

LEJEUNE, M.
1980 Observations on J. HEURGON, A propos de l'inscription 'tyrrhénienne' de Lemnos, *CRAI*, 600-606.
1981a Les six premiers numéraux étrusques. *REL* 59, 69-77.
1981b Un nom étrusque de l'alphabet? *REL* 59, 77-79.
1981c Comment translitérer les sifflantes étrusques? *REL* 59, 79-82.
1981d Procédures soustractives dans les numérations étrusque et latine. *BSL* 76, 241-248.
1985 L'Etrurie et la transmission de l'alphabet. *Atti II Congresso Internazionale Etrusco*, Florence, May-June 1985 (forthcoming).

LIMC *Lexicon Iconographicum Mythologiae Graecae* I-III.

McCARTER, P. K.
1975 A Phoenician Graffito from Pithekoussai. *AJA* 79, 140-141.

MORANDI, A.
1985 CIE 6314-6316, *Quaderni Catanesi di Studi Classici e Medievali VII* 14 (1985) 523-526 (lamina in bronzo, Pirgi, 6313).
1986 Una nuova lettura della grande iscrizione di Velkhas. *Antiqua* XI, 10-13.
1987 Etrusco *ipa*, *Revue Belge de Philologie et d'Histoire* 65, 87-96.

PALLOTTINO, M.
1963 Uno schema greco-anatolico in Etruria, in *Etudes Etrusco-Italiques*. Mélanges pour le 25e anniversaire de la chaire d'Etruscologie à l'Université de Louvain, Louvain, 145-143, pls. 17-18.

1978a *The Etruscans,* Harmondsworth, translation of *Etruscologia,* sixth edition, 1968, Milan, with additions 1973, edited by R. RIDGWAY, 189-234, language; 72-73, 246, Lemnos stele.
1978b La lingua degli Etruschi, in *Popoli e Civiltà dell' Italia antica,* vol. 6, 429-468.
1978c *La langue étrusque. Problèmes et perspectives,* Paris. Translation and introduction by HEURGON of PALLOTTINO 1978b.
1979a *Saggi di antichità,* Rome.
1979b Lo sviluppo socio-istituzionale di Roma arcaica alla luce di nuovi documenti epigrafici, *Studi Romani* 27, 1-14.
1984 *Etruscologia,* seventh edition, Milan, 405-517, language; 97-98, Lemnos stele.
1986 La lingua, in *Rasenna,* Milano.

PELLEGRINI
1985 Review of G. BONFANTE, L. BONFANTE, 1985, in *AGI* 70, 147-151.

PFIFFIG, A.J.
1969 Die etruskische Sprache, Graz.
1972 Zur Förderung nach moderner Sprach betrachtung in der Etruskologie in *Die Sprache* 18, 163-187.
1975a Zum Methodenproblem in der etruskischen Sprachwissenschaft, *Kadmos* 14, 137-145.
1975b *Religio Etrusca,* Graz.
1984 Review of G. BONFANTE, L. BONFANTE, 1983, in *Gnomon* 56, 770-771.

PIAZZA, A.
1988 (with collaboration of N. CAPPELLO, E. OLIVETTI, S. RENDINE), La storia d'Italia letta nel DNA, in *La Stampa,* 1 giugno, *Tuttoscienze,* summary of an article forthcoming in *Annals of Human Genetics* (see fig. 2, *Componente etrusca.*)

PIERI, S.
1969 *Toponomastica della Toscana meridionale,* Siena (edited by Q. GAROSI, G. BONFANTE).

PROSDOCIMI, A.L.
1972 Redazione e struttura testuale delle Tavole Iguvine, in *ANRW* I_2, Berlin-New York, 593-676.
1983a Puntuazione sillabica e insegnamento della scrittura nel venetico e nelle fonti etrusche. *AION* 5, 75-126.
1983b Quarant'anni dopo, Foreword to reprint of DEVOTO 1944.
1984 Storia degli alfabeti etruschi derivati dalle tavole iguvine, con una nota sulla *decifrazione* dell'alfabeto etrusco, in PROSDOCIMI, *Le tavole iguvine* I, Florence, 49-64.

1985a L'etrusco e la *cifra*: riflessioni ad alta voce, in *L'etrusco e le lingue dell'Italia antica,* Atti Pisa 1984 [1985], 53-68.
1985b L'alfabeto come insegnamento ed oralità, *Atti II Congresso Internazionale Etrusco*, Florence, May-June 1985 (forthcoming).

RASENNA
1986 *Rasenna,* Milan 1986.

RASMUSSEN, T.
1984 Review of G. BONFANTE and L. BONFANTE 1983, in *Antiquity* 58, 144-145.

REE *Rivista di Epigrafia Etrusca,* in *Studi Etruschi.*

RICHARDSON, E.
1986 An Archaeological Introduction to the Etruscan Language, in L. BONFANTE 1986, 215-231.

RIDGWAY, D.
1984 *L'alba della Magna Grecia,* Milan.

RIX, H.
1963 *Das Etruskische Cognomen,* Wiesbaden.
1968 Eine morpho-syntaktische Übereinstimmung zwischen Etruskisch und Lemnisch: die Datierungsformel, in *Studien zur Sprachwissenschaft und Kulturkunde. Gedenkschrift für W. Brandenstein,* Innsbruck, 213-222.
1984a Etr. *mech rasnal* = lat. *res publica,* in *Studi di Antichità in onore di G. Maetzke* II, Rome, 455 ff.
1984b La scrittura e la lingua, in *Gli Etruschi. Una nuova immagine,* a cura di M. CRISTOFANI, Florence, 210-238.
1985a Descrizioni di rituali in etrusco e in italico, in *L'etrusco e le lingue dell' Italia antica,* Atti Pisa 1984 [1985], 21-37.
1985b Per una grammatica storica dell'etrusco, *Atti II Congresso Internazionale Etrusco*, Florence, May-June 1985 (forthcoming).

RONCALLI, F.
1980 Osservazioni sui *libri lintei* etruschi, *RendPontAccArch* 51-52 (1978-79, 1979-80), 20-21 of the offprint.
1985 (ed.) *Scrivere Etrusco.* Catalogo della Mostra, Perugia (Milan).
1987 *Etruscan Religious Texts,* unpublished lecture, Perugia.

SILVESTRI, D.
1985 Preistoria linguistica italiana e posizione linguistica dell'etrusco, in *L'etrusco e le lingue dell'Italia antica.* Atti Pisa 1984 [1985], 69-93.

SKUTSCH, F.
1907 in *RE* 9, s.v. *Etrusker,* coll. 770-806.

SOMMER, F.
1930 *Das lydische und etruskische F-Zeichen.* Sitzungsberichte der bayerischen Akademie der Wissenschaften: Phil.-hist. Abteilung, 1-7.

STACCIOLI
1978 Il *mistero* della lingua etrusca, Rome.

STEPHENS, L.D.
1985 review of G. BONFANTE and L. BONFANTE 1983, in *AJP* 106, 133-135.

SWADDLING, J.
1985 (ed.) *Italian Iron Age Artefacts in the British Museum: Papers of the Colloquium*, London.

TATUM, W.J.
1988 The Epitaph of Publius Scipio Reconsidered (*ILLRP* 311), *CQ* 38, 253-258.

ThLE M. PALLOTTINO (ed.), *Thesaurus Linguae Etruscae* I. *Indice Lessicale* (Rome 1978) (=*ThLE*). *Primo Supplemento* (1984). *Ordinamento inverso dei lemmi* (1985).

TLE M. PALLOTTINO (ed.), *Testimonia Linguae Etruscae*, Florence, 1954, 2nd ed. 1968.

TORELLI, M.
1976 Glosse etrusche: Qualche problema di trasmissione, in *Mélanges Heurgon*, Rome, 1001-1008.

1986 History, in L. BONFANTE 1986, 47-65.

VAN DER MEER, L.B.
1987 *The Bronze Liver of Piacenza* (Amsterdam), with reviews by L. BONFANTE, *JRS* 78 (1988) 208-209, and G. BONFANTE, *AGI* (forthcoming).

VETTER, E.
1938 in *RE* 19.2, s.v. *Phersu*, col. 2058.

VINCENT, N.
1985 review of AGOSTINIANI and GIANNELLI, 1983, and of G. BONFANTE and L. BONFANTE, 1985, in *Language* 61, 688-691.

VON BLUMENTHAL, A.
1937 in *RE* 19.1, s.v. *persona*, coll. 1035-1040.

WALDE, A. and HOFMANN, J.B.
1954 *Lateinisches etymologisches Wörterbuch*, Heidelberg, s.v. *persona*, *triumpe* (but not *taberna*, *stilus*, etc.).

FIGURES AND CAPTIONS

ALFABETO ETRUSCO

Alfabeto modello	Arcaico VII-V sec. a.C.	Neo-etrusco V-I sec. a.C.	Pronuncia e trascrizione
			a
			k
			e
			w (v)
			ts
			h
			th
			i
			k
			l
			m
			n
			s
			p
			š (sc)
			k
			r
			s
			t
			u
			s
			ph
			kh (ch)
			f

NUMERALI ETRUSCHI

I (1)

1. Table of Etruscan alphabets and Etruscan numerals (*ThLE* 421-422).

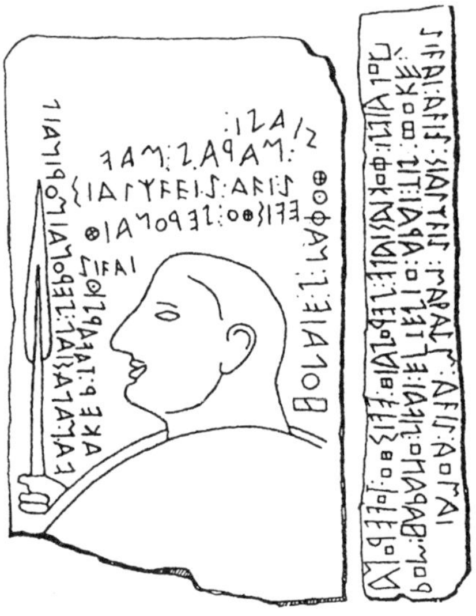

2. Stele from Kaminia, Lemnos.
Athens, National Museum.
Sixth century B.C. (STACCIOLI 1978, fig. 12).

3. Stele of Avle Feluske, from Vetulonia.
Florence, Archaeological Museum.
Ca. 600 B.C. (Drawing by Ana Farkas. *EL*, fig. 14).

4. Stele of Larth Tharnie, from Pomarance (Volterra). 550-500 B.C. Florence, Archaeological Museum (*EL*, fig. 16).

5. Stele of Avile Tite, from Volterra. Ca. 530 B.C. Volterra, Guarnacci Museum (*EL*, fig. 15, corrected).

6. Stele of Larth Ninie, from Fiesole. Ca. 525 B.C. (*EL*, fig. 17).

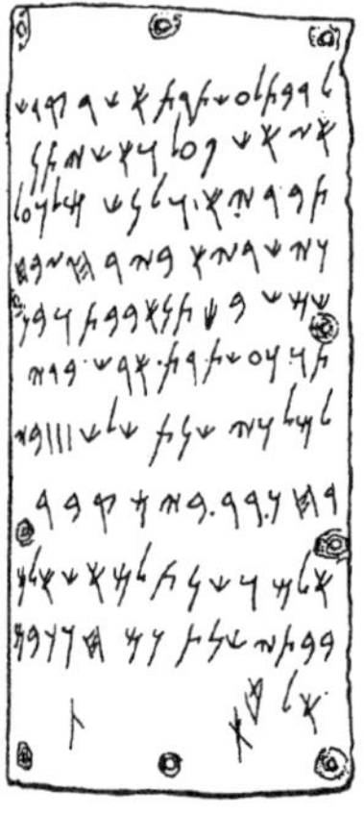

7. Pyrgi tablets with Phoenician and Etruscan inscriptions.Ca. 500 B.C. (PALLOTTINO 1979a, 629-630).

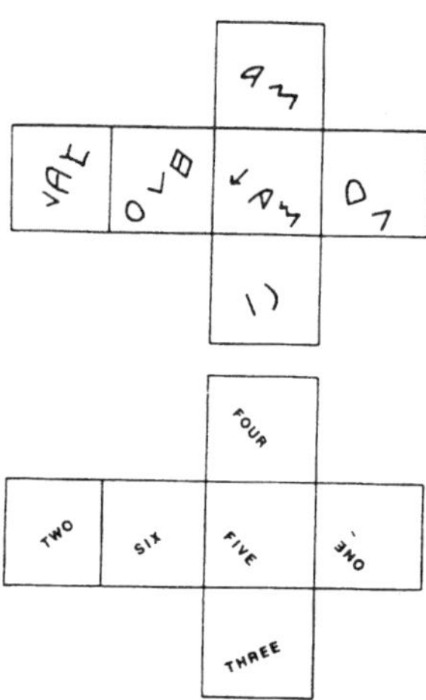

8. Inscribed Etruscan names of numerals on ivory dice, with English translation. Hellenistic period (*EL*, fig. 7).

9. Red-figure crater from Vulci with the farewell of Alcestis and Admetus. Paris, Bibliothèque Nationale, Cabinet des Médailles 918. Fourth century B.C. (DENNIS 1883, vol. 2, frontispiece).

10. Mirror from Volterra, showing Uni nursing Hercle. Florence, Archaeological Museum. Ca. 300 B.C. (*ES* 5.60).

11. Wall painting from the François Tomb, Vulci.
Vel Saties and his assistant, Arnza. Rome, Villa Albani.
Fourth Century B.C.(Drawing, Vatican Museum, copy by Ruspi).

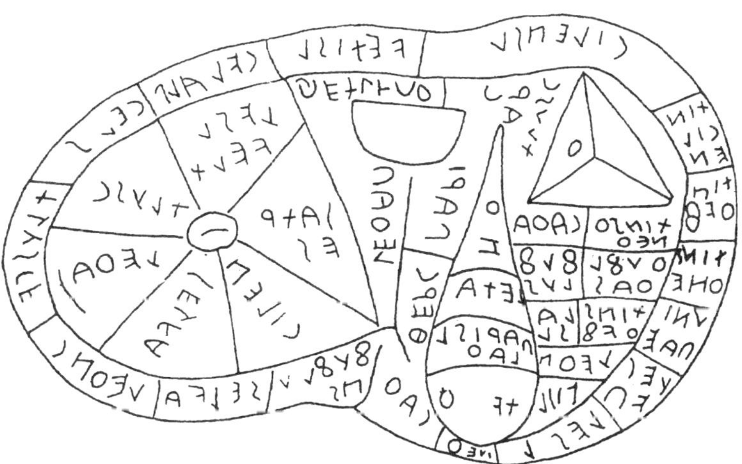

12. Bronze model of a sheep's liver from Piacenza. Piacenza, Museo Civico. Ca. 100 B.C. (VAN DER MEER1987, 10-12).

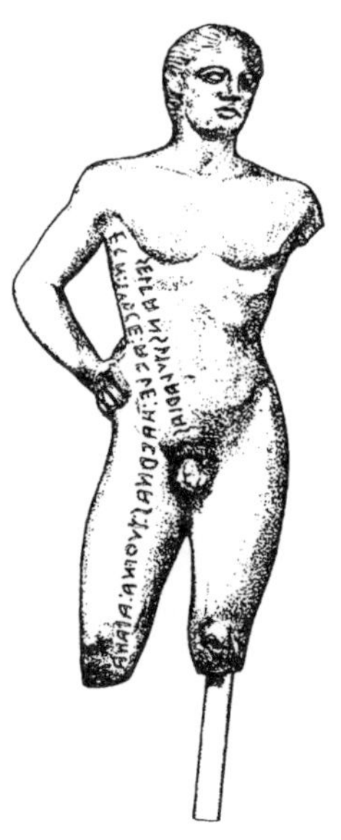

13. Bronze statuette, probably from Bolsena. Private collection.
Ca. 300 B.C. (Drawing by Joann Wood)

Academia Nazionale dei Lincei
Rome, ITALY

Department of Classics
New York University
New York, NY 10003 USA

BCILL 5: *Language in Sociology*, **éd. VERDOODT A. ET KJOLSETH Rn,** 304 pp., 1976. Prix: 760,- FB.
From the 153 sociolinguistics papers presented at the 8th World Congress of Sociology, the editors selected 10 representative contributions about language and education, industrialization, ethnicity, politics, religion, and speech act theory.

BCILL 6: **HANART M.**, *Les littératures dialectales de la Belgique romane: Guide bibliographique*, 96 pp., 1976 (2e tirage, corrigé de CD 12). Prix: 340,- FB.
En ce moment où les littératures connexes suscitent un regain d'intérêt indéniable, ce livre rassemble une somme d'informations sur les productions littéraires wallonnes, mais aussi picardes et lorraines. Y sont également considérés des domaines annexes comme la linguistique dialectale et l'ethnographie.

BCILL 7: *Hethitica II*, **éd. JUCQUOIS G. et LEBRUN R.,** avec la collaboration de DEVLAMMINCK B., II-159 pp., 1977, Prix: 480,- FB.
Cinq ans après *Hethitica I* publié à la Faculté de Philosophie et Lettres de l'Université de Louvain, quelques hittitologues belges et étrangers fournissent une dizaine de contributions dans les domaines de la linguistique anatolienne et des cultures qui s'y rattachent.

BCILL 8: **JUCQUOIS G. et DEVLAMMINCK B.,** *Compléments aux dictionnaires étymologiques du grec*. Tome I: A-K, II-121 pp., 1977. Prix: 380,- FB.
Le *Dictionnaire étymologique de la langue grecque* du regretté CHANTRAINE P. est déjà devenu, avant la fin de sa parution, un classique indispensable pour les hellénistes. Il a fait l'objet de nombreux comptes rendus, dont il a semblé intéressant de regrouper l'essentiel en un volume. C'est le but que poursuivent ces *Compléments aux dictionnaires étymologiques du grec*.

BCILL 9: **DEVLAMMINCK B. et JUCQUOIS G.,** *Compléments aux dictionnaires étymologiques du gothique*. Tome I: A-F, II-123 pp., 1977. Prix: 380,- FB.
Le principal dictionnaire étymologique du gothique, celui de Feist, date dans ses dernières éditions de près de 40 ans. En attendant une refonte de l'œuvre qui incorporerait les données récentes, ces compléments donnent l'essentiel de la littérature publiée sur ce sujet.

BCILL 10: **VERDOODT A.,** *Les problèmes des groupes linguistiques en Belgique: Introduction à la bibliographie et guide pour la recherche*, 235 pp., 1977 (réédition de CD 1). Prix: 590,- FB.
Un «trend-report» de 2.000 livres et articles relatifs aux problèmes socio-linguistiques belges. L'auteur, qui a obtenu l'aide de nombreux spécialistes, a notamment dépouillé les catalogues par matière des bibliothèques universitaires, les principales revues belges et les périodiques sociologiques et linguistiques de classe internationale.

BCILL 11: **RAISON J. et POPE M.,** *Index transnuméré du linéaire A*, 333 pp., 1977. Prix: 840,- FB.
Cet ouvrage est la suite, antérieurement promise, de RAISON-POPE, Index du linéaire A, Rome 1971. A l'introduction près (et aux dessins des «mots»), il en reprend entièrement le contenu et constitue de ce fait une édition nouvelle, corrigée sur les originaux en 1974-76 et augmentée des textes récemment publiés d'Arkhanès, Knossos, La Canée, Zakro, etc., également autopsiés et rephotographiés par les auteurs.

BCILL 12: **BAL W. et GERMAIN J.**, *Guide bibliographique de linguistique romane*, VI-267 pp., 1978. Prix 685,- FB., ISBN 2-87077-097-9, 1982, ISBN 2-8017-099-1.
Conçu principalement en fonction de l'enseignement, cet ouvrage, sélectif, non exhaustif, tâche d'être à jour pour les travaux importants jusqu'à la fin de 1977. La bibliographie de linguistique romane proprement dite s'y trouve complétée par un bref aperçu de bibliographie générale et par une introduction bibliographique à la linguistique générale.

BCILL 13: **ALMEIDA I.**, *L'opérativité sémantique des récits-paraboles. Sémiotique narrative et textuelle. Herméneutique du discours religieux*. Préface de Jean LADRIÈRE, XIII-484 pp., 1978. Prix: 1.250,- FB.
Prenant comme champ d'application une analyse sémiotique fouillée des récitsparaboles de l'Évangile de Marc, ce volume débouche sur une réflexion herméneutique concernant le monde religieux de ces récits. Il se fonde sur une investigation épistémologique contrôlant les démarches suivies et situant la sémiotique au sein de la question générale du sens et de la comprehension.

BCILL 14: *Études Minoennes I: le linéaire A*, **éd. Y. DUHOUX**, 191 pp., 1978. Prix: 480,- FB.
Trois questions relatives à l'une des plus anciennes écritures d'Europe sont traitées dans ce recueil; évolution passée et état présent des recherches; analyse linguistique de la langue du linéaire A; lecture phonétique de toutes les séquences de signes éditées à ce jour.

BCILL 15: *Hethitica III*, 165 pp., 1979. prix: 490,- FB.
Ce volume rassemble quatre études consacrées à la titulature royal hittite, la femme dans la société hittite, l'onomastique lycienne et gréco-asianique, les rituels CTH 472 contre une impureté.

BCILL 16: **GODIN P.**, *Aspecten van de woordvolgorde in het Nederlands. Een syntaktische, semantische en functionele benadering*, VI + 338 pp., 1980. Prix: 1.000,- FB., ISBN 2-87077-241-6.
In dit werk wordt de stelling verdedigd dat de woordvolgorde in het Nederlands beregeld wordt door drie hoofdfaktoren, nl. de syntaxis (in de engere betekenis van dat woord), de semantiek (in de zin van distributie van de dieptekasussen in de oppervlaktestruktuur) en het zgn. functionele zinsperspektief (d.i. de distributie van de constituenten naargelang van hun graad van communicatief dynamisme).

BCILL 17: **BOHL S.**, *Ausdrucksmittel für ein Besitzverhältnis im Vedischen und griechischen*, III + 108 pp., 1980. Prix: 360,- FB., ISBN 2-87077-170-3.
This study examines the linguistic means used for expressing possession in Vedic Indian and Homeric Greek. The comparison, based on a select corpus of texts, reveals that these languages use essentially inherited devices but with differing frequency ratios. in addition Greek has developed a verb "to have", the result of a different rhythm in cultural development.

BCILL 18: **RAISON J. et POPE M.**, *Corpus transnuméré du linéaire A*, 350 pp., 1980. Prix: 1.100,- FB.
Cet ouvrage est, d'une part, la clé à l'Index transnuméré du linéaire A des mêmes auteurs, BCILL 11: de l'autre, il ajoute aux recueils d'inscriptions déjà publiés de plusieurs côtés des compléments indispensables: descriptions, transnumérations, apparat critique, localisation précise et chronologie détaillée des textes, nouveautés diverses, etc.

BCILL 19: **FRANCARD M.**, *Le parler de Tenneville. Introduction à l'étude linguistique des parlers wallo-lorrains,* 312 pp., 1981. Prix: 780,- FB., ISBN 2-87077-000-6.
Dialectologues, romanistes et linguistes tireront profit de cette étude qui leur fournit une riche documentation sur le domaine wallo-lorrain, un aperçu général de la segmentation dialectale en Wallonie, et de nouveaux matériaux pour l'étude du changement linguistique dans le domaine gallo-roman. Ce livre intéressera aussi tous ceux qui sont attachés au patrimoine culturel du Luxembourg belge en particulier, et de la Wallonie en général.

BCILL 20: **DESCAMPS A. et al.**, *Genèse et structure d'un texte du Nouveau Testament. Étude interdisciplinaire du chapitre 11 de l'Évangile de Jean*, 292 pp., 1981. Prix: 895,- FB.
Comment se pose le problème de l'intégration des multiples approches d'un texte biblique? Comment articuler les unes aux autres les perspectives développées par l'exégèse historicocritique et les approches structuralistes? C'est à ces questions que tentent de répondre les auteurs à partir de l'étude du récit de la résurrection de Lazare. Ce volume a paru simultanément dans la collection «Lectio divina» sous le n° 104, au Cerf à Paris, ISBN 2-204-01658-6.

BCILL 21: *Hethitica IV,* 155 pp., 1981. Prix: 390,- FB., ISBN 2-87077-026.
Six contributions d'E. Laroche, F. Bader, H. Gonnet, R. Lebrun et P. Crepon sur: les noms des Hittites; hitt. zinna-; un geste du roi hittite lors des affaires agraires; vœux de la reine à Istar de Lawazantiya; pauvres et démunis dans la société hittite; le thème du cerf dans l'iconographie anatolienne.

BCILL 22: **J.-J. GAZIAUX,** *L'élevage des bovidés à Jauchelette en roman pays de Brabant. Étude dialectologique et ethnographique,* XVIII + 372 pp., 1 encart, 45 illustr., 1982. Prix: 1.170,- FB., ISBN 2-87077-137-1.
Tout en proposant une étude ethnographique particulièrement fouillée des divers aspects de l'élevage des bovidés, avec une grande sensibilité au facteur humain, cet ouvrage recueille le vocabulaire wallon des paysans d'un petit village de l'est du Brabant, contrée peu explorée jusqu'à présent sur le plan dialectal.

BCILL 23: *Hethitica V,* 131 pp., 1983. Prix: 330,- FB., ISBN 2-87077-155-X.
Onze articles de H. Berman, M. Forlanini, H. Gonnet, R. Haase, E. Laroche, R. Lebrun, S. de Martino, L.M. Mascheroni, H. Nowicki, K. Shields.

BCILL 24: **L. BEHEYDT,** *Kindertaalonderzoek. Een methodologisch handboek*, 252 pp., 1983. Prix: 620,- FB., ISBN 2-87'77-171-1.
Dit werk begint met een overzicht van de trends in het kindertaalonderzoek. Er wordt vooral aandacht besteed aan de methodes die gebruikt worden om de taalontwikkeling te onderzoeken en te bestuderen. Het biedt een gedetailleerd analyserooster voor het onderzoek van de receptieve en de produktieve taalwaardigheid zowel door middel van tests als door middel van bandopnamen. Zowel onderzoek van de woordenschat als onderzoek van de grammatica komen uitvoerig aan bod.

BCILL 25: **J.-P. SONNET,** *La parole consacrée. Théorie des actes de langage, linguistique de l'énonciation et parole de la foi*, VI-197 pp., 1984. Prix: 520,- FB. ISBN 2-87077-239-4.
D'ou vient que la parole de la foi ait une telle force?
Ce volume tente de répondre à cette question en décrivant la «parole consacrée», en cernant la puissance spirituelle et en définissant la relation qu'elle instaure entre l'homme qui la prononce et le Dieu dont il parle.

BCILL 26: **A. MORPURGO DAVIES - Y. DUHOUX (ed.),** *Linear B: A 1984 Survey. Proceedings of the Mycenaean Colloquium of the VIIIth Congress of the International Federation of the Societies of Classical Studies (Dublin, 27 August-1st September 1984),* 310 pp., 1985. Price: 850 FB., ISBN 2-87077-289-0.
Six papers by well known Mycenaean specialists examine the results of Linear B studies more than 30 years after the decipherment of script. Writing, language, religion and economy are all considered with constant reference to the Greek evidence of the First Millennium B.C. Two additional articles introduce a discussion of archaeological data which bear on the study of Mycenaean religion.

BCILL 27: *Hethica VI,* 204 pp., 1985. Prix: 550 FB. ISBN 2-87077-290-4.
Dix articles de J. Boley, M. Forlanini, H. Gonnet, E. Laroche, R. Lebrun, E. Neu, M. Paroussis, M. Poetto, W.R. Schmalstieg, P. Swiggers.

BCILL 28: **R. DASCOTTE,** *Trois suppléments au dictionnaire du wallon du Centre,* 359 pp., 1 encart, 1985. Prix: 950 FB. ISBN 2-87077-303-X.
Ce travail comprend 5.200 termes qui apportent un complément substantiel au *Dictionnaire du wallon du Centre* (8.100 termes). Il est le fruit de 25 ans d'enquête sur le terrain et du dépouillement de nombreux travaux dont la plupart sont inédits, tels des mémoires universitaires. Nul doute que ces *Trois suppléments au dictionnaire du wallon du Centre* intéresseront le spécialiste et l'amateur.

BCILL 29: **B. HENRY,** *Les enfants d'immigrés italiens en Belgique francophone. Seconde génération et comportement linguistique*, 360 pp., 1985. Prix: 950 FB. ISBN 2-87077-306-4.
L'ouvrage se veut un constat de la situation linguistique de la seconde génération immigrée italienne en Belgique francophone en 1976. Il est basé sur une étude statistique du comportement linguistique de 333 jeunes issus de milieux immigrés socio-économiques modestes. De chiffres préoccupants qui parlent et qui donnent à réfléchir...

BCILL 30: **H. VAN HOOF,** *Petite histoire de la traduction en Occident*, 105 pp., 1986. Prix: 380 FB. ISBN 2-87077-343-9.
L'histoire de notre civilisation occidentale vue par la lorgnette de la traduction. De l'Antiquité à nos jours, le rôle de la traduction dans la transmission du patrimoine gréco-latin, dans la christianisation et la Réforme, dans le façonnage des langues, dans le développement des littératures, dans la diffusion des idées et du savoir. De la traduction orale des premiers temps à la traduction automatique moderne, un voyage fascinant.

BCILL 31: **G. JUCQUOIS,** *De l'egocentrisme à l'ethnocentrisme*, 421 pp., 1986. Prix: 1.100 FB. ISBN 2-87077-352-8.
La rencontre de l'Autre est au centre des préoccupations comparatistes. Elle constitue toujours un événement qui suscite une interpellation du sujet: les manières d'être, d'agir et de penser de l'Autre sont autant de questions sur nos propres attitudes.

BCILL 32: **G. JUCQUOIS,** *Analyse du langage et perception culturelle du changement*, 240 p., 1986. Prix: 640 FB. ISBN 2-87077-353-6.
La communication suppose la mise en jeu de différences dans un système perçu comme permanent. La perception du changement est liée aux données culturelles: le concept de différentiel, issu très lentement des mathématiques, peut être appliqué aux sciences du vivant et aux sciences de l'homme.

BCILL 33-35: **L. DUBOIS,** *Recherches sur le dialecte arcadien*, 3 vol., 236, 324, 134 pp., 1986. Prix: 1.975 FB. ISBN 2-87077-370-6.
Cet ouvrage présente aux antiquisants et aux linguistes un corpus mis à jour des inscriptions arcadiennes ainsi qu'une description synchronique et historique du dialecte. Le commentaire des inscriptions est envisagé sous l'angle avant tout philologique; l'objectif de la description de ce dialecte grec est la mise en évidence de nombreux archaïsmes linguistiques.

BCILL 36: *Hethitica VII*, 267 pp., 1987. Prix: 800 FB.
Neuf articles de P. Cornil, M. Forlanini, G. Gonnet, R. Haase, G. Kellerman, R. Lebrun, K. Shields, O. Soysal, Th. Urbin Choffray.

BCILL 37: *Hethtica VIII. Acta Anatolica E. Laroche oblata*, 426 pp., 1987. Prix: 1.300 FB.
Ce volume constitue les *Actes* du Colloque anatolien de Paris (1-5 juillet 1985): articles de D. Arnaud, D. Beyer, Cl. Brixhe, A.M. et B. Dinçol, F. Echevarria, M. Forlanini, J. Freu, H. Gonnet, F. Imparati, D. Kassab, G. Kellerman, E. Laroche, R. Lebrun, C. Le Roy, A. Morpurgo Davies et J.D. Hawkins, P. Neve, D. Parayre, F. Pecchioli-Daddi, O. Pelon, M. Salvini, I. Singer, C. Watkins.

BCILL 38: **J.-J. GAZIAUX**, *Parler wallon et vie rurale au pays de Jodoigne à partir de Jauchelette*. Avant-propos de Willy Bal, 368 pp., 1987. Prix: 790 FB.
Après avoir caractérisé le parler wallon de la région de Jodoigne, l'auteur de ce livre abondamment illustré s'attache à en décrire le cadre villageois, à partir de Jauchelette. Il s'intéresse surtout à l'évolution de la population et à divers aspects de la vie quotidienne (habitat, alimentation, distractions, vie religieuse), dont il recueille le vocabulaire wallon, en alliant donc dialectologie et ethnographie.

BCILL 39: **G. SERBAT,** *Linguistique latine et Linguistique générale*, 74 pp., 1988. Prix: 280 FB. ISBN 90-6831-103-4.
Huit conférences faites dans le cadre de la Chaire Francqui, d'octobre à décembre 1987, sur: le temps; deixis et anaphore; les complétives; la relative; nominatif; génitif partitif; principes de la dérivation nominale.

BCILL 40: *Anthropo-logiques*, éd. D. Huvelle, J. Giot, R. Jongen, P. Marchal, R. Pirard (Centre interdisciplinaire de Glossologie et d'Anthropologie Clinique), 202 pp., 1988. Prix: 600 FB. ISBN 90-6831-108-5.
En un moment où l'on ne peut plus ignorer le malaise épistémologique où se trouvent les sciences de l'humain, cette série nouvelle publie des travaux situés dans une perspective anthropo-logique unifiée mais déconstruite, épistémologiquement et expérimentalement fondée. Domaines abordés dans ce premier numéro: présentation générale de l'anthropologie clinique; épistémologie; linguistique saussurienne et glossologie; méthodologie de la description de la grammaticalité langagière (syntaxe); anthropologie de la personne (l'image spéculaire).

BCILL 41: **M. FROMENT,** *Temps et dramatisations dans les récits écrits d'élèves de 5ème*, 268 pp., 1988. Prix: 850 FB.
Les récits soumis à l'étude ont été analysés selon les principes d'une linguistique qui intègre la notion de circulation discursive, telle que l'a développée M. Bakhtine.
La comparaison des textes a fait apparaître que le temps était un principe différenciateur, un révélateur du type d'histoire racontée.
La réflexion sur la temporalité a également conduit à constituer une typologie des textes intermédiaire entre la langue et la diversité des productions, en fonction de leur homogénéité.

BCILL 42: **Y.L. ARBEITMAN** (ed.), *A Linguistic Happening in Memory of Ben Schwartz. Studies in Anatolian, Italic and Other Indo-European Languages*, 598 pp., 1988. Prix: 1800,- FB.
36 articles dédiés à la mémoire de B. Schwartz traitent de questions de linguistique anatolienne, italique et indo-européenne.

BCILL 43: *Hethitica IX*, 179 pp., 1988. Prix: 540 FB. ISBN.
Cinq articles de St. de Martino, J.-P. Grélois, R. Lebrun, E. Neu, A.-M. Polvani.

BCILL 44: **M. SEGALEN** (éd.), *Anthropologie sociale et Ethnologie de la France*, 873 pp., 1989. Prix: 2.620 FB. ISBN 90-6831-157-3 (2 vol.).
Cet ouvrage rassemble les 88 communications présentées au Colloque International «Anthropologie sociale et Ethnologie de la France» organisé en 1987 pour célébrer le cinquantième anniversaire du Musée national des Arts et Traditions populaires (Paris), une des institutions fondatrices de la discipline. Ces textes montrent le dynamisme et la diversité de l'ethnologie chez soi. Ils sont organisés autour de plusieurs thèmes: le regard sur le nouvel «Autre», la diversité des cultures et des identités, la réévaluation des thèmes classiques du symbolique, de la parenté ou du politique, et le rôle de l'ethnologue dans sa société.

BCILL 45: **J.-P. COLSON,** *Krashens monitortheorie: een experimentele studie van het Nederlands als vreemde taal. La théorie du moniteur de Krashen: une étude expérimentale du néerlandais, langue étrangère*, 226 pp., 1989. Prix: 680 FB. ISBN 90-6831-148-4.
Doel van dit onderzoek is het testen van de monitortheorie van S.D. Krashen in verband met de verwerving van het Nederlands als vreemde taal. Tevens wordt uiteengezet welke plaats deze theorie inneemt in de discussie die momenteel binnen de toegepaste taalwetenschap gaande is.

BCILL 46: *Anthropo-logiques* 2 (1989), 324 pp., 1989. Prix: 970 FB. ISBN 90-6831-156-5.
Ce numéro constitue les Actes du Colloque organisé par le CIGAC du 5 au 9 octobre 1987. Les nombreuses interventions et discussions permettent de dégager la spécificité épistémologique et méthodologique de l'anthropologie clinique: approches (théorique ou clinique) de la rationalité humaine, sur le plan du signe, de l'outil, de la personne ou de la norme.

BCILL 47: **G. JUCQUOIS,** *Le comparatisme*, t. 1: *Généalogie d'une méthode*, 206 pp., 1989. Prix: 750 FB. ISBN 90-6831-171-9.
Le comparatisme, en tant que méthode scientifique, n'apparaît qu'au XIXe siècle. En tant que manière d'aborder les problèmes, il est beaucoup plus ancien. Depuis les premières manifestations d'un esprit comparatiste, à l'époque des Sophistes de l'Antiquité, jusqu'aux luttes théoriques qui préparent, vers la fin du XVIIIe siècle, l'avènement d'une méthode comparative, l'histoire des mentalités permet de préciser ce qui, dans une société, favorise l'émergence contemporaine de cette méthode.

BCILL 48: **G. JUCQUOIS,** *La méthode comparative dans les sciences de l'homme*, 138 pp., 1989. Prix: 560 FB. ISBN 90-6831-169-7.
La méthode comparative semble bien être spécifique aux sciences de l'homme. En huit chapitres, reprenant les textes de conférences faites à Namur en 1989, sont présentés les principaux moments d'une histoire du comparatisme, les grands traits de la méthode et quelques applications interdisciplinaires.

BCILL 49: *Problems in Decipherment*, edited by **Yves DUHOUX, Thomas G. PALAIMA and John BENNET,** 1989, 216 pp. Price: 650 BF. ISBN 90-6831-177-8.
Five scripts of the ancient Mediterranean area are presented here. Three of them are still undeciphered — "Pictographic" Cretan; Linear A; Cypro-Minoan. Two papers deal with Linear B, a successfully deciphered Bronze Age script. The last study is concerned with Etruscan.

SÉRIE PÉDAGOGIQUE DE L'INSTITUT DE LINGUISTIQUE DE LOUVAIN (SPILL).

SPILL 1: **JUCQUOIS G.**, avec la collaboration de **LEUSE J.**, *Conventions pour la présentation d'un texte scientifique*, 1978, 54 pp. (épuisé).

SPILL 2: **JUCQUOIS G.**, *Projet pour un traité de linguistique différentielle*, 1978, 67 pp. Prix: 170,- FB.
Exposé succinct destiné à de régulières mises à jour de l'ensemble des projets et des travaux en cours dans une perspective différentielle au sein de l'Institut de Linguistique de Louvain.

SPILL 3; **JUCQUOIS G.**, *Additions 1978 au «Projet pour un traité de linguistique différentielle»*, 1978, 25 pp. Prix: 70,- FB.

SPILL 4: **JUCQUOIS G.**, *Paradigmes du vieux-slave*, 1979, 33 pp. Prix: 100,- FB.
En vue de faciliter l'étude élémentaire de la grammaire du vieux-slave et de permettre aux étudiants d'en identifier rapidement les formes, ce volume regroupe l'ensemble des paradigmes de cette langue liturgique.

SPILL 5: **BAL W. - GERMAIN J.**, *Guide de linguistique*, 1979, 108 pp. Prix: 275,- FB.
Destiné à tous ceux qui désirent s'initier à la linguistique moderne, ce guide joint à un exposé des notions fondamentales et des connexions interdisciplinaires de cette science une substantielle documentation bibliographique sélective, à jour, classée systématiquement et dont la consultation est encore facilitée par un index détaillé.

SPILL 6: **JUCQUOIS G. - LEUSE J.**, *Ouvrages encyclopédiques et terminologiques en sciences humaines*, 1980, 66 pp. Prix: 165,- FB.
Brochure destinée à permettre une première orientation dans le domaine des diverses sciences de l'homme. Trois sortes de travaux y sont signalés: ouvrages de terminologie, ouvrages d'introduction, et ouvrages de type encyclopédique.

SPILL 7: **DONNET D.**, *Paradigmes et résumé de grammaire sanskrite*, 64 pp., 1980. Prix: 160,- FB.
Dans cette brochure, qui sert de support à un cours d'initiation, sont envisagés: les règles du sandhi externe et interne, les paradigmes nominaux et verbaux, les principes et les classifications de la composition nominale.

SPILL 8-9: **DEROY L.**, *Padaśas. Manuel pour commencer l'étude du sanskrit même sans maître*, 2 vol., 203 + 160 pp., 2e éd., 1984. Prix: 1.090,- FB., ISBN 2-87077-274-2.
Méthode progressive apte à donner une connaissance élémentaire et passive du sanskrit (en transcription). Chaque leçon de grammaire est illustrée par des textes simples (proverbes, maximes et contes). Le second volume contient un copieux lexique, une traduction des textes (pour contrôle) et les éléments pour étudier, éventuellement, à la fin, l'écriture nâgarî.

SPILL 10: *Langage ordinaire et philosophie chez le second WITTGENSTEIN. Séminaire de philosophie du langage 1979-1980,* **édité par MALHERBE J.F.,** 139 pp., 1980. Prix: 350,- FB. ISBN 2-87077-014-6.
Si, comme le soutenait Wittgenstein, **la signification c'est l'usage,** c'est en étudiant l'usage d'un certain nombre de termes clés de la langue du philosophe que l'on pourra, par-delà le découpage de sa pensée en aphorismes, tenter une synthèse de quelques thèmes majeurs des **investigations philosophiques.**

SPILL 11: **PIERRET J.M.,** *Phonétique du français. Notions de phonétique générale et phonétique du français,* V-245 pp. + 4 pp. hors texte, 1985. Prix: 550,- FB. ISBN 2-87077-018-9.
Ouvrage d'initiation aux principaux problèmes de la phonétique générale et de la phonétique du français. Il étudie, en outre, dans une section de phonétique historique, l'évolution des sons, du latin au français moderne.

SPILL 12: **Y. DUHOUX,** *Introduction aux dialectes grecs anciens. Problèmes et méthodes. Recueil de textes traduits,* 111 pp., 1983. Prix: 280,- FB. ISBN 2-87077-177-0.
Ce petit livre est destiné aux étudiants, professeurs de grec et lecteurs cultivés désireux de s'initier à la dialectologie grecque ancienne: description des parlers; classification dialectale; reconstitution de la préhistoire du grec. Quatorze cartes et tableaux illustrent l'exposé, qui est complété par une bibliographie succincte. La deuxième partie de l'ouvrage rassemble soixante-huit courtes inscriptions dialectales traduites et accompagnées de leur bibliographie.

SPILL 13: **G. JUCQUOIS,** *Le travail de fin d'études. Buts, méthode, présentation,* 82 pp., 1984. Prix: 230,- FB. ISBN 2-87077-224-6.
Les étudiants se posent souvent la question des buts du travail de fin d'études: quel est le rôle de ce travail dans leur formation, comment rassembler les informations nécessaires, comment les traiter, comment les présenter? Voilà quelques unes des grandes questions auxquelles on tente de répondre

INDEX ET CONCORDANCES DE L'INSTITUT DE LINGUISTIQUE DE LOUVAIN (ICILL).

ICILL 1: **JUCQUOIS,** avec la collaboration de **B. DEVLAMMINCK et de J. LEUSE,** *La transcription des langues indo-européennes anciennes et modernes: normalisation et adaptation pour l'ordinateur*. 1980, 109 pp. Prix: 600,- FB.

ICILL 2: **E. NIEUWBORG et J. WEISSHAUPT,** avec la collaboration de **D. REULEN,** *Concordantielijst van Zuidnederlandse Romans:* **H. CLAUS**, *Natuurgetrouwer; De Zwarte Keizer; Het jaar van de Kreeft*, 1979, 12 pp. + 3.435 pp. en 14 microfiches. Prix: 1.000,- FB.

ICILL 3: **G. JUCQUOIS et B. DEVLAMMINCK,** *Die Sprache I (1949) - 20 (1974):* index des formes, 1979, XVI-301 pp. Prix: 1.000,- FB.

ICILL 4: **E. NIEUWBORG et J. WEISSHAUPT,** avec la collaboration de **D. REULEN,** Concordance de: CESBRON G., *Notre prison et un royaume*. Concordance de *G. BERNANOS, L'imposture*. 1981, 12 pp. + 3.176 pp. en 12 microfiches. Prix: 950,- FB.

ICILL 6: **E. NIEUWBORG et J. WEISSHAUPT,** avec la collaboration de **R. REULEN,** Concordantielijsten van weekbladen en krantentaal (Zuidnederlands taalgebied). 1981, 12 pp. + 2.606 pp. en 11 microfiches. Prix: 800,- FB.

ICILL 11: **E. NIEUWBORG et J. WEISSHAUPT,** avec la collaboration de **R. REULEN,** Concordantielijsten van Zuidnederlandse letterkunde - Hubert LAMPO, *De komst van Joachim Stiller. Er is méér, Horatio*. 1981, 16 × 24, 12 pp. + 2.403 pp. en 10 microfiches. Prix: 800,- FB.